Secrets

of

The Wee Free Men

and

Discworld

ALSO BY
Carrie Pyykkonen and Linda Washington

Inside "The Lion, the Witch and the Wardrobe":
Myths, Mysteries, and Magic from the Chronicles of Narnia
(with James Stuart Bell)

Secrets

of

The Wee Free Men

and

Discworld

The Myths and Legends of
Terry Pratchett's Multiverse

CARRIE PYKKONEN
and LINDA WASHINGTON

St. Martin's Griffin ✺ New York

For Geoff Allen, *a huge Pratchett fan, and his wife—*
our friend Erika—who soon will be.

May your home be filled with Pratchett, Poe, and pets.

SECRETS OF THE WEE FREE MEN AND DISCWORLD: THE MYTHS AND LEGENDS OF TERRY PRATCHETT'S MULTIVERSE. Copyright © 2008 by Carrie Pyykkonen and Linda Washington. All rights reserved. Printed in the United States of America. No part of this book may be used or reproduced in any manner whatsoever without written permission except in the case of brief quotations embodied in critical articles or reviews. For information, address St. Martin's Press, 175 Fifth Avenue, New York, N.Y. 10010.

www.stmartins.com

Book design by Amanda Dewey

Library of Congress Cataloging-in-Publication Data Available Upon Request

ISBN-13: 978-0-312-37243-9
ISBN-10: 0-312-37243-4

First Edition: April 2008

1 3 5 7 9 10 8 6 4 2

CONTENTS

~

Part One:

Pratchett, Parodies, and Plots: The Literary Roots of Discworld

Part Two:

The Few, the Proud, the Inept: Who's Who in Discworld

Part Three:

Power, Police, and Paraphernalia: The Way Things Work in Discworld

ACKNOWLEDGMENTS

Thanks to our editor, Marc Resnick, for once again taking a chance on us. Thanks also to Preston Washington and Gia Washington, for their research assistance, and to Colleen Yang, for her encouragement.

INTRODUCTION

And Now for Something Completely Different . . .

You'd have to be a very strange person to get
all of the jokes. But I hope you'll get between
80 and 90 percent, and the ones you don't get,
you won't actually notice are there.[1]
—Terry Pratchett

Novelist Patrick Rothfuss, when asked "Who do you read?", replied, "Terry Pratchett. He doesn't get enough credit for the superbly believable world he's created. It's internally consistent, well constructed, and his characters behave realistically."[2] Whether you agree with those words or wonder whether Pratchett would agree, one thing is for certain: The influence of Terry Pratchett in the literary world is obvious. If you don't believe that, check out the science fiction/fantasy section at your local bookstore or library.

For a long time, Terry Pratchett was pretty lonely at the very top of the British literary food chain—at least until the arrival of a

---

[1] Terry Pratchett *Bookcase* interview at http://www.lspace.org/about-terry/interviews/book-case.html. The About Terry (and interviews) section of L-Space is maintained by Jamas Enright.

[2] Patrick Rothfuss interviewed by Akiva Cohen in "Pitch-Perfect High Fantasy," *Publishers Weekly*, February 12, 2007, 68.

certain author by the name of J. K. Rowling. But with well over fifty million books sold (as of February 2007, according to Wikipedia, the site that seems to know all), Pratchett is still an international phenomenon and a consistent best seller. His brainchild, as if you didn't know, is the Discworld series, thirty-six books (as of the writing of this book and excluding *Where's My Cow?* and the *Nanny Ogg Cookbook*) strong, and still going like the Energizer bunny. Although this series began as parodies of other works such as *Ringworld*, *Macbeth*, and *The Arabian Nights*, it defies all pigeonholes. Is it science fiction? Fantasy? Mystery? Political intrigue? Romance? (Uh, no to the latter.) It is, to use a phrase often heard on *Monty Python*, something completely different.

If you've been tempted, like many others, to avoid or underestimate the Discworld series because of its parodies and humor, maybe after reading this, you'll reconsider.

READERS OF THE DISCWORLD BOOKS

Okay, so one of the authors of this book (Carrie) is keenly aware that her parents were born the same year as Terry Pratchett was and that she was born the same year as Pratchett's daughter, Rhianna, which in some way creates a connection with the author in a strange, paternal way. (The other author, Linda, has absolutely no comment to make about birthdays.) She is also aware that her parents would never open a Terry Pratchett book, especially not a Discworld book.

So who does read Terry Pratchett? His loyal followers range from nuns (unlike the satanic nuns in *Good Omens*) to the new generation digging into *The Wee Free Men* and *Wintersmith*. Pratchett's audience is hard to fit into a box. Young, somewhat old, Trekkers, *Lord of the Rings* buffs, Harry Potter fans, our strange friend who loves *The Hitchhiker's Guide to the Galaxy* movie that made me (Carrie) fall asleep, hobbits, maybe a teacher or two, and fools. We were even lucky enough to find a Web site giving Christians advice on which Pratchett books were good and which were dangerous.[3] Honestly, it is difficult to really pinpoint what makes a person willing to read Pratchett. Usually the result is to get hooked on the series. Then, of course, the individual tries to read the books quicker than Pratchett writes them (a quite difficult task)!

Discworld is so well received, or at least read, by so many people, because Pratchett is able to make us laugh about everything. He may offend us in one paragraph and then cause us to have a laughing fit in the next, which washes away the initial offense. It is typical for the laughing fit to delay one's reading for many minutes and can be the cause of interesting looks from one's spouse.[4] If you're anything like us, it will be almost impossible to explain to onlookers what was so funny that you fell off the couch and rolled around in hysterics. I have found it is best to not try and explain, especially if it was due to reading *Nanny Ogg's Cookbook*. Oh, and certainly do not try to explain Unseen University's orangutan Librarian.

Someone (perhaps you?) is obviously buying millions of copies of Pratchett's books. If it is not you, we are not quite sure why you picked up this book unless you are Linda's dad or my grandma.

TERRY PRATCHETT IN BRIEF

Terence David John Pratchett was born in 1948[5] and, according to himself, he is still alive.[6] Therefore, if he were an American, he would be considered a baby boomer, which entitles him to our attention. He began his writing career at the age of thirteen, when his short story

---

[3] We will be sure to forward this site to the Pratchett fans who are nuns.

[4] Glares during Pratchett reading are inevitable if they are by a non–Pratchett-reading spouse.

[5] The same year in which Mahatma Gandhi was assassinated in India and the year my parents, Donn and Kathleen Czegus, were born.

[6] This may be debated in certain parts of the world. After all, good definitions of being alive are hard to come by.

"The Hades Business" was published in the school magazine; it was sold to a commercially published magazine when he was fifteen. After leaving school in 1965, he became a journalist with the *Bucks Free Press* and later with the *Western Daily Press* and *The Bath Chronicle*.

While between stints at the *Bucks Free Press*, he published his first novel, *The Carpet People* (1971). He began writing it at the age of seventeen. This was followed by *The Dark Side of the Sun* (1976).

His novel *Strata* (1981) is considered to be the forerunner of Discworld. While he was working as a publicity officer for the Central Electricity Generating Board, he published his first Discworld book, *The Color of Magic* (1983).

We could tell you that he's written well over fifty books, including young adult novels like The Bromeliad Trilogy (*Truckers, Diggers,* and *Wings*), the Johnny Maxwell books (*Only You Can Save Mankind, Johnny and the Dead,* and *Johnny and the Bomb*), and children's books such as *The Unadulterated Cat* and *Where's My Cow?* But you probably already knew that.

WHY WRITE A BOOK ON DISCWORLD?

Call us crazy, but we really like Pratchett's books and are dying to tell you why—hence this book. Collectively, we have read and studied all of Pratchett's Discworld books—except for *Making Money* (October 2007). Our deadline didn't coincide with that one. It is very difficult to read faster than Pratchett writes. By the time our book is published, the prolific writer will probably have at least two more books out. And by the time you find time to read this book, many more titles in the Discworld series will be lining the local bookstores and landing their way on Top Ten readers' lists.

Does writing a book on Discworld make us experts on Pratchett? Hardly. We aren't privy to deep, dark wisdom from Terry and his family, nor did we snoop through his garbage like crazed paparazzi (though we wanted to). Although this book doesn't contain every person, every street, every place, or every event, it *does* explore some of the mythological, scientific, and pop culture building blocks that correlate with Discworld. If you know and love this series, we hope we inspire you to look at it in a fresh way. If you've never read any of the Discworld books, maybe you'll take a chance. Go on. We dare you . . . right after you read this book.

Well, let's get on with it, shall we?

Please Note: In the footnotes throughout, books not attributed to an author were written by Terry Pratchett.

Part One

Pratchett, Parodies, and Plots: The Literary Roots of Discworld

I

⌇

Blueprint for a World

THE ARCHITECT AT WORK

Sometimes old buildings inspire us, sometimes the opposite is true. We look at an old building and ask ourselves, "What on earth were those people thinking of?"
— Witold Rybczynski, *The Look of Architecture*[1]

If you were on an architectural tour of, say, Saint Peter's Square in Rome, maybe your tour guide would say something like, "This is a true example of Italian baroque—one of Giovanni Lorenzo Bernini's finest" in the lilting tone that many tour guides have. Then, while telling you how the architect was inspired to design such a master-piece, he or she might slip in a genteel pun, one certain to be a cut above the if-it-ain't-baroque-don't-fix-it variety that you might hear and chuckle at out of pity back home.

---

[1] *The Look of Architecture* by Witold Rybczynski (Oxford: Oxford University Press, 2001), 48. Not like "The Look of Love," but still entertaining.

We brought that up for two reasons: (1) A fantasy writer like Terry Pratchett is an architect of sorts, but on a much grander scale than an Italian baroque master like Bernini or his rival, Francesco Borromini. After all, he had a whole world to design. Bernini and Borromini only had to influence Italy and several generations of would-be architects. (2) In this chapter, we're about to take you on an architectural tour of the Discworld, but one without the lilting tone or even remarks (at least not many remarks) about the *actual* architecture, such as Unseen University. (You would've bought *The Discworld Mapp* or *The Streets of Ankh-Morpork* for that, wouldn't you?) Instead, we'll discuss words—the building blocks of Discworld. Like the furniture in the office of Ladislav Pelc, the Professor of Morbid Bibliomancy in *Going Postal*, Discworld is a world designed out of books. It is a veritable library of literary allusions. By the end of the tour, you might feel like A. Clarence Shandon in *Silverlock* by John Myers Myers—as if you've walked through literary history.

And since we're discussing Discworld, where characters named Flatulus (the god of winds, of course) abide, we'll throw in puns for free. Let's get write to it, shall we? (Feel free to ask questions while on the tour. We'll do our best to answer them. No question is considered dumb.)

Since this is not a short chapter, maybe you should send out for pizza. We like pepperoni. . . .

DISCLAIMER (or in honor of Discworld, Disc-Claimer):
This tour is by no means exhaustive. You might easily think of some aspects or allusions not noted here. We won't hold that against you.

Like any good architect's, Pratchett's work should be judged by whether it fulfills the three purposes of good architecture, namely: (1) to shelter people; (2) to be durable against the elements and gravity; (3) to be beautiful or delightful.[2] Judging by the millions of fans, shelves of books written over decades, awards, and several Discworld conventions (the first North American one coming in 2009!), we would venture to say that Discworld fulfilled all three.

If you read *Strata*, you caught the gleam of Discworld in Pratchett's eye. But if you read *Ringworld* by Larry Niven, you caught the inspiration for that gleam. After all, *Strata* is considered a parody of *Ringworld*, Niven's 1970 sci-fi classic detailing the discovery of a 600-million-mile, ring-shaped world by an intrepid, eclectic collection of explorers. (In comparison, the Disc is only 10,000 miles wide.)[3]

But the world beginning with *The Color of Magic* didn't just spring into being in 1983, or two years previous to that when *Strata* appeared, or even when *Ringworld* was read. If you look even further back, you'll find other elements that went into the blueprint of Discworld. There's a little bit of this and that in Pratchett's design.

INSPIRATION FROM THE PAST

Throughout our history we have clung to elements of our past as carriers of our culture. . . . Where we can, we need to preserve its triumphs and occasionally its follies, the best and even sometimes the mundane examples of how our society lived, worked, worshiped, and played.
—John George Vanderbilt Henry Spencer-Churchill[4]

An architect can look at an old building, with its crenellations or cornices, its Gothic or baroque style, and find inspiration to design

---

[2] According to Sir Henry Wotton, a man writing in 1642 (and he would know), discussed in *The Look of Architecture*, 4–5.

[3] Made you look.

[4] Quote from the 11th Duke of Marlborough in *Palm Beach: An Architectural Legacy* by Polly Anne Earl (New York: Rizzoli International Publications, Inc., 2002), 7. And we're pretty sure the duke was never a "Marlborough Man."

something new to wow a twenty-first-century population. Or he or she, for the love of a particular time period (say, the 1920s), might design a building to revive a style of the past.

Terry Pratchett looked at several old myths and was inspired to create Discworld.

Greek, Roman, and Norse Mythology: Pratchett Mines the Myths

Pick any of the Discworld books at random and you'll soon know that Terry Pratchett is very familiar with Greek, Roman, Norse, and Celtic mythology. Go on. We dare you. First, look at the Disc itself. In the world of Norse mythology, Earth is a flat disc in the branches of a tree called Yggdrasil. (Not a name you'd stick on a baby these days.) In Pratchett's world, the earth is a flat disc mounted on the backs of four elephants standing on a humongous turtle traveling through the multiverse (rather than the universe). That turtle is based on a myth he read as a child. More on that myth later.

Second, check out the population. As you remember from high school or even middle school if you went to a fancy one, in Greek and Roman mythology, there are creatures like centaurs, fauns, satyrs, naiads, dryads, nymphs. But intervening or interfering in their lives are gods/goddesses such as Zeus, Hera, Minerva/Athena, Ares, and so on, who live on Mount Olympus. (Yeah, yeah. Like in the old *Xena: Warrior Princess* and *Hercules: The Legendary Journey* shows.) In Norse mythology, the gods/goddesses Odin, Thor, Eir, and so on live in Valhalla. Let's begin our population examination (it won't hurt) with the Discworld pantheon.

The Gods Must Be Crazy. In the pantheon of Discworld, there's a smidgen of Greek and Roman mythology, plus a smattering of Norse as well. Instead of the two-eyed chief god Zeus (Jupiter in

Roman mythology); Thor, the Norse thunder god; or even Thor's father, Odin, the one-eyed chief of the Aesir gods in Norse mythology, Blind Io, the thunder god, is the chief of the Discworld gods. Instead of Bacchus, the Greek god of wine, there's Bibulous, the god of wine and things on sticks. Instead of Loki, the trickster god kicked out of Valhalla, there's Hoki the Jokester. Instead of Aphrodite/Venus, the goddess of love, there's Astoria (like the hotel). And who can forget Pratchett's Fedecks—the messenger of the gods? ("When it absolutely has to be there overnight," as a FedEx advertising slogan proclaimed.) He can give Hermes, the messenger god (Mercury in Roman mythology), a run for his money. And of course, Discworld has minor deities similar to those in Greek and Roman mythology: Vulcan (the Greek Vulcan) and Hephaistos (the Greek Hephaestus).

Pratchett includes unique gods and goddesses as well, like Anoia, the minor goddess of things that stick in drawers (and also lost corkscrews and things that roll under furniture), and Aniger, the goddess of squashed animals. (She must work overtime.)

Although we said we wouldn't talk about architecture, we can't help mentioning one place—Dunmanifestin, the place where the gods apparently were *done manifesting*. In *The Last Hero*, Ghengiz Cohen (a.k.a. Cohen the Barbarian with a bit of Genghis Khan, the Mongolian conqueror of the thirteenth century) and his posse, the Silver Horde, argue with the Valkyries who want to take them to the Halls of the Slain in Dunmanifestin on Cori Celesti. Well, Dunmanifestin is referred to as "the stuccoed Valhalla" in *Guards! Guards!*[5] (The Valkyries, the female warriors who take the dead to Valhalla, come from Norse mythology.)

According to *Fairies and How to Avoid Them* by Miss Perspicacia Tick (a book mentioned in *Hat Full of Sky*), the Nac Mac Feegles believe that Earth is like Valhalla.

---

[5] *Guards! Guards!* (New York: HarperTorch, 1989), 292.

Other Stories (But the Gods Are in Them, Too). Not content to tweak just the gods of Greek myths, Pratchett tweaks other people or their situations to include in Discworld. For example, you know the story of King Midas, right? An allusion to the greedy king's story appears early in *Witches Abroad*, which seems to be a veritable "*glod*mine" of allusions. Instead of King Midas, there is Seriph Al-Ybi, whose curse by a god with poor spelling causes everything he touches to turn to a dwarf named Glod.

And how about the story of Daedalus and Icarus? It gets a send-up in *Jingo* and *The Last Hero*. Leonard of Quirm, Pratchett's answer to Leonardo da Vinci (more on them in chapter 19), has a similar goal of perfecting the art of flying, but not airline food.

And of course, there is the story of Prometheus, the Titan and creator of man (according to the Greek myth) who dared to steal fire from the gods and suffered for it by having his liver eaten by an eagle every day. (But not with bacon or onions.) He's Mazda in Discworld and his theft is the inspiration for *The Last Hero*, where Ghengiz Cohen and the Silver Horde try to return fire to the gods by blowing them up. (A weird way of saying thanks. Flowers would've been better.)

At this point, we have to mention another place—the Underworld, or realm of the dead. The Greeks and Romans had it in their mythology. This kingdom is ruled by Hades and surrounded by rivers that include Acheron, Styx, and Lethe. A three-headed dog named Cerberus guards this realm.

Discworld not only has an Underworld, it has an inferno similar to the one described in *The Divine Comedy* by Dante Alighieri. But we're getting ahead of ourselves. (See "The Devil Made Me Do It" later in the chapter.) In *Wintersmith*, the Nac Mac Feegles and Roland de Chumsfanleigh journey through the Underworld to wake up the Summer Lady and meet an unnamed, overcharging ferryman. Pratchett cleverly reminds us where they are by having one of the Feegles shout, "We're right oot in the Styx noo!"[6] The three-headed dog, however, meets its end thanks to the loads of boggles in the Underworld.

As the Feegles explain, a trip through the Underworld is traditional for heroes, because a number of heroes in classical mythology journeyed through it. We're told of a myth of Ephebe—the rescue of Euniphon by Orpheo,[7] which is an allusion to two Greek myths: (1) The story of Orpheus and Eurydice. Orpheus, the son of Apollo (the god of fine arts) and Calliope (a muse), was a poet and musician known especially for playing the lyre. (In Pratchett's book, a lute and a lyre are mentioned.) He sorrowed so much when his wife, Eurydice, died, that Hades allowed her to return to Earth with him on one condition—that Orpheus not look back until he returned above ground. (In *Wintersmith*, Rob Anybody cautions Roland in a similar manner.) But in a move like that of Lot's wife in the Bible, Orpheus looked back and Eurydice returned to the Underworld. (2) The story of Persephone, whose enforced stay in the Underworld caused winter on earth. But in Discworld, the rescue is all about the return of summer—hence the Summer Lady's stay in the Underworld.

As we read this journey, we couldn't help thinking of Odysseus, whose trip through the Underworld to seek the aid of Tiresias, a blind prophet, is chronicled in *The Odyssey* by another architect of worlds—Homer (but not Simpson).

Speaking of Homer (still not Simpson), both of his epics, *The Iliad* and *The Odyssey*, and Virgil's *The Aeneid* have a place in Discworld mythology. In *Eric*, the Trojan Wars from *The Iliad* and *The Aeneid* are the Tsortean Wars in which the Ephebians (the Greeks) fight the Tsorteans (the Trojans), because of Elenor, the Helen of Troy of the story. Lavaeolus, the Odysseus of the story, is trying to return home.

---

[6] *Wintersmith* (New York: HarperTempest, 2006), 295.
[7] Ibid., 275.

The Tsortean Wars are woven even tighter into the fabric of Discworld mythology when Nanny Ogg refers to them (and an Achilles's heel situation) in *Witches Abroad*.

Lest we forget, Roland de Chumsfanleigh is an allusion to Roland, the hero of *Chanson de Roland* (Song of Roland) the twelfth-century French epic by Turoldus.

A Nod to the Norse Myths. Moving on to Norse mythology, some of its population find equal opportunity in Discworld, namely elves, dwarfs (or dwarves, as Tolkien popularized), trolls (the faithful Sergeant Detritus), werewolves (of sorts), and Valkyries.

The large number of werewolves prowling around Uberwald owe their fictional lives to the long history of werewolf stories, starting with Loki's wolf son, Fenrir—who was so fearsome that the other gods had to bind him to prevent him from killing them—and continuing with "White Wolf of the Harz Mountains," an 1839 story by Frederick Marryat, and the 1941 Lon Chaney movie *The Wolf Man*. (More on werewolves in chapter 4.)

European Folklore and History

I Dream of Jenny with the Light Green Teeth. Although *The Lord of the Rings* was meant to be a mythology of sorts for England, many folktales already existed around the British Isles. Some of these folktales derived from tales elsewhere in Europe and the world. Take, for example, the tale of Jenny Green-Teeth, whom Pratchett mentions in *The Wee Free Men*. Jenny, a hag of the river and a "Grade 1 Prohibitory Monster"[8] according to Miss Tick (see chapter 6), was known to lure children to their doom—a fate that nearly befalls Tiffany's sticky brother, Wentworth. She's a sort of antiondine or undine—a water elemental of folklore

---

8 *The Wee Free Men* (New York: HarperTrophy, 2003), 56.

based on Ondine, a water nymph in German myths, who fell in love with a faithless human. (Reminds you of "Little Mermaid," doesn't it?) Whereas water nymphs are said to be beautiful and helpful (if helping suits their needs), Jenny's the Ugly Betty of the water spirit world. She's not so much concerned about gaining a soul, which undines seek (if you read Hans Christian Andersen's "Little Mermaid," you know that was the goal). She just wants lunch, as other famous child-eating witches (Baba Yaga, the witch of Russian folklore, or the witch in "Hansel and Gretel") could relate to.

Freaks and Geats, Plus Arthur—Warts and All. Pratchett admits to reading *Beowulf*, the thousand-year-old Anglo-Saxon epic, as a boy. Beowulf, the great Geat hero with amazing strength, had the gumption to fight the monster Grendel with his bare hands. And who doesn't know the story of King Arthur, told in a cycle of medieval stories? *Beowulf,* supposedly written by a monk, and the legend of King Arthur—realized by Sir Thomas Malory (*Le Morte d'Arthur*, based on French and English tales) and T. H. White in *The Once and Future King* and *The Book of Merlyn*—set the standard for heroic tales.

Carrot Ironfoundersson, who was named after a guy with red hair who worked on Pratchett's house, has both the manner of a Beowulf-type hero and the legacy of a King Arthur, even though he considers himself a dwarf. Like King Arthur, formerly known as Wart in *Once and Future King*, Carrot is an orphan who is probably the rightful king of the land. Both have heirloom swords. Unlike Arthur, Carrot was raised by dwarfs and is content to remain a simple watchman for now, rather than rule over corrupt Ankh-Morpork.

In *The Fifth Elephant*, Carrot agrees to fight a werewolf with his bare hands. Shades of the Beowulf–Grendel match perhaps? Only Pratchett knows. But a direct allusion to the monsters in Beowulf occurs in *Guards! Guards!* when one hero says to another, "Monsters are getting more uppity, too. I heard where this guy, he killed this monster in this lake, no problem, stuck its arm up over the door. . . . Its mum come and complained."[9]

An allusion to the King Arthur legend occurs in *Wintersmith*, when Roland throws his sword into the river while in the Underworld. The sword is caught in a manner similar to that of the Lady of the Lake in the King Arthur stories, who caught the sword, Excalibur, when it was returned to her—her stipulation upon granting Arthur the sword.

Historical Hijinks. Another building block of Discworld involves Alexandre Dumas, a nineteenth-century French writer you probably read in high school, who used the drama of seventeenth-century France to tell his musketeer stories. In *The Truth*, an allusion to *The Man in the Iron Mask* is made when Lord Havelock Vetinari is asked about the fate of his doppelgänger, an unfortunate man named Charlie. Is he "in a deep cell, and made . . . [to] wear a mask all the time, and have all his meals brought by a deaf and dumb jailer?"[10] Philippe, the unfortunate mask-wearing prisoner of *Man in the Iron Mask*, was taken away from the Bastille in a carriage manned by a "deaf and dumb" postilion arranged by ex-musketeer Aramis.

Folklore of the East

If any one should be asked . . . what is it that solidity and extension adhere in, he would not be in a much better case than the Indian before mentioned who, saying that the world was supported by a great elephant, was asked what the elephant rested on; to which his answer was- a great tortoise: but being

---

[9] Ibid., 123.
[10] *The Truth* (New York: HarperTorch, 2000), 338.

> *again pressed to know what gave support to the broad-backed*
> *tortoise, replied- something, he knew not what.*
>
> —John Locke, British philosopher in chapter XXIII of
> *An Essay Concerning Human Understanding,* written in
> 1690,[11] a time when everyone talked like this.

Perhaps when you're eating *aloo gobi* or watching a Tony Jaa film (*The Protector!*) you don't think about myths from such countries as Thailand, China, or India. (Maybe you will next time.) But Pratchett folds some of the myths of the East into his cultural stew.

Terrifying Tortoises and Powerful Pachyderms. If you happen to know Hindu mythology, you know about Akupara, the tortoise carrying a world on its back. English philosopher and empiricist John Locke was certainly aware back in the seventeenth century. We've already said Pratchett was aware; hence his inclusion of the Great A'Tuin, the giant turtle upon which the four elephants (Great T'Phon, Tubul, Jerakeen, and Berilia) carrying the Disc ride. (A fifth elephant, discussed in *The Fifth Elephant,* is just a legend.)

Elephants play a big role in Hindu mythology. Not only does the Hindu god Indra ride one (Airavata—the first elephant created), elephants supposedly are the mounts of choice for the guardian gods at the eight points of the compass. (Some people prefer horses as destriers.) So, it's only fitting that elephants, like Atlas the Titan in Greek mythology, hold up the world.

A'Tuin isn't the only chelonian mentioned in Discworld (although it is the largest, being a star turtle). The Great God Om (*Small Gods*) is a small tortoise for much of the time (and a grumpy one at that) until more people believe in him.

---

[11] Posted at the Enlightenment Web site: http://enlightenment.supersaturated.com/johnlocke/BOOKIIChapterXXIII.html.

And Yet There's the Yeti. You've undoubtedly heard stories of the yeti, the ape-man creatures loping around the Himalayas and supposedly leaving their scalps around monasteries. (We don't make these things up.) These are "the abominable snowmen" of many stories. (The Tibetans have the yeti. In North America, we have Bigfoot and Sasquatch.) But only Pratchett (see *Thief of Time*) mentions the "sword trick"—cutting off a yeti's head and having it come back to life.

Are yeti real or mythological? Scientists aren't really sure, even after several expeditions to track them. The jury's still out on Bigfoot, as well.

Stories? She's Got a Thousand of 'Em. The stories woven through one master storyteller, Scheherazade, in *The Arabian Nights* or *The 1001 Arabian Nights*, are myths from Persia (now Iran), Asia, India, and Arabia and were written in the tenth through the fourteenth centuries. Maybe you read the collection of stories compiled by Andrew Lang (usually relegated to the kids' section of the library) or the complete tales found in the nonfiction section of the library. Pratchett, like Scheherazade, wove several stories (or allusions to stories) from *The Arabian Nights* into one book: *Sourcery*. Check it out: The cowardly Rincewind's journey to Al Khali, a city in Klatch, his dealings with Creosote, the Seriph of Al Khali, and Abrim the evil vizier who instigates the Mage Wars (see also chapter 7)—all are reminiscent of stories in the *Arabian Nights* collection, particularly "Aladdin and the Wonderful Lamp," "The Three Princes and the Princess Nouronnihar," and the Haroun al-Raschid, Caliph of Baghdad, stories. A major nod to *The Arabian Nights* comes through the mention of a flying carpet and a magic lamp from the seriph's treasury. Contrary to the 1992 Disney movie *Aladdin* (which drew some inspiration from *The Thief of Bagdad*, a movie from 1940), the flying carpet comes from "The Three Princes and the Princess Nouronnihar."

Another oblique nod (we think) to *The Arabian Nights* is the character of Rincewind who, like Sinbad, the intrepid sailor of seven voyages, journeys around the world and encounters many dangers. Unlike Sinbad, however, who at least *wanted* to go on some of the voyages, Rincewind is dragged kicking and screaming.

By the way, Creosote is an allusion to Croesus—the king of Lydia in 560–546 B.C., who was known for being wealthy, hence the idiom "rich as Croesus." Of course, you knew that.

DISCWORLD: AN IDEAL ENVIRONMENT?

The decision as to what form the house shall take is made on sociocultural grounds—way of life, shared group values, and "ideal" environment sought.

Amos Rapoport, *House Form and Culture*[12]

An architect also has to be an anthropologist of sorts in order to make his or her designs functional and culturally relevant. Terry Pratchett is an anthropologist as well—perhaps not in degree, but in his experience as a journalist and in the stories from other cultures he has read. The curios and connections he gained through stories added to the crucible in which Discworld was born.

Discworld has several people groups, some of which have a changing cultural identity based on the region they're in. For example, the dwarfs in Shmaltzberg might act a little differently than do the dwarfs in Ankh-Morpork. Angua, a werewolf from Uberwald, opposes some of the practices of her family back home. But Pratchett still keeps the basic cultural identities of dwarfs and werewolves found in literature. Werewolves are still people who transform into wolves (or, in the case of the yennork, a werewolf who doesn't

---

[12] Amos Rapoport, *House Form and Culture* (Englewood Cliffs, NJ: Prentice Hall, Inc., 1969), 104.

change at all). Witches are still witches. Immortals (personifications), while they may work as milkmen at times (e.g., Ronny Soak, alias Kaos) or look like men (the Wintersmith), are still, well, elementals. It's elementary. (Just keeping up with our end of the bargain concerning the bad puns.)

So, how does Pratchett give shape to the cultural identities of his people/creature groups? Some classic stories inspire him.

Full of Fairy Tales . . . and Classic Tales

If you made the trek to see any of the *Shrek* movies, chances are you probably liked fairy tales as a kid (and still do, if you're honest with yourself; we know you record *The Fairly OddParents* on TiVo). The fairy-tale collections of Charles Perrault in seventeenth-century France, the Brothers Grimm (Jacob and Wilhelm) from Germany, Peter Christen Asbjørnsen and Jørgen Moe from Norway in the eighteenth century, and Scotsman Andrew Lang in the nineteenth influenced many fantasy writers, including Terry Pratchett.

"Little Red Riding Hood," a story all three collections have in common, also finds its way into Pratchett's *Witches Abroad*—one of the Lancre witch novels featuring Granny Weatherwax, Nanny Ogg, and Magrat Garlick. Perrault's "Cinderella" story also is integral to the plot. Since the novel deals with the fulfillment of stories, it includes a plethora of nods to other well-known fairy tales from the three collections: "Sleeping Beauty" (also alluded to in *Mort*), "The Frog Prince," "Goldilocks and the Three Bears," "Hansel and Gretel" (also alluded to in *The Light Fantastic*), "Snow White and the Seven Dwarfs," and "Rumpelstiltskin."

In each of Pratchett's allusions, the characters behave in a way readers can easily recognize from fairy tales. But he places his own spin on the situations. Although fairy godmothers still provide pumpkin coaches, Magrat winds up turning everything into pumpkins at first. Black Aliss is the wicked witch shut up in the oven in a

Hansel and Gretel–like way. The frog prince (really a *duc*—French for "duke" and "horned owl"—go figure), who is hardly a Prince Charming, tries to marry the Cinderella of the story.

In *Thief of Time*, Pratchett alludes to *Grimm's Fairy Tales* when Jeremy Clockson reads *Grim Fairy Tales*, which contains such stories as "The Old Lady in the Oven" (gotta be a Hansel and Gretel story) and "The Glass Clock of Bad Schüschein."

The Amazing Maurice and His Educated Rodents is one large allusion to the Pied Piper of Hamelin story, a story the Grimm brothers included and one that inspired poet Robert Browning. Pratchett also mentions the story of "Puss in Books" from Charles Perrault's collection and "Dick Livingstone and his wonderful cat"—an allusion to Dick Whittington, a story Andrew Lang collected (which is partially based on the life of Richard Whittington the Lord Mayor of London), and Ken Livingstone the Leader of the Greater London Council until 1986. He became Mayor of London in 2002.

Every culture has folktales. Pratchett is undoubtedly familiar with the folktales of Norway, judging by his allusion to *East of the Sun, West of the Moon* in *Lords and Ladies*. That story comes from the fairy-tale collection of Peter Christen Asbjørnsen and Jørgen Moe published in 1845, another volume of which was published in 1879.

The Devil Made Me Do It. As you may or may not know, *Faust*, the epic by Johann Wolfgang von Goethe, featuring a Job-like agreement and a contest of wills between Faust and Mephistopheles, is parodied in *Eric*. Instead of the pious Doktor Faust, there's Eric, a fourteen-year-old who wants to meet the most beautiful woman in the world, have mastery over the kingdoms, and live forever—apt goals according to some in our world. Having a huge amount of gold would be nice, too. But instead of summoning someone like Mephistopheles, Eric summons Rincewind.

In *Faust*, Mephistopheles tried and failed to gain Faust's soul through similar temptations—the pleasures of life, the search for the most beautiful woman in the world (Helen of Troy), a desire for power. As we mentioned earlier, Helen is Elenor in *Eric*.

As the scenery of Pandemonium—the place to which Eric journeys—is described, we can't help also seeing the influence of *The Divine Comedy*, the fourteenth-century Dante Alighieri classic, and *Paradise Lost*, John Milton's epic take on the temptation and fall of man, published in 1667. The city Eric comes to, which is surrounded by a lake of lava, has "unparalleled views of the Eight Circles"[13]—like the nine circles of Dante's *Inferno*, the first cantica of *The Divine Comedy*. The name Pandemonium is a reference to Lucifer's palace of the same name in *Paradise Lost*.

In *Inferno*, you see some elements similar to Greek mythology in the use of the River Acheron and Charon the ferryman. In the journey through the Underworld described in *Wintersmith*, the taciturn river ferryman is like Charon and the river is like Acheron.

A Book to Sink Your Teeth Into. Bram Stoker's 1897 classic novel *Dracula* is the great-great-grandfather of many a vampire story, even though it wasn't actually the first vampire story written. (John William Polidori wrote "The Vampyre," published in 1819. But even that wasn't the first, although it started the tradition of the vampire story in literature.) As Pratchett gives shape to the fortified communities of Uberwald, a land "with no real boundaries and lots of forest in between"[14] plus plenty of howling wolves, you see echoes of the Transylvania the unfortunate Jonathan Harker saw in *Dracula*, with its howling wolves and mile after mile of forested land.

Pratchett's vampires run the gamut from bloodthirsty (the de Magpyrs of *Carpe Jugulum*) to black ribboners (Lady Margolotta

---

[13] *Eric* (New York: HarperTorch, 1990), 35.
[14] *The Fifth Elephant* (New York: HarperTorch, 2000), 15.

von Uberwald in *The Fifth Elephant*, Lance-constable Sally von Humpeding in *Thud!*, Otto Chriek in *The Truth* and other books, Maladict/Maladicta in *Monstrous Regiment*) who have taken the pledge to avoid the usual diet of vampires, to wannabes (Doreen Winkings—Countess Notfaroutoe in *The Reaper Man* and *Thud!*—who isn't really a vampire, but acts as if she is).

In *Carpe Jugulum*, the name Magpyr is an allusion to the Magyars—Hungarians in western Transylvania in the nineteenth century. Vlad is an allusion to Vlad Tepes also known as Vlad the Impaler, the fifteenth-century ruler of Walachia known for impaling prisoners. Of course, you knew that. Stoker used Tepes as a model of sorts for Count Dracula. Not content to stop at that reference, Pratchett references a character known as Griminir the Impaler, a female vampire who merely bit people but did not suck their blood.

The name Notfaroutoe is an allusion to the movie adaptations of *Dracula*, namely the 1922 silent movie *Nosferatu*, directed by F. W. Murnau and its 1979 remake *Nosferatu the Vampyre* by Werner Herzog.

"That's Fronck-en-shteen" Mary Shelley's creation came "to life" in 1818 and spawned Frankenstein movies as well as the Igor tradition in Discworld. Although there is no character named "Igor" in Shelley's book, an Igor appears in many of the films based on the book (like Mel Brooks's classic, *Young Frankenstein*, starring Gene Wilder where Igor—or rather, Eye-gore—is played by Marty Feldman).

While visiting Lord Byron in 1816, Shelley (then Mary Wollstonecraft Godwin), John William Polidori (the physician of Lord Byron), and Shelley's then husband-to-be, poet Percy Bysshe Shelley, were encouraged by Byron to each write a scary story. Shelley wrote *Frankenstein*. Polidori wrote "The Vampyre." And thus history was made.

Jeremy Clockson plays a sort of Victor Frankenstein–like creator in *Thief of Time*. Instead of using lightning to bring life to a creature amassed out of corpses' body parts, he uses it to bring the ultimate clock to life. It's apt that he's assigned an Igor (yes, there's more than one) to help him, since Igors usually work for vampires, mad scientists, and other criminally insane individuals.

Throughout Discworld, the Igors carry on the Victor Franken-stein tradition by operating on themselves and others as well as recy-cling spare body parts. Just doing their bit to help the environment.

Ringing in the New. Moving along on this architectural tour, we come to one of the pillars of fantasy fiction. J. R. R. Tolkien is widely considered the father of twentieth-century fantasy. Prat-chett read Tolkien's trilogy during his childhood, and describing how he felt when he first read the trilogy, Pratchett remarked in an essay, "I can remember the vision of beech woods in the Shire . . . I remember the light as green, coming through trees. I have never since then so truly had the experience of being inside the story."[15]

Maybe that's why several allusions to Tolkien's works became part of the Discworld makeup. In *Equal Rites*, Gandalf's single state gets a shout-out in the second paragraph of the first chapter. In *Lords and Ladies*, witches are referred to as having minds "like metal"[16]— reminiscent of Treebeard's description of Saruman in *The Two Tow-ers*: "He has a mind of metal and wheels."[17] A scene in *Witches Abroad* provides an allusion to aspects of *The Fellowship of the Ring* and *The Hobbit*. Perhaps you caught it. While on their way to Genua by boat, Granny Weatherwax, Nanny Ogg, and Magrat Garlick spy with their little eyes a "small gray creature, vaguely froglike" on a log, who is whispering of his "birthday."[18] As you know, in *The Hob-*

---

[15] From "Cult Classic" by Terry Pratchett, one of the essays in *Meditations on Middle-Earth*, edited by Karen Haber (New York: St. Martin's Press, 2001), 78. Worth a read.

[16] *Lords and Ladies* (New York: HarperTorch, 1992), 6.

[17] *The Two Towers* by J. R. R. Tolkien (Boston: Houghton Mifflin, 1954, 1965, 1966), 462.

[18] *Witches Abroad* (New York: HarperTorch, 1991), 66.

bit Gollum referred to the ring as his birthday present. And in *Fellowship*, Frodo, Sam, and Aragorn noticed that Gollum used a log to follow them while they traveled on the river Anduin. And of course, the *draco nobilis* in *Guards! Guards!* sitting on a hoard of gold brings to mind Smaug from *The Hobbit*.

In *Wintersmith*, during the Underworld journey, Roland recalls his time as the prisoner of the queen of the elves, an event that takes place in *The Wee Free Men*: "I could hardly remember anything after a while. Not my name, not the feel of the sunshine, not the taste of real food."[19] His words are an allusion to Frodo's words in *Return of the King* in response to Sam's question concerning the rabbits Frodo and Sam ate in Ithilien, earlier in their journey (*The Two Towers*): "I know that such things happened, but I cannot see them. No taste of food, no feel of water, no sound of wind, no memory of tree or grass or flower, no image of moon or star are left to me."[20]

A-Head of His Time. If you saw *Sleepy Hollow*, the 1999 movie starring Johnny Depp (directed by Tim Burton), you're undoubtedly familiar with "The Legend of Sleepy Hollow," the short story written by American author Washington Irving, published in 1820. The story is a staple in many elementary school curricula, especially around Halloween. The setting is Sleepy Hollow, an area near Tarrytown, New York, a place of "haunted spots, and twilight superstitions"[21]—the home of the legendary Headless Horseman, the so-called ghost of a Hessian soldier killed during the Revolutionary War, who frightened the ill-fated schoolmaster, Ichabod Crane. His fright, however, was due to the shenanigans of Brom

---

[19] *Wintersmith*, 297.

[20] *The Fellowship of the Ring* by J. R. R. Tolkien (New York: Ballantine Books, 1955, 1965), 238.

[21] From "The Legend of Sleepy Hollow" by Washington Irving. Originally published in *The Sketch Book of Geoffrey Crayon, Gent.* Posted at http://www.bartleby.com/310/2/2.html. Check it out.

(Bones) Van Brunt—his rival for the affections of Katrina Van Tassel.

A headless horseman makes an appearance in *The Wee Free Men* and thus provides another building block for Discworld. Too bad Ichabod Crane didn't have the Nac Mac Feegles (see chapter 10) on his side. They prove to be a huge help to Tiffany Aching who encounters the headless horseman.

"Phantastic" Voyage. George MacDonald is another author who helped inspire a cornice or two in Discworld. If you read his novel *Phantastes*, you read of Anodos, a man who wakes up to discover himself in Fairy Land. As with many "Otherworld" trips, there is delight mixed with horror.

Pratchett's Fairyland, a place you travel through in *The Wee Free Men*, is a ramped-up Neverland, where everything tries to harm you instead of just one jealous pixie like Tinker Bell. Traveling through it is like taking a trip through an evil version of Wonderland or the everyday version of the Matrix (i.e., evil) where Agent Smiths abound. But there is wonder as well, however, with talking daisies (reminiscent of the talking flowers of *Alice's Adventures in Wonderland*). However, creatures like the dromes, grimhounds, and bumblebee women take the joy out of the journey.

An Oz Encore. Perhaps you think of Oz only in terms of the prison drama on HBO from 1997–2003. Another building block of Discworld comes from L. Frank Baum's classic children's series of that name. Some aspects of the 1939 movie based on Baum's first book (*The Wizard of Oz*) are alluded to in *Witches Abroad*. The witches fly on broomsticks, a reminder of an image Dorothy saw during the tornado: the evil Miss Gulch turning into a wicked witch flying on a broomstick. Later, when a farmhouse falls on Nanny Ogg and a "dwarf " asks for Nanny Ogg's red boots but doesn't know why he asks for them, you can't help thinking of the scene in the Munchkins'

Country (or Munchkinland as the movie refers to it) where Dorothy's farmhouse fell on the Wicked Witch of the East and Dorothy gained the ruby slippers (silver in the book). It's only fitting that the fate of one witch befall another (one decidedly nicer, however).

When Granny Weatherwax and Magrat argue (an inevitability when they get together), each deciding that a person needs more brain or more heart (page 165 of the paperback edition of *Witches Abroad*), you can't help thinking of what the Scarecrow and Tin Man each thought he needed.

During the argument, Nanny notices that the road to Genua is paved with yellow bricks—an allusion to the yellow brick road leading to the Emerald City of Oz. Genua even sparkles like the Emerald City.

Still another nod to *The Wizard of Oz* comes in *Moving Pictures*, where an actor describes the plot of the click—or movie—he's working on as "going to see a wizard. Something about following a yellow sick toad."[22]

But an oblique reference to *The Wizard of Oz* (possibly) can be found in *Pyramids*, when the Sphinx tells young Teppic, "Thou art in the presence of the wise and the terrible." The fake wizard of Oz described himself as "Oz, the Great and Terrible."[23]

∽

Even with such building blocks, Pratchett still needs the best patching materials—his imagination, skill, and humor—to ensure that the three purposes of good architecture are fulfilled.

That concludes this leg of the tour. Please notice the tip jar on your way out.

---

[22] *Moving Pictures* (New York: HarperTorch, 1990), 156.
[23] *Pyramids* (New York: HarperTorch, 2001), 264–65. See also L. Frank Baum, *The Wonderful Wizard of Oz* (New York: HarperTrophy, 1987 [afterword]; originally published in 1899), 154.

Fully Realized Worlds

Discworld works because it takes itself seriously. The people in Ankh-Morpork don't think they're being funny.

—Terry Pratchett at an October 12, 2006, book signing (Anderson Bookshop, Naperville, Illinois)

Some fantasy worlds can seem as real as your backyard—almost like you could step into it the moment you open the book. Worlds like . . .

The Star Wars Galaxy (various planets "a long time ago, in a galaxy far, far away")

The incredibly popular film series created by George Lucas chronicled the rise of the Galactic Empire and spawned many series of books written by authors as disparate as Terry Brooks, Jude Watson, Elizabeth Hand, Troy Denning, Kathy Tyres, R. A. Salvatore, Michael Stackpole, and many more.

Lucas came up with the mythology of the various planets (Tatooine, Naboo, Alderaan, Dagobah, and others), cultures, and characters like Luke Skywalker, Anakin Skywalker, Yoda, Han Solo, C3PO, and so on, and revolutionized the movie industry as well as science fiction in general.

Middle-earth

In his quest to develop a mythology for England, Tolkien created a mythical place that seems like an actual place in history. The moment you walk into Bilbo Baggins's hobbit hole in the Shire and trek through the region of Eriador all the way through Mordor, you get a sense of being in a believable world. (And after the movies, beautifully realized by Peter Jackson and hundreds of craftspeople, Middle-earth seems even more real.)

Like Pratchett, Tolkien was inspired by Norse mythology. Middle-earth is Midgard—the home of men in Norse mythology.

Pern

Anne McCaffrey has multiple series that take place on Pern, a planet in the Rukbat System. This planet's Earth-like environment came at a price for settlers, thanks to the threat of Threadfall—the silver spores deposited by an orbiting planet, Red Star. Because the Thread attacked all organic matter, the technologically advanced society returned to a medieval state. Only dragonfire could stop the Thread.

Kahrain, Araby, and Cathay were just a few of the provinces established in the first landing. The society became divided among the weyrs (the homes of the dragons and their riders), the holds (lord-ruled lands), and the halls (those of craftspeople). The series continues under the pen of McCaffrey's son, Todd.

Arrakis/Dune

Frank Herbert's award-winning epic series (now known as "classic Dune") of political intrigue in space took place on the desert planet Arrakis, a fiefdom run by the House Atreides. Arrakis, populated by Fremen and sandworms, was the place for melange, a spice valued throughout the universe. The Fremen searched for their Messiah—Muad'Dib—while House Atreides and House Harkonnen battled each other for control of Arrakis.

The series began in 1965 and after Herbert's death was continued by his son, Brian, and Kevin Anderson.

Earthsea

Ursula LeGuin's archipelago of islands (Gont, Roke, Karego-At, Atuan, Havnor, etc.) is the setting where magic and mayhem abound. In *A Wizard of Earthsea* to *The Other Wind* and books of Earthsea short stories, LeGuin showed the history of Earthsea from the Creation of Eá through Ged's birth and rise from wizard to archmage to Tenar's adoption of Therru/Tehanu the dragon/child, who reached adulthood.

With Ged's wandering tendencies, readers tour the islands from Roke to the farthest shore where dragons fly and the dead walk. In this series, prepare to see dragons, creatures of the Old Powers, and plenty of feats of magic.

The Hyborian Age of Conan

Robert E. Howard's creation, Conan the Barbarian, a.k.a. Conan the Cimmerian, lives on thanks to such writers as L. Sprague de Camp, Lin Carter, Robert Jordan, and Dale Rippke.

Conan lived in the Hyborian Age, supposedly after Atlantis sank but before other civilizations sprang into being. Kingdoms like Nemedia, Ophir, Zamora, Brythunia, Hyperborea, and Aquilonia sprawled across this mythical form of Earth. Hyperborea, from Greek mythology, was the original happiest kingdom on earth (way before Disney World)—a vacation spot for Apollo. Some believed that Hyperborea was Great Britain.

Having been a warrior, a thief, a mercenary, and a pirate, Conan later became king of Aquilonia—the most powerful kingdom. Not your average hero. When you read the exploits of Cohen the Barbarian in *Interesting Times* and *The Last Hero*, you can't help but see the parody.

The books spawned two Conan movies, starring Arnold Schwarzenegger, one in 1982 and the other in 1984.

Hogwarts and the London of Harry Potter

J. K. Rowling, the only author who outsells Terry Pratchett in Britain and possibly every other author in the world, created an instantly memorable character in Harry Potter and the other students and faculty of Hogwarts School of Witchcraft and Wizardry. Although the stories take place in modern-day England, Rowling's world of wizards and witches is almost an alternate universe, where Muggles are not allowed.

The movies bring to life the Hogwarts of our imaginations with its gloomy edifice surrounded by rolling hills and eerie forest. Inside the castle, the ghosts, moving stairways, dark passages, and "live" pictures are all there—as is the incredible danger Harry and his friends face.

Star Trek's Worlds

The old television series, created by Gene Roddenberry in 1966, spawned other series and well over one hundred books. In the twenty-third century after a third world war, Captain James T. Kirk and his intrepid crew traveled from planet to planet "boldly going where no man has gone before." The governing body for humans and aliens was the United Federation of Planets. (Kind of reminds you of the Republic, doesn't it?)

The first series was written by James Blish until his death. But many, many writers, including Margaret Armen, Larry Niven, Gordon Eklund, Walter Koenig, Michael Jan Friedman, and Diane Duane, contributed to the series. Then came other TV series and books: *Star Trek: The Next Generation*; *Star Trek: Deep Space Nine*; *Star Trek: Voyager*; and *Star Trek: Enterprise*.

Midkemia/Kelewan

Raymond Feist's Riftwar Saga covered the wars with the Tsurani, an alien race of beings from Kelewan. Pug, one of the main characters of the series, lived on Midkemia, a planet with three continents established by feudal societies, where dukes and princes lived peacefully or at war with elves, dark elves (moredhel), and dwarves. As with many fantasy lands, magic abounded. Oh, and there were dragons and dragonlords, too.

The Tsurani society had a Far East flavor while the Midkemians went the medieval Europe route. Other series followed such characters as Arutha and Pug beyond the Riftwar drama.

The World of the Wheel of Time

Robert Jordan's massive Wheel of Time series might seem like *The Lord of the Rings* upon first glance with its Emond's Field, the Shire-like village from which Rand al'Thor and his friends (Mat, Egwene, Perrin) hailed. After all, we know we're in the midst of a society like something out of a Renaissance fair. The world opened much wider as Rand traveled with his friends and the Aes Sedai—a female channeler or mage—and later went their separate ways (a breaking of the fellowship). With its Westlands, city states (Tar Valon), blighted areas, and seas, you feel as if you live there.

2

Terry Pratchett: Man of Mystery

A CONVERSATION IN THREE ACTS

Act I, Scene I: In Which the Players Are Discussed

Setting: Your home or wherever you happen to be now.

Us: Take a street-smart detective/cop/medieval monk/nosy British aristocrat/bounty hunter/little old lady well versed in psychology and an impossible case, and what do you have? A definitive work of mystery fiction by the likes of Terry Pratchett, P. D. James, Ed McBain, J. A. Jance, Lawrence Block, Janet Evanovich, Sue Grafton, Agatha Christie, Lilian Jackson Braun, Arthur Conan Doyle, Raymond Chandler, Dashiell Hammett, Wilkie Collins, Edgar Allan Poe, Ellis Peters, Dorothy Sayers, Sara Paretsky, Ross Macdonald, Ruth Rendell, Patricia Cornwell, Robert Parker, Ngaio Marsh, Ken Follett, Tony Hillerman, Margery Allingham, Georges Simenon, Donald Bain/Jessica Fletcher, and many others.

You: Terry *Pratchett? Discworld* Terry Pratchett?

Us: Glad you asked.

You: I really didn't. I'm just reading this.

Us: Since you asked, consider the mysteries solved by Commander Samuel Vimes and other members of the Watch.

Every great work of mystery fiction needs at least two ingredients: (1) an intriguing mystery, many times involving a formidable adversary, and (2) someone to solve it. In a mystery subgenre such as police procedurals, a team of experts are put to the test. But many whodunit mysteries rest on the personality of the leading detective—amateur or professional.

The City Watch miniseries has many of the elements of mystery subgenres (classic whodunits, private-eye novels, cozies, police procedurals, suspense, thrillers) and defies them all.[1] For that reason, we'd dub Pratchett's main detective—Sam Vimes—the "Hardest-Working Crime Solver" in mystery fiction. Wondering why?

You: Not really, no. But I'm sure you'll tell me.

Us: We will in the next scene. We have a lot of lines in that one.

DISC-CLAIMER:
Plot spoilers ahead. Read at your own risk.

Act I, Scene II: In Which Mystery Subgenres Are Discussed

Us: First, some handy definitions of mystery subgenres:

---

[1] The legal mystery is another subgenre. But since none of Pratchett's City Watch stories take place in a courtroom setting, we left that subgenre off the list. However, we're sure Pratchett would put his own spin on that one as well.

Whodunits

Who took the countess's priceless diamond bracelet? Who killed the blackmailer? With mysteries like these, the main question, naturally, is "Whodunit?" The whodunit subgenre is the largest of the mystery subgenres. In books of this ilk, "great ingenuity may be exercised in narrating the events of the crime, usually a homicide, and of the subsequent investigation in such a manner as to conceal the identity of the criminal from the reader until the end of the book, when the method and culprit are revealed."[2] This group includes "cozies" (see page 32), "locked room" mysteries, and "aristocop"[3] mysteries. (For more on "aristocop" mysteries, see "The Titled Crime Solvers: It's in the [Blue] Blood," page 41.)

With classic whodunits such as *The Woman in White* and *The Moonstone* by Wilkie Collins, "The Murders in the Rue Morgue" by Edgar Allan Poe (considered the first published detective story), or *Bleak House* by Charles Dickens, you might think of the well-crafted plots faster than the characters' names.

You: *Bleak House* is on DVD. Let's see, there's Esther Summerson, Lady Dedlock, Mr. Tulkinghorn, and there's . . .

Us (*interrupting*)**:** The Sherlock Holmes novels, on the other hand, are classic whodunit detective novels. You might read them *because* of Sherlock Holmes, rather than the plot specifically. (For more about that, don't miss "Vimes versus Holmes: The Smackdown" in Act II, Scene I.)

You: My favorite Sherlock Holmes novel is—

Us: Let's move on to private-eye novels. These are nonpolice detective novels. The characters are realistic rather than eccentric. These mysteries are populated by "old school" characters like Sam Spade, Philip Marlowe, Nick and Nora Charles, Lew Archer, or the

---

[2] Definition from http://en.wikipedia.org/wiki/Detective_fiction—Wikipedia, the free encyclopedia. (Not *The Wee Free Men Encyclopedia*. If you come across one, let us know.)

[3] Title used at http://www.mysteryguide.com/classic-whodunit.html. (Please note: Although the site was in operation during the writing of this book, it was missing in action later on.)

Continental Op and "the next generation": V. I. Warshawski, Matthew Scudder, Kinsey Millhone, Stephanie Plum, or the erudite Spenser (no revealed first name). (If you're confused about which author wrote which character, see the end of the chapter for a list.)

This is where personality counts. Many private eyes in fiction have similar traits. They're tough (they have to be, to solve the grisly crimes in their beat), jaded, hard drinkers (or at least alcoholics on the mend), and have enough determination to stay with a case even after someone tries to run them over or push them out of a window. Most are good at what they do, or at least keep at a job until the truth is revealed.

Cozies. According to an article written by mystery writer Stephen P. Rodgers,[4] a cozy mystery is "a mystery which includes a bloodless crime and contains very little violence, sex, or coarse language. By the end of the story, the criminal is punished and order is restored to the community."

With cozy mysteries, you might think of such characters as Hercule Poirot, Jane Marple, Lord Peter Wimsey, Jessica Fletcher, Jim Qwilleran/ Koko/Yum Yum. (You can't get much cozier than two cats.) Rather than ranked as strictly amateur sleuths, characters like Hercule Poirot and Lord Peter Wimsey are considered criminologists and are regularly consulted by the police. (And Poirot *is* a former cop.)

Police procedurals. According to a definition posted at the Mystery Guide site, "police procedurals must be realistic depictions of official investigations. They emphasize teamwork, methodical pavement-pounding, lucky breaks, administrative hassles, and endless paperwork."[5]

---

[4] Posted at http://www.writing-world.com/mystery/cozy.shtml.
[5] Posted at http://www.mysteryguide.com/police-procedural.html. Obviously, we like this site.

If you're a fan of such shows as *Prime Suspect, CSI,* or *Law and Order* (with all of its spin-offs)—

You: What has this got to do with Terry Pratchett?

Us (*as if you hadn't spoken*):—you probably like your mysteries by the book, according to realistic police procedures. This is the form popularized in America by the late Ed McBain, Patricia Cornwell, Tony Hillerman, J. A. Jance, Joseph Wambaugh, and many others. But looking at the European police scene, you'll find such characters as Roderick Alleyn, Adam Dalgliesh, Endeavour Morse, the world-weary Jules Maigret, Reginald Wexford, and the forensics experts Brother Cadfael or Kay Scarpetta. These crime solvers walk a grisly beat.

Suspense. Sometimes suspense and thrillers are lumped together. In suspense stories, the focus is on whether the villain will be caught before he or she strikes again. These are the edge-of-your-seat mysteries, many of which involve females as lead characters— the kind who can't help investigating even when the body count climbs. When you think of suspense, you might think of writers like Mary Higgins Clark (*Moonlight Becomes You*), Nancy Atherton (*Aunt Dimity Goes West*), or Anne Perry (*The Cater Street Hangman*). We would add Terry Pratchett to that list, even though Vimes has never shown his feminine side.

You: I see. I would've preferred a chart, though. Visual aids rule, you know.

Us: Moving on to the *thriller,* the focus is on fast-paced action where chase scenes and technology abound. The villains may be megalomaniacs bent on taking over the world or simply average joes gone postal. With thrillers, the main element is time. The clock is ticking to catch that kidnapper before the victim is killed or the bomb explodes. Writers like Tom Clancy, Ken Follett, and Elmore Leonard are well known in this subgenre.

Act I, Scene III: The Plot Thickens

Whodunits

Us: The Pratchett novels *Men at Arms* and *Feet of Clay* can be described as "who-or-what-dunits," thanks to the fact that you never know what species (dragon, dwarf, werewolf, vampire, golem, troll, etc.) might have done the crime. Even so, both novels have the same "whodunit" elements as do classic works by Wilkie Collins, Charles Dickens, and Edgar Allan Poe. See for yourself as we compare *Feet of Clay* to Collins and Dickens's novels.

You (*happily*): A chart! (*See charts on pages 36 and 37.*)

Us: *The Fifth Elephant* also has a locked-room mystery element as Vimes investigates the theft of the famed Scone of Stone from a locked museum and a mysterious death that took place in a locked area.

Act II, Scene I: Enter . . . the Detective

Vimes versus Holmes: The Smackdown

Us: Sherlock Holmes is unquestionably the most famous detective in fiction.

You: No question about that.

Us: But Holmes is the kind of clue-analyzing detective who rubs a clue-hating cop like Vimes the wrong way. A discussion of methods might result in a *Smackdown* battle of Vimes and Holmes. We can't help but wonder who would win in a battle of the minds. Maybe it would go like this.

You: Will Holmes and Vimes enter from stage left or stage right?

Us (*brightly, because we always agree with you*): Uh, thanks for sharing that. Take it away, Holmes and Vimes.

Holmes: "How often have I said . . . that when you have eliminated

	FEET OF CLAY	**"THE MURDERS IN THE RUE MORGUE"**
Setting?	Various places in Ankh-Morpork	A locked apartment in Paris
Is the mystery the heart of the story or just an element of the story?	The heart of it	The heart of it
What is the problem(s) to be solved?	Who poisoned Vetinari? Who killed Father Tubelcek and Mr. Hopkinson?	Who murdered two women in the Rue Morgue?
Who tries to solve the mystery(ies)?	The Watch, led by Vimes	An amateur sleuth, C. Augustine Dupin
Who are the prime suspects?	Vimes for poisoning Vetinari, Dorfl (a golem) for murder	Adolphe Le Bon
So, whodunit?	If you want a hint, read chapter 15.	We'll never tell. Read the book!

THE MOONSTONE	BLEAK HOUSE	THE WOMAN IN WHITE
Country house in Yorkshire	London	London; a country house (Limmeridge) in Cumberland
The heart of it	A large part of it	The heart of it
Who stole Rachel Verinder's legendary diamond, the Moonstone?	Who is Lady Dedlock's daughter? Who is Nemo and what is his connection to Lady Dedlock? (Hint: He's not the clown fish of the movie.) Who shot Tulkinghorn?	Who is the woman in white? Are the accusations against Sir Percival Glyde true? What is Count Fosco up to?
Sergeant Cuff, whose reputation is well known, but who is underestimated	Mr. Bucket, a "detective officer,"[6] and a scheming lawyer, Mr. Tulkinghorn	Walter Hartright, Marion Halcombe
Rosanna Spearman (housemaid)	Lady Dedlock	Sir Percival
We'll never tell. Read the book!	We'll never tell. Read the book!	We'll never tell. Read the book!

---

[6] *Bleak House* by Charles Dickens (New York: Bantam Books edition, 1983. Originally published in 1852–53), 285. We first read this in college. Not that you had to know that.

the impossible, whatever remains, *however improbable*, must be the truth?"[7]

Vimes: "The real world was far too *real* to leave neat little hints. It was full of too many things. It wasn't by eliminating the impossible that you got at the truth, however improbable; it was by the much harder process of eliminating the possibilities."[8]

Holmes: "I have a lot of special knowledge which I apply to the problem, and which facilitates matters wonderfully. Those rules of deduction . . . are invaluable to me in practical work. Observation with me is second nature."[9]

Vimes: "Every real copper knew you didn't go around looking for Clues so that you could find out Who Done It. No, you started out with a pretty good idea of Who Done It. That way, you knew what Clues to look for."[10]

Holmes: "There is no branch of detective science which is so important and so much neglected as the art of tracing footsteps."[11]

Vimes: "I never believed in that stuff—footprints in the flower bed, tell-tale buttons, stuff like that. People think that stuff's policing. It's not. Policing's luck and slog, most of the time."[12]

Pratchett and the Private Eye

Us: Although Vimes isn't a private investigator, he's asked to turn in his badge a number of times during the course of the series, which forces him to act like one. (See *Jingo* and *Guards! Guards!*) So, how does he fit in the hard-edged world populated by the likes of Kinsey Millhone, Philip Marlowe, and Sam Spade?

---

[7] From *A Study in Scarlet and the Sign of Four* by Arthur Conan Doyle (New York: Berkley Books edition, 1975), 173.

[8] From Vimes's musings in the narration of *Feet of Clay* (New York: HarperTorch, 1996), 174.

[9] *Scarlet*, 24.

[10] From Vimes's musings in the narration of *Feet*, 234.

[11] *Scarlet*, 127–28.

[12] *Men at Arms* (New York: HarperTorch, 1993), 344.

	VIMES	MILLHONE	MARLOWE	SPADE
Carries a weapon?	You betcha. A crossbow comes in handy in the mean streets of Ankh-Morpork.	When necessary	Check	Has his own and will even grab some-one else's
Nearly killed during the course of an investigation?	Usually	Usually	Usually	Usually
Has a cast-iron stomach?	Living in Ankh-Morpork, anyone would.	Yes. Anyone who eats peanut butter and pickle sandwiches must have.	Yep. Comes with the territory	Ditto
Smokes?	Cigars	No . . . well, smoked cigarettes and "spice cigarettes" in high school.	Cigarettes	Ditto
Drinks?	Like a fish at first, but is on the wagon	No more than anyone else who investigates crime for a living	Like a fish	Like a fish

(continued)

Table (continued)

	VIMES	MILLHONE	MARLOWE	SPADE
Keeps a bottle handy (like, in a desk drawer)?	Always (now as a test)	Keeps one in a fridge	Keeps one in a desk drawer	Keeps one in a desk drawer
Well dressed or a slob?	A slob unless Lady Sybil has something to say about it	Does okay for herself, having the one dress and all	"I was everything the well-dressed private detective ought to be."[13]	Does okay for himself
Street-smart or book-smart?	Street-smart	Both	Street-smart	Street-smart
Crossed in love?	Supposedly (or so the rumor in *Guards! Guards!* goes)	Often	Often	Often
Regularly annoys those in authority (civic leaders, cops, etc.)?	Of course	Of course	Of course	Of course

---

[13] *The Big Sleep* by Raymond Chandler in *The Raymond Chandler Omnibus* (New York: Alfred A. Knopf, Inc., 1939), 4.

You: Uh, you'll use another chart, perhaps?

Us: Good idea! (*See chart on page 39–40.*)

Us: Vimes may be hard-boiled like this lot, but he's also slightly cracked, thanks to living in Pratchett's world. Like Marlowe, he can be insubordinate, even though he can never one-up Vetinari, Ankh-Morpork's Patrician. Like Sam Spade, Sam Vimes is quick with an elbow when it comes to a fight. And, like Sam Spade, he fights dirty.

Like all classic fiction private eyes, Vimes works cheap—more than Carrot's $43 per month, plus allowances (the *Last Hero* rate). (Marlowe earns $25 dollars a day, plus expenses, and Archer gets $50 a day, plus expenses.)

Murder with a Cozy Feel

Us: Although many of Pratchett's mysteries take place within the teeming sprawl of Ankh-Morpork, some have a cozy element. So, while Pratchett might mention that a man has been beaten to death with a loaf of dwarf bread (and that's easy to believe if you know about the consistency of dwarf and other battle breads), you won't actually see the crime take place or see any (at least *much*) blood.

You: You mean like in *Saw IV*?

Us (*as if you hadn't spoken*)**:** While Fletcher and Marple have the edge on coziness, Vimes at least is a contender.

The Titled Crime Solvers: It's in the (Blue) Blood

Us: During a period known as the "Golden Age" of mysteries in Great Britain (between World War I and World War II), such writers as Agatha Christie, Ngaio Marsh, Margery Allingham, and Dorothy Sayers wrote their novels. They were the "queens" of English detective mysteries, the creators of the upper-class detectives Roderick Alleyn (Marsh), Albert Campion (Allingham), and Peter Wimsey (Sayers).

	VIMES	POIROT	MARPLE	FLETCHER
Crimes take place in a cozy setting?	If a dark Dwarf Bread Museum or an embassy in Uberwald counts, then yes!	Always (cozy seaside, cozy manor)	Always (St. Mary Mead, etc.). She's the ultimate in coziness.	Cabot Cove wrote the book on coziness.
Brags about his/her ability to solve cases?	Never	Always	Never	Never
Uses coarse language or is around those who do?	Yes, and sometimes encourages it	No. He's a gentleman.	What? Never! But she sometimes overhears things . . .	Not one to indulge
Has a lovable sidekick?	Errol the dragon (briefly), Nobby, Colon, Cheery, Detritus	Hastings	Her nephew	Anyone in Cabot Cove
Is a nosy old lady?	No	No	Yes!	Yes!

If they're the queens, Pratchett must be the joker.

You (*shifts uneasily at your current location on Earth*): No comment.

Us: Pratchett plunks his square-peg character into the round hole of this gentlemen's league of suave, well-dressed, and well-educated detectives—a description no one would dream of using for Vimes.

Here's how he measures up to the other members of the gentlemen's league.

Us: Vimes would be the first to admit that, unlike his esteemed

	VIMES	ALLEYN	WIMSEY	CAMPION
Cop or private investigator?	Cop (watchman, actually)	Cop	PI	PI
Rank or reputation in society?	Knight, Duke of Ankh-Morpork	Brother of a baronet (Sir George)	Brother of the Duke of Denver	Supposedly related to royalty
Title(s)	Commander Vimes; Sir Samuel; His Grace; His Excellency, the Duke of Ankh-Morpork	Mostly known as Chief Detective Inspector	Lord Peter	Mr. Campion. Since the name Campion is an adopted pseudonym (his real name is Rudolph), we can't really know for sure. He's a gentleman, though.

(continued)

Table (continued)

	VIMES	ALLEYN	WIMSEY	CAMPION
Married to . . . ?	Lady Sybil Ramkin, renowned raiser of swamp dragons and at the top of Ankh-Morpork society	Agatha Troy, renowned painter, who is equally at home in society	Harriet Vane, renowned writer and rebel	Lady Amanda Fitton, renowned aircraft engineer and society maven
An officer and a gentleman?	Officer only	Both	A gentleman who served during the war	A gentleman who served during the war
Keeps a manservant?	Well, there's a butler, Willikins, who came with Lady Sybil.	Vassily, a "Russian carry-over from a former case"[14]	Bunter, who butles exceptionally well (and takes great photos)	Magersfontein Lugg. He's coarse, but you can't help but love the big lug.
Clothes make the man?	No way. Prefers boots with holes to new boots	Adores a fedora; usually well dressed	Savvy about Savile Row tailors	Knows his way around evening wear
Can tell a lobster fork from a tuning fork?	Wouldn't care	Yes	Of course	Definitely

---

14 *Death in a White Tie* by Ngaio Marsh (New York: Jove, 1938), 314.

	VIMES	ALLEYN	WIMSEY	CAMPION
Plays nicely with others?	No; he even annoys the people under his command.	Yes. He's always polite, even to murder suspects.	Yes. Often construed as silly, but makes friends easily	Yes. Like Wimsey, he is considered silly, but isn't.
Has friends in high places?	No; he has friends in low places.	Always travels in the right circles	Has friends in high and low places	Has friends in high and low places
A user of fisticuffs or words?	Fists mainly; words occasionally	Words mostly. Won't shy away from a fight, though	Both	Both

colleagues, he's no gentleman, nor the son of a gentleman. Thrust into society, thanks to his marriage to Lady Sybil and promotions for services rendered, Vimes is the thorn in everyone's side. Vimes's problem is that he can't stop annoying the upper crust—Lords Selachii, Rust, and others, many of whom happen to be the assassins hired to kill him or Vetinari. If he encountered Alleyn, Wimsey, or Campion, Vimes might be tempted to stick him with a lobster fork rather than pass him one.

Police Procedurals: Murder by the Book

Us: With ex-magistrate/employees of the British Home Office (P. D. James), you would expect accurate details about police procedures. But what of Pratchett?

	VIMES	MORSE
Rank in the force?	Constable to Captain to Commander (promotions during the course of the series)	Detective Chief Inspector
Officers under his command?	Carrot, Nobby, Colon, Cheery, Angua, etc.	Detective Sergeant Lewis
Beat?	Ankh-Morpork or wherever he happens to travel (like Bonk)	Oxford
Reports to	Vetinari	The Chief Superintendent
Manner?	Taciturn; the nickname "Old Stoneface" is apt; yet he's compassionate.	Taciturn
Usually right or wrong?	Usually wrong, but comes right in the end	Usually wrong, but comes right in the end
Favorite crime-solving method?	Walking the streets of Ankh-Morpork	Drinking beer with Lewis or suspects

DALGLIESH	WEXFORD	ALLEYN	MAIGRET
Chief Superintendent to Commander (promotions during the course of the series)	Chief Detective Inspector	Chief Detective Inspector	Chief-Inspector to Superintendent Commissaire
Massingham, Miskin, Tarrant, and others	Inspector Burden (whose name is apt)	Inspector Fox, Bailey, etc.	Lucas, Janvier, Lapointe
London (or wherever he happens to travel)	Kingsmarkham	London (or wherever he happens to travel)	Paris
Politicians—whoever hands him the "sensitive case"	Chief Superintendent	The Superintendent	The Director
Calm, unhurried	Taciturn	Well mannered	Patient, compassionate, weary
Usually right	Usually right	Usually right	Usually persistent until he gets it right
Asking the right questions, like "Why did you lie to me?"	Yelling at someone (e.g., Burden)	Talking with Troy or Fox	Smoking his pipe; using his intuition

(continued)

Table (continued)

	VIMES	**MORSE**
Relationship to those in authority	Tenuous; claims to hate Vetinari, yet saves his life time and again	Has enemies

You: Yeah, what of him?

Us: Thanks to his journalism background, you get the feel of the mean streets, even if they're fictional. Here's how Pratchett's copper compares to the others. (Go back to page 46 and read the table . . . until you're back here.)

Harrowing Horror and Subtle Suspense

Us: Every good suspense story needs a page-turning plot to keep you on the edge of your seat. Although he does not churn out suspense novels in the purest sense of the genre, Pratchett ratchets up the suspense quotient in most of the books about the Watch. His books might aptly be called horror suspense *Buffy the Vampire Slayer/ Exorcist/Underworld* style. After all, Vimes has stared down dragons (*Guards! Guards!*), negotiated with golems (*Feet of Clay*), wrestled and escaped from murderous werewolves (*The Fifth Elephant*) and a venomous vampire (*Feet of Clay*), and been influenced by evil entities such as the Summoning Dark (*Thud!*) and the gonne, a whispering weapon invented by Leonard of Quirm (*Men at Arms*) which destroyed the life of assassin Edward d'Eath.

Vimes has fallen out of windows, down mineshafts and water-

DALGLIESH	WEXFORD	ALLEYN	MAIGRET
Maintains good connections	Okay	Annoys his superior, who is envious of his connections (e.g., his brother George who curries favors for him)	Annoyed by his superior

falls, and escaped by the skin of his teeth, all for the sake of keeping our pulse rates up and our lights burning far into the night as we follow his exploits and those of the officers under his command—the always unsettling Angua, the courageous Captain Carrot, and "dumb and dumber" Colon and Nobby.

You: They're more Laurel and Hardy–esque.

The Thrill of the Chase

Us: If you haven't read much of the Discworld series—

You: I've read most of them.

Us (*again as if you had not spoken*):—you might envision Ankh-Morpork's quaint cobblestone streets, clacks towers, and stagecoaches as a low-tech world far different from that of *The Hunt for Red October* and other Tom Clancy creations. But for a plot that combines technology Pratchett-style (which Vimes refers to as "technomancy"; for more about that, read chapter 19) and political shenanigans—the kind a writer like Clancy or Frederick Forsyth would discuss—look no further than *Jingo*. It has a *Day of the Jackal*-meets-*Hunt for Red October* element with a side order of *JFK* and *Lawrence of Arabia*. The technology kicks in with the introduction of various Burleigh and

Stronginthearm's weaponry (the Shureshotte Five and the ominous-sounding Streetsweeper) and Leonard of Quirm's Going-Under-the-Water-Safely-Device, a.k.a. the Boat, which is really a submarine.

The thrill and danger of the chase is the focus of *The Fifth Elephant*, when Vimes runs for his life from werewolves playing "the game," and of *Night Watch*, when Vimes chases Carcer, a psychopathic killer, through time.

Act II, Scene II: The U(nu)sual Suspects

"If the point of your story is 'whodunit,' the culprit needs to be worth the finding. Often the nature of the villain, and how absorbing a character he or she is, will affect the flavor of the whole rest of the story."[15]

You: Where'd that come from?

Us: You'll have to check the footnote. A good mystery needs a worthy adversary who makes the detective earn his or her pay. Sherlock Holmes has criminal genius Professor Moriarty (*The Final Problem*, *The Valley of Fear*), Jack Stapleton (*The Hound of the Baskervilles*), Irene Adler Norton ("A Scandal in Bohemia"), and others. Sam Spade and Philip Marlowe have various double-crossing clients. Poirot has a slew of murderers and thieves foolish or egotistical enough to match wits with him.

You: A *slew* of murderers? Is that a collective term like a muster of peacocks or a murder of ravens? A murder of murderers perhaps?

Us (*hastily*): But what of Vimes?

You: My cue to say, "Yeah, what of Vimes"?

Us: In a Pratchett-created world populated by werewolves, dragons, vampires, assassins, golems, dwarfs, and trolls, the sky's the limit for unusual suspects.

---

[15] "Vivid Villains" by Sandra Scoppettone in *Writing Mystery: A Handbook by the Mystery Writers of America* (Cincinnati: Writer's Digest Books, 1992), 66.

Pratchett is adept at juxtaposing unusual villains with the evils of the everyday. (For more on villains, see chapter 12.) Vimes's prime adversary is himself, followed a close second by the "politicians"—guild leaders and Vetinari, who is incredibly skilled at mind games. And then there's everyone and everything else: corrupt cops and a psychopath (*Night Watch*); dwarfs, werewolves, and vampires with political agendas (*The Fifth Elephant*); corrupt civil servants and a confused but dangerous dragon (*Guards! Guards!*); assassins with diabolical weapons (*Men at Arms*); a crazed golem and a vampire with an agenda (*Feet of Clay*); the corrupting evils of war and bureaucracy (*Jingo* and *Thud!*); and ancient supernatural evil (*Thud!*). Even a street-smart detective like Sam Spade or a cop like J. P. Beaumont would be hard-pressed to last in the minefield of Ankh-Morpork.

You: Not sure I agree with that. If they were born in Ankh-Morpork—

Us: Now let's move on to the end.

You: Finally! (*pauses*) You get it? Finally . . .

Act III: The Denouement—All's Well That Ends Well?

Us: Every good mystery needs a satisfactory ending.

You: That goes without saying. . . . Speaking of endings, I never finished what I started to say about Ankh-Morpork at the end of the last scene.

Us: In some mysteries, a dramatic showdown occurs between the villain and the hero/heroine. In others, the truth is revealed in a dramatic fashion by the detective. ("At eight o'clock precisely in the drawing room, I will reveal the murderer's identity.") In Pratchett's mysteries, you may find your views overturned as to who the villain really is. Is Dee, the ideas taster of the Low King, really all "he" says "he" is in *The Fifth Elephant*? Is a golem a tool or a person (*Feet of Clay*)? If it is a tool, can it commit murder?

You: I wouldn't mind having a golem to be my slave.

Us (*nod, but move on quickly*): Sometimes, although a mystery is solved, some things, like bureaucracy, still continue, to Vimes's chagrin.

Not content to bring their mystery story to a satisfactory conclusion, some writers attempt to end their creations, and thus begin a new chapter of their literary lives. Arthur Conan Doyle tried to end his famous character by sending him over the Reichenbach Falls with Moriarty. Simenon, too, tried to end the celebrated Maigret.

Pratchett thought he was done with Vimes after *Guards! Guards!* But the fans responded positively. Now Vimes is a favorite of Pratchett's, as he revealed at a book signing in Naperville, Illinois. He's a favorite with us, too, obviously.

That's our argument for why Vimes is the hardest-working detective in mystery fiction. Any questions?

You: I'm sure you'll think of some that I would have asked.

 # Mystery Scorecard

Confused about which mystery writer is responsible for which character? This handy list will help. For more on Vimes and the Watch, see chapter 16, "Why the Watch Works."

AUTHOR	DETECTIVE/CRIME SOLVER
Bain, Donald, and Jessica Fletcher	Jessica Fletcher
Block, Lawrence	Matthew Scudder
Braun, Lilian Jackson	Jim Qwilleran/Koko/Yum Yum

AUTHOR	DETECTIVE/CRIME SOLVER
Chandler, Raymond	Philip Marlowe
Christie, Agatha	Jane Marple, Hercule Poirot, Tommy and Tuppence Beresford
Cornwell, Patricia	Kay Scarpetta
Dexter, Colin	Endeavour Morse
Doyle, Arthur Conan	Sherlock Holmes
Evanovich, Janet	Stephanie Plum
Grafton, Sue	Kinsey Millhone
Hammett, Dashiell	Sam Spade, the Continental Op, Nick and Nora Charles
James, P. D.	Adam Dalgliesh
Jance, J. A.	J. P. (Beau) Beaumont
Marsh, Ngaio	Roderick Alleyn
Parker, Robert	Spenser
Peters, Ellis	Brother Cadfael
Pratchett, Terry	Sam Vimes
Rendell, Ruth	Reginald Wexford
Sayers, Dorothy	Lord Peter Wimsey
Simenon, Georges	Inspector Maigret

3

Lights, Camera, Chaos

Your Quest stands upon the edge of a knife.
Stray but a little and it will fail, to the ruin of all.
—Galadriel in *The Fellowship of the Ring* by J. R. R. Tolkien[1]

Each of our acts of observation will in some way disturb
the universe and we must accept full responsibility
for the consequences of these actions.
—F. David Peat, *From Certainty to Uncertainty*[2]

THE MAKINGS OF A DISASTER MOVIE

- The earth's inner core stops rotating. The eroding magnetic field will mean the deaths of billions. *Chaos?*
- Frog DNA used to complete the DNA strand causes uncontrolled breeding in dinosaurs, including vicious raptors. *Chaos?*
- An iceberg looms out of the darkness. A huge luxury liner strikes it. *Chaos?*

---

[1] *The Fellowship of the Ring* by J. R. R. Tolkien (New York: Ballantine Books, 1955, 1965), 422–23. Obviously, we like this book.
[2] F. David Peat, *From Certainty to Uncertainty: The Story of Science and Ideas in the Twentieth Century* (Washington, D.C.: Joseph Henry Press, 2002), 134. Science nicely done.

Many think of chaos as any of the above—a chain of events gone horribly wrong. In other words, the ingredients of a thriller/disaster movie such as *Core*, *Jurassic Park*/*The Lost World*, and *Titanic*. But chaos is many things. It's certainly the "I don't know what could happen if things keep going the way they're going" factor in a chain of events. It is a quest standing on the edge of a knife, as Galadriel said in *Fellowship*—one that could end in disaster if the quest fails. It's the slow unraveling of order—like a key thread pulled out of a sweater. (It's also anytime Carrie's cat, Sassie, gets angry with Carrie's border collie, Wilfred. But that's another story.)

Chaos as a theory in science evolved in the twentieth century. You know the buzzwords: fractals (patterns that repeat a particular design), time evolution, dynamical systems, nonlinear behavior, *the butterfly effect*. (Yes, that *was* the name of the Ashton Kutcher movie from 2004.) Chaos is often discussed in terms of entropy, the second law of thermodynamics ("The total entropy of any isolated thermodynamic system tends to increase over time, approaching a maximum value"[3]), since entropy is a way to measure the chaos or order of a system.

You can find loads of references to chaos throughout Discworld, which we'll get to shortly. But first, what *is* chaos? For an answer to that, we have to start at the beginning.

Roll credits. . . .

In the beginning, there was Chaos . . .

. . . according to the Greeks, particularly the Greek poet Hesiod. Chaos was a god who ruled over the shapeless, preuniverse mass. Some would say he personified this void. Supposedly out of Chaos came Nyx (Night). Nyx was the wife of Chaos; they had a son, Erebus (Darkness). But then Erebus decided that Nyx would make a good wife for *him*. (We would call that incest.) Their union produced two offspring: Ether (Sky), and Hemera (Day). Hesiod had lots to say

---

[3] Posted at http://en.wikipedia.org/wiki/Entropy.

about that in his *Theogony*. But Ovid, a Roman poet, believed that Chaos was matter without form (sort of like a movie with a weak storyline and tacky sets). In his narrative poem *Metamorphoses* (which reminds us of the title of that Kafka story usually read in high school—"The Metamorphosis"), we read, "A lifeless lump, unfashion'd, and unfram'd,/Of jarring seeds; and justly Chaos nam'd."[4]

But the theory of chaos evolved from a gleam in the eye of Henri Poincaré, a mathematician, physicist, and philosopher who hoped to solve the tricky two- or three-body problem in physics and astronomy. What's the three-body problem? We have to go to Newton's theories for that.

And then there was Newton . . .

As you learned in physics or earth science, British physicist/mathematician Sir Isaac Newton came up with three laws of motion:

I. Every object in a state of uniform motion remains in that state of motion unless an external force is applied to it.

II. The relationship between an object's mass m, its acceleration a, and the applied force F is $F = ma$.

III. For every action there is an equal and opposite reaction.[5]

According to Newton, this creates a sort of built-in regularity in the universe (tides, sun rising and setting, eclipses) like that of the mechanism of a clock. Pratchett alludes to this in *Thief of Time* as "the fabled 'tick of the universe.'"[6] But other scientists wondered about the effects of small irregularities in pull (also known as "perturbations"—disturbances in the pattern) when the moon goes around the Earth or the Earth orbits the sun. This is a three-body

---

[4] From Book the First of *Metamorphoses*, "The Creation of the World," posted at http://classics.mit.edu/Ovid/metam.1.first.html.

[5] Posted at http://www.spaceandmotion.com/Physics-Sir-Isaac-Newton.htm.

[6] *Thief of Time* (New York: HarperTorch, 2001), 19.

problem: "How do three or more bodies move under their mutual attractions of gravity?"[7]

Some astronomers came up with a theory known as the "perturbation theory," which meant shifting the calculation of an orbit to account for tiny irregularities. But even that created more irregularities. That was the problem Henri Poincaré tried to solve.

And then there was Poincaré, a bunch of mathematicians and scientists, Edward Lorenz, and such writers as Michael Crichton . . .

Along came Poincaré, toward the end of the nineteenth century, with the germ of chaos theory. He started with the issue of the buildup of tiny irregularities known as "resonance." When resonance upon resonance occurs, instability can occur—something you can't always predict. This is chaos.

Mathematicians later theorized that repetition in some cycles can cause repetitive changes in other cycles. This is known as "iteration"—using the output of one equation as input for the next. They were one step closer to the theory. But it needed computers to come to fruition. In 1963, Edward Lorenz, a meteorologist, used computers to experiment with iterations in weather prediction and came up with a chaos breakthrough that other mathematicians and scientists have since refined.

They discovered that tiny changes within a system can "perturb" the system—one dependent on a certain set of conditions—into wildly different behavior—the butterfly effect. This is why attempts by Evan (Ashton Kutcher's character in *The Butterfly Effect*) to make changes in his life in the past wildly affected his life in the future (the present). Famed author H. G. Wells discussed this aspect over a century before in *The Time Machine*.

The "attractor" is an active ingredient in this system. Attractors

---

[7] *From Certainty to Uncertainty*, 119.

are patterns within a system that push the system toward a certain point (kinda like some boyfriends we've had). In other words, they run a stable system. "Strange attractors" (also like some boyfriends we've had) are attractors within a chaotic system that take a system to a different place and show a kind of order. (Sort of like the well-mannered psychopath Hannibal Lecter in *Silence of the Lambs*.) You can thank Lorenz for the term "strange attractors" and for the butterfly effect, which came from the butterfly shape of his charted pattern of a strange attractor in weather. But the butterfly analogy is from ancient China.

Now some systems are "self-organized"—able to return to a semblance of order. Think of a city like Chicago or Paris. Order is maintained even through bouts of chaos (riots, traffic, wars). Attractors (police, laws) are at work there as well.

With a new theory in science like chaos floating around, book authors and Hollywood were bound to take notice. You've already seen the results if you saw *The Butterfly Effect* or any of the adaptations of *The Time Machine*. But before that, Michael Crichton's 1990 novel *Jurassic Park* (also a 1993 Steven Spielberg movie—yeah, ages ago) featured a chaos-theory-spouting mathematician, Ian Malcolm (played by Jeff Goldblum in the movie), who predicted the chaos of the dinosaur experiment. If you read the various iterations of the experiment in the book or saw the movie, you know dinosaurs ran amok, thus proving Malcolm's point.

But what about Pratchett? Drumroll, please . . .

And then there was Pratchett . . .

In many of his Discworld novels, Pratchett pushed the conflict to the point of chaos and beyond. Since his created universe is constantly destroyed and rebuilt anyway, as we're told in *Thief of Time*, chaos is constant.

In cracking the code on Discworld chaos, let's start with some allusions. You can find them in *Witches Abroad, Interesting Times, The*

Last Continent, and *Wintersmith*. At the beginning of *Witches Abroad*, we're in the world of chaos where the butterfly exists. In *Interesting Times*, we're told about "the butterfly of storms," "the fractal nature of the universe," "Freak Gales Cause Road Chaos," and the butterfly with "mandelbrot patterns" on its wings—Mandelbrot being a reference to Benoit Mandelbrot, a real-life mathematician and fractal geometry guru.[8] In *The Last Continent*, the wizards discuss how treading on an ant or making any changes in the last continent (Fourecks) could change their future existence (shades of *The Time Machine*). In *Wintersmith*, the Summer Lady talks of resonance—the fact that she looks like Tiffany and Tiffany acts like her. Tiffany's insertion of herself in the Morris dance causes this resonance. And the intrepid Commander Vimes in *Men at Arms* muses that wizards occasionally "took the canoe of reality too close to the white waters of chaos."[9]

Magic is a frequent contributor to chaos in Discworld. Unseen University, particularly the High Energy Magic Building and the library, contains enough ingredients to provide endless calamities. Think about the chaos caused in *Guards! Guards!* by *The Summoning of Dragons*, a book stolen from Unseen University's library. Think of the wizards themselves and their inept attempts to send Rincewind anywhere.

We talked about attractors earlier. Azrael (the Death of Universes), Granny Weatherwax, Tiffany Aching, Lord Vetinari, Sergeant Jackrum (*Monstrous Regiment*), Carrot Ironfoundersson, Death, and other characters behave as attractors—those who pull others to a certain point. They work overtly or behind the scenes. Azrael has to be the biggest attractor of them all, since he's known as "the Great Attractor" (*Reaper Man*, 321). Ha! Ha! Actually, a "great attractor" in space is a large mass about the size of thousands of galaxies

---

[8] Quotes from *Interesting Times*, 4.
[9] *Men at Arms* (New York: HarperTorch, 1993), 319.

with an enormous amount of gravitational pull. That's Azrael all over. Just a big charming lump, really.

While characters such as Vimes and Susan are at the forefront of the action in their stories, they're often reactors to the attractor or the strange attractor who comes on the scene and attempts to take the system to a different place. Think about it. In *Thief of Time*, Death inspires Susan to action by mentioning that someone like her was involved in building the clock. Vetinari often manipulates Vimes into action by telling Vimes what he *shouldn't* do. And Carrot, possibly the rightful heir to the throne of Ankh-Morpork, is the one responsible for Vimes being the commander and knight that he is.

In the wizard miniseries, when chaos happens, Rincewind's usually in the thick of things. Check it out.

DISC-CLAIMER:
Plot spoilers ahead. Read at your own risk.

Tiffany is unique in that she's an attractor *and* a system bordering on chaos. When the queen of the fairies (the strange attractor) steals Tiffany's brother, Wentworth, and tries to take over Tiffany's world in *The Wee Free Men*, Tiffany acts to pull the system back into order. In *A Hat Full of Sky*, she repels another strange attractor—an invading entity (the hiver) that attempts to pull her mind into chaos. In *Wintersmith*, Tiffany gains the attention of still another strange attractor—the Wintersmith—after leaping into the Morris dance, thus setting in motion a change in the pattern that will ultimately bring chaos (endless winter). Once again, she is a system bordering on chaos as she slowly gains the power of the Summer Lady but isn't sure what to do with it.

Thief of Time is another novel with strong elements of chaos. The villainous Auditors (more on them in chapter 12) hire Jeremy

BOOK	STRANGE ATTRACTOR(S)	MOMENT OF CHAOS
The Color of Magic	Twoflower, the naive tourist	Rincewind and Twoflower wind up off Discworld.
The Light Fantastic	Great A'Tuin	Great A'Tuin goes on a collision course for a red star. Only the eight great spells in the *Octavo*, a book in the wizards' keeping, can stop it. But one is lodged in Rincewind's head.
Sourcery	Coin the sourcerer who attracts magic; the archchancellor's hat, which, unlike the sorting hat in Harry Potter, is manipulative and evil.	Coin takes over Unseen University and completely changes things there. Conina, the daughter of Cohen the Barbarian, steals the archchancellor's hat, which falls into the hands of Abrim, the wicked vizier. The Mage Wars result. And Rincewind's right in the middle of it.
Interesting Times	Twoflower again (through his pamphlet, *What I Did on My Holidays*)	Rincewind travels to the Agatean Empire and is believed to be a powerful wizard/revolutionary. As usual, whenever Rincewind is present, war is the result.

(continued)

Table (continued)

BOOK	STRANGE ATTRACTOR(S)	MOMENT OF CHAOS
The Last Continent	Rincewind and the wizards	The presence of Rincewind and the wizards of Unseen University on the continent of Fourecks, still in its formative stages, causes changes that affect the fabric of the land.
The Last Hero	Cohen the Barbarian and the Silver Horde	The Silver Horde takes a bomb to Dunmanifestin— the home of the gods— which goes off. Rincewind's on hand as well.

Clockson to build a clock to stop all clocks and trap Time (personified as a female—more on her in chapter 9). The Auditors usually behave as the strange attractors—beings who present a kind of order in chaos. They believe the universe would run smoothly without humans or immortals like Death and the Hogfather and use chaos to achieve that goal. But Lady LeJean (a.k.a. Unity) is an Auditor who becomes an attractor and tries to stop the other Auditors.

As we mentioned before, the "tick of the universe" is an allusion to Newton's clock. In a universe governed by magic and chaos, regulating the universe according to Newton's clock would bring a reverse form of chaos. (That would be order, wouldn't it?)

Not only is chaos there, Kaos is there as well. The fifth horseman of the Apocalypse is mild-mannered (until provoked) Ronnie Soak, a.k.a. Kaos (not to be confused with KAOS—the secret organization of criminals on *Get Smart,* the 1960s TV spoof of James Bond movies). He's a milkman, which is fitting for someone who once dealt with the primordial milk of creation, so to speak. It takes Kaos, the Monks of History, Lobsang Ludd (son of Time), and the intrepid Susan Sto Helit to make things right. Achieving balance—entropy—is the key. The procrastinators—the machines the monks monitor and use—are the symbols of balanced time. They're also an example of the perturbation theory—how irregularities are compensated for to balance the equation. (For more on procrastinators, see chapter 19.)

For other moments of chaos in Discworld (this list is by no means exhaustive), see the chart on pages 64 and 65.

And soon there was order out of chaos . . .

Not content to leave everything in a mess, Pratchett shows how order comes from chaos. This is also known as resolving the conflict.

So in *The Last Hero,* Carrot's heroic intervention, like Alan Ladd's in *High Noon* or like any of the X-Men's (except for the Phoenix), helps prevent total chaos. This is also why Granny Weatherwax, another attractor, can help Tiffany set things right in *Wintersmith* or any other book in which Granny Weatherwax appears. This is why the Monks of History soldier on, helping to repair the universe every time it is destroyed.

And this is why Vetinari, the ultimate attractor as the Patrician in Ankh-Morpork, maintains power in a city like Ankh-Morpork. . . .

Fade to black. . . .

BOOK	STRANGE ATTRACTOR(S)	MOMENT(S) OF CHAOS
Equal Rites	Drum Billet	Having given his staff to what he assumes is a male child, Billet inadvertently creates the first female wizard—Eskarina.
Mort	Mort	By saving Princess Keli from assassination, Mort messes with the fabric of time and reality. (Nice going, Mort.)
Wyrd Sisters	Duke Felmet and his wife	Granny makes time speed up fifteen years to allow Tomjon, the rightful king of Lancre, to grow up. But the murderous duke still refuses to give up the throne. What's more, Tomjon doesn't want to be king.
Reaper Man	The Auditors	Death is fired and marked for termination, which causes an increase in Life, which means Ankh-Morpork will be destroyed.
Lords and Ladies	The Dancers	Diamanda, a young witch, leaps between the Dancers, a circle of stones (see chapter 14), causing the Fairy Queen and her elves to invade Lancre.

BOOK	STRANGE ATTRACTOR(S)	MOMENT(S) OF CHAOS
Jingo	The island of Leshp	When Ankh-Morpork and Klatch both claim it, war is declared.
Night Watch	Quantum interference (the weird lightning)	Sam Vimes and the psychopathic Carcer are sent back in time. Their actions make the future uncertain.
Going Postal	Moist von Lipwig	Moist's boasts and lies spin everything into chaos (Post Office burns to the ground; he boasts that he can get a package to Genua before the clacks).

4

The Discworld Tapestry: Can They All Get Along?

Can we all get along?
—Rodney King

> The principal aim of the tapestry, obviously, was to cover the walls of a given room completely, and to provide a homogeneous decoration which related to both the walls and the furniture.[1]

This is a chapter about a tapestry, but not like the Unicorn Tapestries, one of the most famous sets of tapestries in the world, dating back to 1500. We're talking about the tapestry of humanity. (Already, you're probably thinking, *I've heard the tapestry analogy before. Cliché.* But bear with us.)

A tapestry is designed to cover a wall. A human tapestry covers a world. In our world, the human tapestry consists of people of various races. You know them. We don't have to list them. If you saw the video for "We Are the World" ages ago, attended a meeting at

---

[1] *The Book of Tapestry: History and Technique* by Pierre Verlet, Michael Florisoone, Adolf Hoffmeister, and François Tabard (New York: The Vendome Press, distributed by Viking Press, 1965), 13.

the UN, or looked at Carrie's pets, you'd see colors as varied as the threads of a medieval tapestry. (Well, Carrie's pets are only somewhat varied color-wise. Two have a mostly black and white color scheme. Sassie, the orange tabby, is in the minority. But the other two do not discriminate.)

The people and species of creatures of Discworld form a unique tapestry with threads from throughout literature. In chapter 1, we discussed how various myths informed Pratchett's choice of people or beings to populate his series. But how do those people and beings fit together? What are the warp and weft of their relationships?

In a tapestry, the various threads work together to show the whole picture. In the Discworld tapestry, the "threads" often try their best to pull out the other threads. It's the same in our world. Let's face it—we don't always get along. Hatred and prejudice wear a very human face. You can probably easily think of books and movies that deal with the reality of tense racial situations. For example, *To Kill a Mockingbird*, *A Time to Kill*, *To Sir with Love*, *The Defiant Ones* (the Tony Curtis/Sidney Poitier movie from 1958), *West Side Story*, *Guess Who's Coming to Dinner* (old and new), *Amazing Grace*, *Amistad*, *The Interpreter*. Some of these tensions are played out in wars that stain the human tapestry.

With such an explosive situation, maybe that's why many sci-fi and fantasy writers use alien races or even differing types of robots or androids in their stories as a metaphor for race relations. Think of the Vulcans and Romulans in the first *Star Trek* series. Think of the Daleks and Cybermen in the most recent *Doctor Who* series on BBC One. (Well, the Daleks and Cybermen hate everyone but themselves. And they're not all robot, either. Cybermen have human brains and the Daleks are bad-tempered small aliens in armored suits. No wonder prejudicial thoughts occur.)

Although there are no "aliens" per se in Discworld, Pratchett shows race relations among humans and between humans and other species. Let's look at the human factor first.

> **DISC-CLAIMER:**
> Plot spoilers ahead. Read at your own risk.

PATTERN I: THE HUMAN FACTOR

We have met the enemy and he is us.

—Walt Kelly,[2] creator of *Pogo* comic strip

Klatch vs. Ankh-Morpork

*I have a dream that my four little children will one day live in a
nation where they will not be judged by the color of their skin
but by the content of their character.*

—Martin Luther King

In *Jingo*, a mysterious island rich in treasures (or so the rumor goes)
is a hotbed of contention between the people of Klatch and of
Ankh-Morpork. Pratchett weaves the threat of war in with moments of slapstick. But more than that, we see the attitudes of the
people of Ankh-Morpork and of Klatch toward each other, especially when Vimes is asked to explain a derogatory remark leveled
at a visiting prince from Klatch. And even Vimes has to explore his
attitude toward 71-hour Ahmed, the clove-eating cultural attaché
and bodyguard. (But then, Vimes never pretends to be PC.)

The island ownership issue sparks race-related skirmishes in
Ankh-Morpork. We've certainly heard about or experienced those
in our country. During the civil rights movement in the 1950s and
1960s, riots broke out in Chicago, Birmingham, and other places.
The death threats during Prince Cadram's diplomatic visit to

---

[2] Posted at http://www.igopogo.com/we_have_met.htm.

Ankh-Morpork reminded us of the threats Martin Luther King received while organizing nonviolent protests—threats that culminated in his assassination in 1968. But race riots didn't end there. The verdict after the trial of police officers caught on video beating Rodney King sparked a three-day riot in Los Angeles in 1992.

War over a piece of land is a familiar tune played over centuries. In the United States as the West was settled, soldiers fought Native Americans over the plains. The Battle of the Little Bighorn in June 1876 (a.k.a. Custer's last stand) was fought over the Black Hills of South Dakota. Miners wanted the area for the gold they found. The Lakota Sioux, who had a reservation there as well as a treaty signed by the government, considered the land sacred. General George Armstrong Custer was sent to deal with the situation. Custer's troops faced the combined forces of Lakota Sioux and Northern Cheyenne warriors and lost. Fatally.

At least in *Jingo*, the war is averted. But not so with the duchy of Borogravia and its Zlobenian antagonists in *Monstrous Regiment*. Prince Heinrich wants control of the duchy. Pratchett alludes to Walt Kelly's poignant statement with Polly Perks's thought, *We have met the enemy and he is nice*.[3] But such thoughts don't keep her from fighting.

Agatean Empire vs. Ankh-Morpork with Rincewind on the Side

As we look at this wall—we do not want any walls of any kind between peoples.

—Richard Nixon[4]

---

[3] *Monstrous Regiment* (New York: HarperCollins, 2003), 86.
[4] Posted at the BBC site: http://news.bbc.co.uk/1/hi/world/asia-pacific/1821104.stm.

They're, well . . . foreign over there.
— Archchancellor Ridcully about the Agatean Empire[5]

Diplomacy is a way of weaving the threads of two countries together. (It's also a way to forge powerful alliances with bigger countries with better weaponry.) In *Interesting Times*, Rincewind's enforced diplomatic trip to the Agatean Empire (a country with some aspects of China and Japan) in the Counterweight Continent reminded us of former president Richard Nixon's historic visit to the People's Republic of China in 1972, a trip that paved the way for a new foreign policy. No other U.S. president had visited China before. First time for everything. While we take for granted today that anyone can visit China (we visited China thirty years after Nixon's trip; no albatrosses were dispatched to encourage the visit), the fact that anyone can go there is probably due to Nixon's trip.

Just before that trip, then national security officer Henry Kissinger visited Beijing. But before that, an American Ping-Pong team paved the way for the visit—hence the "ping-pong diplomacy" designation for Nixon's trip.

Relations between the U.S. and China had been strained at best. But China's weakened alliance with Russia strengthened U.S. resolve to visit the country. Nixon met with Prime Minister Zhou Enlai and Communist party leader Mao Zedong. So, what did they talk about? Now that the notes from their meetings have been declassified, we know they talked about the Vietnam War, Taiwan (would it become independent?), and the Chinese leaders' fears about Japan—whether it would continue to expand.

Discworld's Lord Hong is no Mao Zedong. Hong comes from a wealthy family. Mao Zedong was the son of a peasant who rose to wealth. Mao became the leader of the Red Army (now the People's Liberation Army)—the revolutionaries. Lord Hong wants the Red

---

[5] *Interesting Times* (New York: HarperPrism, 1994), 10.

Army—the revolutionaries of the story—to fail. But the incredibly large Chinese Red Army, begun in 1927, has similarities not only in size but also to the history of the PLA.

Unfortunately, Lord Hong doesn't factor in the chaos a Rincewind and a Cohen the Barbarian could cause. (More on chaos in chapter 3.) No one ever does. Suffice it to say that there's no army big enough to stop them.

Omnians vs. The Ephebians: Jihad Discworld-style

A nation's culture resides in the hearts and in the soul of its people.

—Mohandas Gandhi[6]

Religious wars and persecution are still other ways the threads of the tapestry try to pull each other out. In *Small Gods*, Deacon Vorbis, the Quisition head, instigates war against Ephebe and anyone else who refuses to believe in "the right" god—Om—a god that Vorbis doesn't really believe in. The Islamic term "jihad"—"holy war"—immediately leaps to mind. Vorbis also wants to persecute anyone who claims to be a devotee of the "turtle movement"—those who believe that the world is carried on the backs of four elephants standing on a giant turtle. In his opinion, the very thought is ridiculous!

It's all a matter of perspective.

You can see the similarities between the turtle movement and early Christians who had secret signs and calls to alert or encourage one another in times of persecution. And, of course, the Quisition is like the Spanish Inquisition, a tribunal begun by King Ferdinand II of Aragon and Queen Isabella I of Castile (a.k.a. the "Catholic

---

[6] Quoted at http://www.brainyquote.com/quotes/authors/m/mohandas_gandhi.html.

King and Queen") in the fifteenth century in reaction to suspicions concerning the conversion of Jews to Christianity. The inquisitor general (Vorbis's office in *Small Gods*) headed the Inquisition. The idea was to maintain Catholicism in the kingdom of Castile. One way to do this was to stamp out what inquisitors believed were heretical ideas (i.e., Protestant beliefs) through the use of trials and torture. You've probably heard the saying "Nobody expects the Spanish Inquisition," a saying popularized in a *Monty Python* sketch. This was because no one knew exactly when the inquisitors would roll into town. Everything was hush-hush.

Vorbis's trip to Ephebe and the war that almost results also bring to mind the Crusades, starting at the end of the eleventh century. The Crusades were a counter-jihad of sorts fought in Palestine and Syria, after Muslims tried to take back Christianized areas. The fighting went on for centuries.

Sadly, we're all well acquainted with the consequences of the jihad of our day: war in Iraq, suicide bombings, buildings toppling in New York on September 11, 2001, and so on, thanks to the efforts of Muslim extremists. As a counter-jihad to the trauma of 2001, U.S. troops were dispatched to Afghanistan beginning in 2003. It's déjà vu all over again.

To the Muslim, jihad isn't just a war against a perceived enemy, it is a duty. Think of the jihad of the Fremen led by their Messiah— Muad'Dib/Lisan al-Gaib in Frank Herbert's *Dune* (classic *Dune*). As Daniel Pipes of *The New York Post* put it, "Jihad is thus unabashedly offensive in nature, with the eventual goal of achieving Muslim dominion over the entire globe."[7]

Vorbis would agree.

---

[7] Posted at http://www.danielpipes.org/article/990, December 31, 2002.

Males vs. Females: Gender Politics

I usually make up my mind about a man in ten seconds;
and I very rarely change it.

—Margaret Thatcher[8]

Another rip in the tapestry is the war between the sexes. In *Equal Rites*, Pratchett addresses the issue with Eskarina's quest to become a wizard—a quest opposed by the wizards and even, for a time, Granny Weatherwax. Granny pooh-poohs the notion of women using wizard's magic (fireballs and such) not only in *Equal Rites*, but also in *Wintersmith*.

The only women the wizards gladly admit to the hallowed halls of Unseen University are Mrs. Whitlow the housekeeper, a woman they admit they're afraid of, and her staff. Occasionally Susan drops by via the rite of AshkEnte when subbing for Death. To the wizards, women aren't capable of "high" magic. They're only good for, well, womanly things like birthing babies. Hmmm.

While the Discworld series is no *Feminine Mystique*, the seminal work by Betty Friedan, it is chock-full of strong female characters trying to overcome the limitations set for them in predominantly male environments. In *Monstrous Regiment*, Polly Perks and other members of Sergeant Jackrum's regiment learn a hard fact of life that female dwarfs in Discworld already know: to get ahead in a male-dominated society, disguising one's femininity is sadly necessary. Dee learns to play the game of politics by acting and looking like a male dwarf. And Polly Perks learns the value of a well-placed pair of socks, as well as a well-aimed knee when accosted by frisky enemy troops.

There's Conina, the daughter of Cohen the Barbarian, who may

---

[8] Quoted at http://www.quotationspage.com/quote/25727.html.

look like a helpless female but is just as deadly as Cohen. Several thugs in *Sourcery* find this out the hard way. And there's Ptraci the handmaid half sister of Teppic in *Pyramids*. Ptraci isn't your stereotypical happy harem girl. (See chapter 11 for other strong women in the Discworld.)

Pratchett provides other moments of feminine enlightenment, all the while tweaking gender stereotypes. In *Thud!* Sally von Humpeding, the vampire Watchperson, tries to school Angua after seeing Angua trailing after Carrot with puppy eyes. In turn, Sally, Angua, and Cheery Littlebottom, the forensics recruit on the Watch, do the same for Nobby's girlfriend Tawneee, who is perfectly willing to stand by her . . . man. (You can't help pausing when the words "man" and "Nobby" are used together.)

But for the ultimate in feminine enlightenment, there's Nobby, who dresses as a woman in *Jingo* and has a heart-to-heart chat with a group of women who complain about a man. He gets so into his role, he starts to complain about Colon's gender stereotyping.

PATTERN II: THE MYTHOLOGY FACTOR

The designer of the cartoons for the tapestries was strongly influenced by other works of art.

—John Williamson, *The Oak King, the Holly King, and the Unicorn*[9]

Dwarfs vs. Trolls

Trolls. Dwarfs of Northern mythology, living in hills, underground in caverns or beneath; they are represented as stumpy, misshapen,

---

[9] John Williamson, *The Oak King, the Holly King, and the Unicorn* (New York: Harper & Row, 1986), 7.

and humpbacked, inclined to thieving, and fond of carrying off human children and substituting their own.[10]

Dwarfs. Dwarfs . . . generally dwelt in rocks, caves, and recesses of the earth, were the guardians of its mineral wealth and precious stones, and were very skillful in the working of these.[11]

In Discworld, prejudice isn't just about one human looking down on another. Pratchett throws in other species (trolls, vampires, werewolves, golems, and zombies) to add to the malcontent mix.

As we mentioned in chapter 1, Pratchett is strongly influenced by other works of literature. In Discworld, he includes the good and the bad, with his own special tweaks. With dwarfs and trolls, you find the good, the bad, and the sometimes ugly.

In Discworld, the dwarfs and trolls are ancient enemies, a fact shown through the Battle of Koom Valley—discussed especially in *Thud!*—and their uneasy relations in Ankh-Morpork. When a dwarf is murdered, a troll is the fall guy. But friendships between dwarfs and trolls, like the friendship between Lance-constable Detritus and Lance-constable Cuddy in *Men at Arms*, also occur, which serve as a mirror of sorts for times in this country and others when relationships between members of different races were deemed "shocking."

In mythology and its fantasy offspring, trolls are considered stupid, strong, and rarely on the side of good. Think way back to childhood when you heard the tale of "The Three Billy Goats Gruff," a tale from the collection of Peter Christen Asbjørnsen and Jørgen Moe. Who was the bad guy? The troll under the bridge. Or consider *The Hobbit*. Bilbo Baggins and the dwarves encountered a

---

[10] Definition from *Brewer's Dictionary of Phrase and Fable* by E. Cobham Brewer (New York: Tess Press), 823.

[11] Ibid., 277.

group of hungry but easily fooled trolls, who tried to snack on them. And in *The Lord of the Rings*, trolls fought on Sauron's side.

Discworld trolls (which, it should be noted, are huge and made of rock) have the same "stupid and strong" reputation. They have a watchdog committee—the Silicon Anti-Defamation League— headed by troll thug Chrysophrase. (Watchdog organizations in our world: the NAACP, the ACLU, the Jewish Defamation League.)

Dwarfs, on the other hand, have a better reputation, but are some- times seen as avaricious because of their love of silver and gold, as *The Hobbit, The Lord of the Rings*, and other books attest. They have the same reputation in Discworld. Exhibit A: "Gold, Gold, Gold"—a popular dwarf song. They're a dual-society people (Copperhead and Ankh-Morpork), like many immigrants in America who try to assim- ilate into American society while maintaining roots back home. Like the trolls, dwarfs also have a watchdog committee—the Committee for Equal Heights.

Werewolves vs. Vampires vs. Humans

Even a man who is pure in heart . . . May become a wolf when the wolfbane blooms.
> —Poem from *The Wolf Man*[12]

Look! It's a black chicken! Get it!
> —A hungry family, trying to catch Dracula
> in bat form in *Love at First Bite*[13]

In *Underworld* and *Underworld: Evolution*, the werewolves (lycans) and vampires have been at war for ages. The two movies show a touch of forbidden love in the vein of *West Side Story* and *Romeo*

---

[12] Posted at http://www.amazon.com/Wolf-Man-Claude-Rains/dp/B00001TZ6Q.
[13] Posted at http://horror.about.com/od/quotablequotes/a/qq_vampire.htm.

and Juliet (the play that inspired West Side Story) with the relationship between Selene (Kate Beckinsale), a vampire Death Dealer who kills werewolves, and Michael (Scott Speedman), a werewolf/vampire. (With that combination—werewolf vs. vampire—you can't win.) So, why the animosity? Because werewolves are the only species vampires fear—or so we're told in some stories. Werewolves can kill vampires.

So is it any wonder that in Discworld, vampires and werewolves find getting along difficult? Angua, the resident werewolf on the Watch, can't stand vampires and cringes at being forced to work with Lance-constable Sally von Humpeding, the Watch's first vampire. But Angua's animosity goes all the way back to life in the old country—Uberwald, where werewolves and vampires only work with other species when plotting misery to others they hate more.

Human animosity toward vampires is just as deeply ingrained. Few people on the Disc are fond of vampires, as Carpe Jugulum, The Fifth Elephant, and Thud! make abundantly clear. Vimes's antipathy toward them, in just about every book he's in, shows the standard human response.

It's the same in our world. What's the first thing you think of when the subject of vampires comes up? Is it a warm and cheery thought? Y'know, I'd like a vampire to drop by for dinner someday. No matter how appealing they might seem (e.g., Constantine in Sunshine by Robin McKinley, Selene—Kate Beckinsale's character in the Underworld movies, Wesley Snipes's hybrid vampire in the Blade movies, Angel in Buffy the Vampire Slayer, Edward in the Twilight series by Stephenie Meyer), you would still give them a wide berth, as Angua tries to give Sally, even if they claim to hunt other vampires. After all, they can't help looking at you the way Hannibal Lecter looks at a human—as an entrée to go with the fava beans.

In the past, literature and movies painted a dark picture of the vampire. After Bram Stoker, many authors, including Stephen King

(*Salem's Lot*), and screenwriters showcased these creatures of the night as the enemy (think of *From Dawn till Dusk*). But nowadays, they've been given a new status as angst-ridden "sexy beasts"— tortured souls just lookin' for love (or as Eddie Murphy in an old *Saturday Night Live* skit said, "Wookin' pa nub") and tryin' to survive the best way they can. Exhibit A: Anne Rice's Vampire Chronicles. Exhibit B: the *Underworld* movies. Exhibit C: just about any young adult series involving vampires, including Meyer's *Twilight*, *New Moon*, and *Eclipse*, and Ellen Schreiber's *Vampire Kisses*. Oh, and let us not forget Christopher Moore's books about Jody the vampire—Exhibit D. Lastly, Exhibit E: hundreds of books listed on Amazon about finding love with a vampire. With vampires like these, potential victims almost beg to be bitten. (I [Linda] admit to a partiality for Meyer's series, thanks to strong, likable characters. But I'd still go "Tiffany Aching" all over any who came my way— frying pan and a good stake well done. Clang! I prefer my blood in my body, thank you.)

And werewolves or werewolf-of-sorts movies? Consider special effects–laden movies such as *An American Werewolf in London*, *The Howling* (which spawned seventy-five thousand sequels—okay, a slight exaggeration), *Wolfen*, *Van Helsing* (Kate Beckinsale again), the *Underworlds*, and *Brotherhood of the Wolf*. (The Beast of Gevaudan in the last movie is not really a werewolf. But this movie has the essence of the werewolf movie.) Although we pity the victim of the werewolf's bite who undergoes a painful metamorphosis when the moon is full, werewolves are portrayed as ravenous, untrustworthy creatures—just a cut above vampires. They simply can't help killing! While werewolves are viewed with sympathy in *Blood and Chocolate* by Annette Curtis Klause, the element of being somewhat out of control when the full moon hangs in the sky is there.

Werewolves in Discworld are tolerated more than vampires are, particularly on non-full-moon nights, but are not much liked. The undead have that effect on people. Like the *Underworld* saga, the forbidden love between Angua and Carrot serves as a way to bridge the gap created by the uneasy relations between humans and the undead.

Zombies vs. Humans

I always look for an intense experience, an intense ride. There is nothing better than a good zombie movie where you run crazy and blow at monsters!

—Sarah Polley, actress in *Dawn of the Dead* (2004 version)[14]

If you've seen Peter Jackson's movie *Braindead*, George Romero on a zombie roll (*Day of the Dead, Night of the Living Dead, Dawn of the Dead*), *Re-animator, The Fog, Army of Darkness, Shaun of the Dead, Resident Evil, Dawn of the Dead* (2004), or any of the score upon score of other zombie movies out there (including the not-really-zombies-but-still-murderous-crazies in *28 Days Later* or its sequel), you've seen the normal reaction to zombies (i.e., destroy them). After all, who wants to cozy up to something homicidal and hungry (Hannibal Lecter, anyone)?

But in Pratchett's world, zombies are a beleaguered minority. Watchman Reg Shoe is a self-described advocate, combating prejudice toward the Discworld dead, while Mr. Slant takes the route of assimilation by heading the guild of lawyers in society.

Wizard Windle Poons briefly experiences the aversion of others when he dies and becomes a zombie in *Reaper Man*. But Reg's Dead Rights group (the Fresh Starters) are there to succor and protect him.

But then there's Saturday, the murdered baron of Genua, who comes back as an avenging zombie. Saturday, which is an allusion to Baron Samedi, a voodoo figure, is the right-hand man of Mrs. Gogol,

---

[14] Posted at http://www.brainyquote.com/quotes/authors/s/sarah_polley.html.

the voodoo witch in *Witches Abroad*. While Saturday thirsts for vengeance, he's still polite about it. No chewing on humans for him! But he will kill them if necessary.

Golems vs. Humans

Golem: *I feel so guilty! I've mangled and maimed thirty-seven people and I told a telemarketer I was busy when I wasn't! I'm not a good man.*
Lisa Simpson: *He sure is neurotic for a monster.*[15]

We shall overcome someday.

—Lyrics adapted from a gospel song
written by Charles Tindley

If you've played video games such as *Warcraft III* or *Enchanted Arms*, you've seen golems at work and probably already know that golems are from Jewish folklore. In one tale, Rabbi Judah Loew created a golem when the Jews in Prague were persecuted during the nineteenth century. But these animated beings created from clay are treated as mindless slaves in Discworld. Hmm. You can't help thinking about Gollum in *Lord of the Rings*, who was a slave to the ring.

In Discworld, golems are given the worst tasks to do and have no rights whatsoever—a situation reminiscent of human slavery, especially the enslavement of African Americans in the seventeenth through the nineteenth centuries in America. Golems are viewed as little more than chattel—something that can be sold or destroyed at an owner's whim. The golems could probably hum a bar or two of "We Shall Overcome."

---

[15] Quote from *The Simpsons*: "Treehouse of Horror XVII" episode posted at http://www.tv .com/the-simpsons/treehouse-of-horror-xvii/episode/728361/trivia.html.

Isn't it interesting that stories of golems flourished during times of persecution in Jewish history? While the golem has the protector role in Jewish folklore, it has the hunting-down-the-humans-to-destroy-them role in video games—a role not far from that of a robot or a cyborg like the terminators of the *Terminator* movie series.

According to Jewish folklore, a person who had a golem was considered wise, especially since golems were created with a sacred word attached to their foreheads like a phylactery. The Discworld golems (Dorfl, Mr. Pump, Anghammerad, etc.) have those sacred words, which Carrot later uses to free Dorfl in *Feet of Clay*.

The golem legend might have inspired Mary Shelley to create *Frankenstein*. It certainly inspired such writers as Michael Chabon (*The Amazing Adventures of Kavalier & Clay*), Jorge Luis Borges, Jonathan Stroud, and Isaac Bashevis Singer.

Banshees vs. Humans

Banshee. The domestic spirit of certain Irish or Highland Scottish families, supposed to take an interest in its welfare, and to wait at the death of one of the family.[16]

The howl of the banshee is supposed to drive a person crazy. Maybe that's because the banshee's scream is the signal that death is coming for you. But if you're in Discworld, perhaps the banshee's methods won't drive you crazy—not if the omen comes on a slip of paper thrust under your door by Mr. Ixolite.

Banshees, like vampires and werewolves, have their place in Discworld. Although Mr. Gryle's murderous actions might give them a bad name, for the most part all's quiet on the western front. Ixolite

---

[16] Definition from *Brewer's Dictionary of Phrase and Fable* by E. Cobham Brewer (New York: Tess Press), 64. Pratchett recommended this book to the audience at his Naperville book signing. He contributed to a volume of *Brewer's* (the millennium edition), which was much more expensive than the one we have.

is part of Reg Shoe's Fresh Starters group, which means that for the banshee there's some perception of mistreatment. It's difficult to want someone around who screams piercingly at you. (Well, Mr. Ixolite, a shy banshee with a speech impediment, wouldn't.)

In folklore, banshees were of the female persuasion, since the name means "woman of fairyland." But if you're an *X-Men* fan, you know that the Banshee (Sean Cassidy) was male and had a piercing sonic scream. Guess Pratchett decided to buck tradition as well, by making his banshees male.

∽

In a skillfully woven tapestry, you don't notice so much the individual threads as you notice the picture as a whole. In Discworld, no thread seems out of place.

5

The Play's the Thing

The play's the thing wherein I'll catch
the conscience of the king.
—*Hamlet*, act 2, scene ii, lines 633–34

ACT I: IN WHICH WE EXAMINE SHAKESPEARE

Where There's a Will(iam Shakespeare), There's a Way

When you read Shakespeare, what do you think of besides descriptions like *clever* or *boring* or memories of the fifth-period English teacher or college prof who nauseated you? Depends on the play, right? If you read *Macbeth* ("the Scottish play"—see the sidebar on page 90) or saw it performed, maybe you remember certain lines, especially since many of them are quoted in fantasy books or scripts as disparate as old *Star Trek* (the "classic" series) reruns or *Harry Potter* films. If you read *Hamlet,* or even if you didn't, you can probably recall some of the "to be or not to be" soliloquy, since it's quoted often. And if you read *A Midsummer's Night Dream* or saw the 1999 movie of the same name that starred Christian Bale, Kevin Kline,

Rupert Everett, Michelle Pfeiffer, Sophie Marceau, and Calista Flockhart, well, who knows what you probably thought during that!

For Pratchett, reading Shakespeare was the catalyst to a Discworld plot or some aspect of Discworld mythology. But not just Shakespeare. There's also Andrew Lloyd Webber (*The Phantom of the Opera*), Richard Wagner (the Ring Cycle), and other composers and authors.

DISC-CLAIMER:
Plot spoilers ahead. Read at your own risk.

Just *As You Like It*: A Big MacMess with a Side Order of Ham(let)

If you read *Wyrd Sisters* and some of the other Lancre witch novels (*Maskerade*, for example), you revisited some aspects of the plot and some of the lines of *Macbeth*. But not just *Macbeth*. There's also a smattering of *As You Like It*, one of Shakespeare's comedies, and *Hamlet*—probably his most well-known tragedy. You know—it's the one where Hamlet learns that his mother's new husband, Claudius, killed Hamlet's father. (A therapy session just waiting to happen.)

The plot of *Macbeth*, in short, is this: After three witches (the weird sisters) predict that Macbeth, thane of Glamis and lately of Cawdor, will become king of Scotland (and that his friend Banquo will be the father of kings), the henpecked Macbeth is encouraged by his wife to "screw his courage to the sticking-place"[1]—a line Gaston sang in *Beauty and the Beast*—and murder Duncan (the king, a guest in their castle), thus taking over the throne of Scotland. Lady Macbeth plants the daggers on the king's servants. But

---

[1] William Shakespeare, *The Tragedy of Macbeth* (New York: Signet Classics, 1963), line 60, p. 57.

when Macduff, yet another thane, visits and discovers the murder, Macbeth murders the servants.

The late king's sons, Malcolm and Donalbain, flee to England and Ireland respectively and are suspected of the deed. But Macduff suspects Macbeth. During his exile from Scotland, Macduff resolves to bring one of the king's sons back to rule.

Meanwhile back at the ranch, or rather, castle, Macbeth then hires two murderers to off Banquo and his son, Fleance, who escapes. Banquo's ghost makes a guest appearance at Macbeth's home. Macbeth then visits the three witches, and hears a ghost prophesy that none of woman born will harm him. Ha, ha! No one should ever trust that line, as the Witch King in *Return of the King* could tell you. Wait. He can't. Eowyn finished him off, thanks to a similar prophecy.

Back to *Macbeth*: The witches also tell him that he'll be defeated if forces unite at Birnam Wood. Macbeth then sends the murderers to deal with Macduff. But he's not home. Just so the trip isn't a total loss, they murder Macduff's family and servants.

The guilt over the murder of Duncan and subsequent crimes sends Lady Macbeth over the edge. She later dies, undoubtedly by her own hand.

Malcolm brings forces from England to usurp the throne. During the war, Macduff, who fights on Malcolm's side, kills Macbeth. Before doing so, Macduff smugly announces that he was taken from his mother's womb earlier than normal (possibly by Caesarean). Another prophecy is fulfilled.

In *Wyrd Sisters* (an obvious play on "weird sisters" or the Fates), Duke Felmet and his lady are, of course, the Macbeth and Lady Macbeth of the story. By murdering King Verence, Duke Felmet usurps the throne of Lancre. But Granny Weatherwax, Magrat Garlick, and Nanny Ogg take on the roles of the three witches as well as of Macduff when they rescue the king's son (Tomjon) and try to get his throne back for him.

The duke is a little more insane and the duchess a lot less so than are the couple in Macbeth. And Felmet's wife is much more calculating and vicious, with no moral guilt.

The opening line of *Macbeth*, spoken by the First Witch ("When shall we three meet again?"), appears at the beginning of *Maskerade* and *Wyrd Sisters*. (Well, in *Maskerade*, "we two" appear, instead of three.) The "rule of three" witches that Granny enforces in *Maskerade* harks back to *Macbeth*'s three witches as well as to the three archetypes of women: the maiden, the mother, and the crone, and the three Fates in Greek mythology—Clotho, Lachesis, and Atropos. Three witches are deemed more powerful together than one.

Plays written by Hwel (shades of Will?) the dwarf, a friend of Tomjon, are parodied lines from *Macbeth* and *As You Like It*.

PRATCHETT	SHAKESPEARE
King: Is this a ~~duck-knife~~ dagger I see ~~behind beside in front of~~ before me, its ~~beak~~ handle pointing at my hand?[2]	Macbeth: Is this a dagger which I see before me, the handle toward my hand? (*Macbeth,* act II, scene i, lines 33–34)
All the Disc it is but an Theater, Ane alle men and wymmen are but Players.[3]	All the world's a stage, And all the men and women merely players. (*As You Like It,* act II, scene vii, lines 139–43)
The very soil cries out at tyranny.[4]	Macduff: Bleed, bleed, poor country: Great tyranny, lay thou thy basis sure (*Macbeth,* act IV, scene iii, line 38)

---

2 *Wyrd Sisters* (New York: HarperTorch, 1980), 193.
3 Ibid., 170.
4 Ibid., 234.

The title of one of Hwel's plays—*Please Yourself*—is an allusion to *As You Like It*—a romantic comedy concerning love at first sight (Orlando for Rosalind), banishment (Orlando and Rosalind again), cross-dressing (uh, Rosalind), and betrayal (Rosalind again; just kidding—this time it's usurping brother Frederick against his brother, Duke Senior). Love wins out, of course.

The duchess's suggestion to use a play to cause the people of Lancre to hate the witches reminds us of Hamlet's hope that a play will "catch the conscience" of his murderous uncle, Claudius. A more direct allusion to Hamlet comes when Vitoller (theater manager and surrogate father of Tomjon) says, "The pay's the thing" but then switches to "the play's the thing."[5]

An earlier allusion to *Hamlet* (possibly) comes when Granny, Nanny, and Magrat attend a play in the hopes of choosing a surrogate family for Verence's son, whom they rescued from a murderous guard. During the play, Granny is appalled by and confused about the scene she sees—a murder and the murderer's speech concerning his sorrow over the murder. Could this be an allusion to Hamlet's murder of Polonius in act III, scene iv of *Hamlet*?

Since we're on the subject of foolish behavior, let's move on to fools. Even though there is a Fools and Joculators guild in Ankh-Morpork, Verence's profession as a fool harks back to Touchstone the fool in *As You Like It*, as well as to lines spoken by Jaques, a depressed character. A fool's capering lightens Jaques's mood, as he describes in act II, scene vii. Also, the fact that Verence (or the Fool, as he is known for much of *Wyrd Sisters*) constantly uses the language of the day ("marry," "prithee") fits the Shakespearean mode.

---

[5] Ibid., 188.

A Slumber Party, Lords and Ladies

Next up in the playbill: *Lords and Ladies* (*LL*). While Pratchett's *LL* is not a parody of *A Midsummer Night's Dream*, Shakespeare's tale of erroneous match-ups among lovers, it has some similarities. Verence II, the king of Lancre, and Magrat Garlick are on the eve of their wedding (one that will take place on Midsummer Day), just as Duke Theseus (yes, that Theseus—the Greek hero) and Hippolyta in *Dream* are. There's even to be a special play that takes place on Midsummer's Eve to commemorate the wedding of Verence and Magrat. And whaddya know—a play is held at the wedding feast of Theseus and Hippolyta in *Dream*. Unlike "the story of the Queen of the Fairies"[6] that Jason Ogg describes in *LL*, in *Dream* a group of Athenian laborers—Quince the carpenter, Snug the joiner, Bottom the weaver, Starveling the tailor, Snout the tinker, and Flute the bellows-mender—perform the love story of Pyramus and Thisbe, a reference to a story in *Metamorphoses* by Ovid and one that parallels the situation with Lysander and Hermia.

Of course, we can't help comparing the list of these laborers to the Lancre Morris Men in *LL*. Pratchett mentions Carter the baker, Weaver the thatcher, Baker the weaver, Tailor "the other weaver," Carpenter the poacher, Thatcher the carter, Tinker the tinker, and Jason Ogg the blacksmith, who call themselves "Rude Mechanicals" (*LL*, page 140)—an allusion to Puck's description of the Athenian laborers in *Dream*: "a crew of patches, rude mechanicals that work for bread upon Athenian stalls."[7]

"The fair folk"—the elves/fairies or "lords and ladies" as Granny

---

[6] *Lords and Ladies* (New York: HarperTorch, 1992), 83.

[7] Shakespeare, *A Midsummer Night's Dream* (New York: Washington Square Press, 1993), lines 9–10, p. 83.

and Nanny call them—almost ruin "the course of true love" (*Dream*, act I, i, 136) with their antics, just as in *Dream*. In *LL*, the Fairy Queen's desire for a mortal husband (even though she already has an immortal one) mirrors Titania's flirting, as Oberon her King of the Fairies husband, would attest. The Long Man, the husband of the Fairy Queen, has to help set things right, just as Oberon has to do in *Dream*.

Even though he has antlers, the Long Man reminds us of Pan, the Greek god of shepherds and flocks, who had goat horns and hooves. (If you saw *Pan's Labyrinth*, an Oscar-winning film from 2006, directed by Guillermo del Toro, you've seen a portrayal of Pan.) But the name is an allusion to the Long Man of Wilmington, the male figure carved into Windover Hill in Sussex, England. No one knows who carved the figure, which is outlined by painted concrete blocks. It may have been done in the twelfth century.

And what of the elves? They are mischievous like Puck in *A Midsummer Night's Dream*. But their mischief goes beyond flinging a love potion or giving someone a donkey's head. We've more to say about that in chapter 12. They only look like Legolas and the other noble elves of *Lord of the Rings* because of the glamour they cast on unsuspecting humans—the belief that they are beautiful.

If you're into Brian Froud at all, you know that he illustrated a number of books on fairy creatures (*Giants*; *Faeries*, co-illustrated with Alan Lee; *Good Faeries/Bad Faeries*). Pratchett's elves would fall under the bad faeries category. Pratchett's Fairy Queen, like Titania, is self-centered but less pliable than Titania. Unlike Gloriana, the fairy queen of Edmund Spenser's epic, *The Faerie Queen*, Pratchett's queen is iceberg-cold emotionally, colder than Hans Christian Andersen's Snow Queen. In *The Wee Free Men*, where we meet her again (first in *Lords and Ladies*), she at least has some maternal instincts, as shown through her kidnapping of children (another allusion to the Snow Queen). But she really doesn't understand children and thinks nothing of ordering her elves to shoot to kill any humans who get in her way. Can't imagine Galadriel doing that!

Hwel the playwright makes a guest appearance in a footnote at the end of *LL* with the mention of two titles for the same play: *The Taming of the Vole* and *Things That Happened on a Midsummer Night*. We don't have to tell you that these titles are allusions to Shakespeare's *The Taming of the Shrew* and *A Midsummer Night's Dream*. Whoops. Guess we already did.

This is a great opportunity to take a ten-minute intermission. We expect you back in your seats when the lights flash.

 ## The Scottish Play: A Superstition

In some theatrical circles, actors perform "the Scottish play," rather than *Macbeth*. This is all due to the Macbeth superstition—the fear that performing the play will cause horrible things to happen to the actors or others on the set. In particular, those who even say the name of the play or use the words of the witches' chant (act IV, scene I) could have an accident or die.

Rumors of terrible things that happened to theatrical companies caused this superstition to flourish. So, how did this superstition begin?

Many companies on the wane would perform *Macbeth* at the end of their season, hoping to stay in business, knowing that the crowds loved the play. But even the ticket sales for *Macbeth* couldn't keep them afloat. So they closed, thus inspiring the fear that performing *Macbeth* would cause terrible things to happen.

ACT II: IN WHICH WE EXPLORE MUSICAL THEATER

A Grand Day at the Opera

When was the last time you saw *Phantom of the Opera?* We've seen the stage production a combined total of about seven times. *Maskerade* revisits the world of the *Phantom of the Opera.* But Andrew Lloyd Webber's stage hit wouldn't have been made had it not been for the book written by Gaston Leroux and serialized in 1909–10. Leroux was inspired to write books because of the well-known mysteries of Arthur Conan Doyle and Edgar Allan Poe. Although Leroux said that the inspiration for *Phantom* was the Paris opera house and an accident that took place in 1896, when the counterweight of a chandelier dropped on the audience (ouch), it also may have been inspired by *Trilby*, a popular novel by George du Maurier, published in 1894. The protagonist is Trilby, a tone-deaf young woman who can't sing but who is hypnotized into doing so by Svengali, a musician and mesmerist.

Leroux's world is populated by opera ingénue Christine Daaé, her aristocratic childhood friend Raoul, opera diva Carlotta, opera managers Richard and Moncharmin, Madame Giry, and Erik, the misshapen "opera ghost"/"angel of music" whose murderous antics overshadow all. A man known as the Persian witnesses the story's events.

Erik vows to make Christine a great opera singer if she remains in his control and loves only him. He's also not above extorting money from the previous managers of the opera house and occasionally killing anyone who gets in his way. (As a criminal, he is an overachiever.) But Raoul falls for Christine, who reciprocates his love, which raises the ire of Erik, who tries to coerce Christine into giving up Raoul, by first kidnapping her and then torturing Raoul and the Persian to rid himself of his rival. But Christine later talks Erik into letting them go.

Opera, of course, plays a major part in the story, with the mention of performances of Gounod's opera *Faust* (based on Goethe's epic) and Erik's own composition—*Don Juan Triumphant*.

Leroux's book wasn't exactly a smash hit when it hit the shelves. But a 1925 Lon Chaney movie helped it gain more attention. Other film versions soon followed, including one in 1943 with Claude Rains and Nelson Eddy. (We didn't see either one.)

Andrew Lloyd Webber's stage production of *Phantom,* which first opened in London in 1986, became the *Phantom* most people remember. As of the writing of this book, it is the longest-running show on Broadway in history. It spawned a movie adaptation of its own—a 2004 production directed by Joel Schumacher and produced by Webber.

Pratchett stepped into the *Phantom* world with *Maskerade,* a title that plays on the masquerade taking place during the course of Leroux's story and the stage play and Poe's story "The Masque of the Red Death"—from which Erik's Red Death costume in the book and musical is derived. (Got all that? There will be a quiz later. . . . Just kidding.)

A Christine inhabits the Pratchett *Phantom* world, but so does an Agnes Nitt, the would-be member of Granny Weatherwax's trio of witches, whose voice is used for Christine's opera debut. Instead of Paris, the venue is Ankh-Morpork. Instead of Buquet, the murdered scene-stealer in Leroux's story, there is Mr. Bucket, the owner of the opera house. (A scene-stealer *does* make an appearance in *Maskerade.*) And instead of Erik the solitary phantom, there are two opera ghosts: Walter Plinge and Salzella, the musical director. But per Webber's production, there is an André. But instead of being the owner/manager of the house, he is an undercover cop as well as a piano player.

Not content to parody the plot of *Phantom,* Pratchett alludes to several operas, not to mention the one-two combo of a title like *The Joye of Snacks* (Nanny Ogg's racy cookbook), which parodies in content and title both *The Joy of Cooking* and *The Joy of Sex*. But let's stick with opera.

PRATCHETT OPERAS	THE OPERAS TO WHICH PRATCHETT ALLUDES
Cosí fan Hita	*Così fan tutte*, composed by Wolfgang Amadeus Mozart
Die Meistersinger van Scrote	*Die Meistersinger von Nürnberg* (The Mastersingers of Nuremberg), composed by Richard Wagner
Lohenshaak	*Lohengrin*, composed by Wagner
La triviata	*La traviata* (The Fallen One), composed by Giuseppe Verdi
Il Truccatore (The Master of Disguise)	*Il trovatore* (The Troubadour), composed by Verdi
Die Fleiderliev	*Die Fledermaus* (The Bat), composed by Johann Strauss II
The Ring of the Nibelungingung	*Der Ring des Nibelungen* (The Ring of the Nibelung), composed by Wagner
The Barber of Pseudopolis	*Il barbiere di Siviglia* (The Barber of Seville), composed by Gioacchino Rossini
The Enchanted Piccolo	*Die Zauberflöte* (The Magic Flute), composed by Mozart

Other theatrical productions mentioned in *Maskerade*:

PRATCHETT MUSICALS	THE MUSICALS TO WHICH PRATCHETT ALLUDES
Guys and Trolls	*Guys and Dolls*, composed by Frank Loesser and adapted from Damon Runyon's short story by Jo Swerling and Abe Burrows, opened in 1950.
Hubward Side Story	*West Side Story*, an updated *Romeo and Juliet*, was composed by Leonard Bernstein with lyrics by Stephen Sondheim and a book by Arthur Laurents, opened in 1957.
Miserable Les	*Les Misérables*, written by Claude-Michel Schönberg and Alain Boublil, who based it on the novel by Victor Hugo, opened in Paris in 1980. It is the third-longest running show on Broadway (behind *Cats* and *Phantom*).
Seven Dwarfs for Seven Other Dwarfs	*Seven Brides for Seven Brothers*, a 1954 movie directed by Stanley Donen, with lyrics by Johnny Mercer and music by Saul Chaplin and Gene de Paul.

With Discworld's parodies, the play's the thing and the play's cha-ching for Pratchett. For another musical parodied, see chapter 13. But for now, please exit to your right. And don't forget your playbill.

Ringside Seats

In *The Fifth Elephant*, Sam, Sybil, and the rest of the diplomatic team travel to Shmaltzberg in Uberwald and see a performance of the dwarf opera *Bloodaxe and Ironhammer*. This opera, we're told, is from the Koboldean Cycle—a series of operas usually performed over five weeks. Well, that's an allusion to Richard Wagner's opera series *Der Ring des Nibelungen* (The Ring of the Nibelung)—which is about as grand as opera can get. Many people just call it the Ring Cycle.

The four operas of the Ring Cycle are *Das Rheingold, Die Walküre, Siegfried,* and *Götterdämmerung*. This opera series is usually shown over four nights and takes about fifteen hours to perform. (If you're tempted to sneer at that, consider the fact that many people watched all three *Lord of the Rings* extended editions in marathon showings at theaters—almost twelve hours of viewing, not to mention a marathon of all five Best Picture Oscar nominees for 2007 at AMC theaters.)

Maybe you're not into opera as grand as that. But many fantasy writers, including Pratchett, Tolkien, Stephen R. Donaldson, and the Wachowski Brothers (the *Matrix* trilogy), were familiar with the story.

The Ring Cycle, which is based on Norse mythology, is about a magic ring a dwarf named Alberich forged out of Rheingold stolen from the Rhine that grants power to rule the world. (So, it's fitting that the Koboldean Cycle is performed by dwarfs!) Everyone who gains it has great difficulty giving it up. Sound familiar? Wotan (Odin), the chief god, steals the ring, thus prompting Alberich to curse it. All who obtain it come to grief as Wotan soon finds out. (Sméagol in *Lord of the Rings* found that out as well.) Siegfried—a

(continued)

hero not unlike Achilles in that he's part god, part human, with one weakness (his back instead of his heel)—obtains it, to his doom. If you saw *Matrix Revolutions*, you saw a funeral as grand as that of Siegfried's in *Götterdämmerung*.

After that, the ring finally returns from whence it came, just as the ring in *Lord of the Rings* returns to Mount Doom. Kinda gets you all choked up, doesn't it?

Part Two

The Few, the Proud, the Inept: Who's Who in Discworld

6

~

Witchy Woman

Wooo hooo witchy woman,
See how high she flies.
—"Witchy Woman" by the Eagles from *The Eagles*
album (1972), lyrics by Don Henley[1]

Witches are just plain meaner than wizards.
—Professional wizard/detective Harry Dresden in *Storm Front*[2]

BEWITCHED

What words or images does the word "witch" conjure in your mind? (Ha ha. Pun intended.) Bad-tempered? Evil? Scary? Warty? An image of someone mysterious like the woman in the song above, even though that song is really not about a witch, per se? It is one that conflicts many people—us included. Traditionally, witches in literature have not been viewed as positively as warlocks or sorcerers have. Think of the image of Ged (Ursula LeGuin's Earthsea series) or Merlin (for more on them, see the next chapter) versus Ged's aunt in *A Wizard of Earthsea*. Whereas Ged becomes a learned man well versed in high magic, the magic-wielding aunt walks in ignorance and battles the suspicions of others. Or think of *The Crucible*, Arthur Miller's

---

[1] Posted at http://www.cowboylyrics.com/lyrics/eagles/witchy-woman-16012.html.
[2] Jim Butcher, *Storm Front*, book 1 of The Dresden Files (New York: Penguin, 2000), 21.

classic play about the Salem witch hunt, as a symbol for McCarthyism. (Or maybe you wish to forget that.) Consider the fears, prejudices, and ignorance of the townspeople and how the accusation of witchcraft became a tool in the hands of manipulative individuals.

Let's get back to image. Many of the books and movies written today have tried to shake up the image of the witch we're used to in fairy tales. In the 1960s, there was Samantha Stephens, the suburban housewife/witch played by Elizabeth Montgomery in the TV show *Bewitched*, which you can still see on TV Land. You know—the one with the annoying mother, Endora, and the mortal husband, Darrin (played by two different actors—Dick York and Dick Sargent). Samantha made a comeback in the 2005 movie starring Nicole Kidman and Will Ferrell. (Perhaps you wish to forget that, as well.) Just before the movie *Bewitched*, TV shows and movies like *Charmed, Sabrina the Teenage Witch*, and *The Craft* featured younger witches. And of course, there's the Harry Potter book and movie series, and *Wicked*—first the book, then the hit play.

As you know, witches in traditional fairy tales tend to come in oven door–slamming sizes, ride broomsticks, have warts, and cackle. They're wicked (the Wicked Witches of the West and East from Oz), like to snack on children (Baba Yaga in Russian fairy tales; the witch in "Hansel and Gretel"), are fond of cats, and wouldn't win any beauty contests. But sometimes witches are beautiful, but still evil at heart, like the White Witch in *The Lion, the Witch and the Wardrobe*, C. S. Lewis's classic tale, Morgan Le Fay in the King Arthur tales, or the queen in "Snow White and the Seven Dwarfs," the Brothers Grimm fairy tale used in the 1937 Disney movie. The queen was also of the stepmother variety and you know what fairy tales have to say about them. (See *evil* above.)

But in the Harry Potter series, Hermione Granger is one of the heroines and doesn't have a wart. She is fond of cats, though. And then there's Professor McGonagall, the head of Gryffindor House—a stern but noble woman, who can turn herself into a cat, and Professor Trelawney, who's ditzy. In Robert Jordan's Wheel of Time series, Moiraine Damodred, Egwene al'Vere, Nynaeve al'Meara and many others are Aei Sedai—female channelers of power—who behave heroically, but sometimes make mistakes. None of them have warts, either. And let's not forget the Bene Gesserits—the witches of the Dune series. Like Jessica, the mother of Paul (Muad'Dib), they can be manipulative. (Some would call that assertive.) But no warts there, either.

So, what are witches like in Discworld? Well, they are . . .

. . . Powerful.

At Hogwarts, Hermione Granger is touted as the best witch of her generation. So, what does that mean exactly? Well, she's the smartest girl at school, for one thing. (Well, in book 7 this aspect changed to a degree.) Esmeralda (Granny) Weatherwax is possibly the best witch in Discworld. In other words, she's the Ged or Merlin of her world. (Although we wonder if Tiffany Aching may someday eclipse her.) Her brand of "headology" (she makes *you* do the work instead of her) may seem like a bunch of hooey or psychobabble, but it helps her reserve power. She unleashes it from time to time to help save Discworld.

She's a borrower—but not like the Clocks in Mary Norton's classic children's series The Borrowers. She can delve into the mind of an animal. This is different from actual transformation into an animal, as wizards such as Ged or Merlin achieve with the right word of power. After all, Granny leaves her body behind, usually with a sign reminding others that she's alive.

With a troll-given name Aaoograha hoa ("She Who Must Be Avoided"—see *Maskerade*—or the dwarf-given name K'ez'rek d'b'duz ("Go Around the Other Side of the Mountain"—also in *Maskerade*), you know that others see her as intimidating. (Maybe right now, you're thinking of "He Who Must Not Be Named"—Lord Voldemort of the Harry Potter series. Well, *Maskerade* came first.) And Granny's good at psyching out opponents in Cripple Mr. Onion—the preferred card game of Discworld. Only a fool would bet against her.

Imagine what being the best at something is like. (Perhaps you don't have to imagine—you are.) Like a gunslinger, you wait for someone to come along and challenge your position. Only when that person comes, you know that being the best might mean killing or being killed, severely wounded, dethroned, or humiliated. That's Granny's position. When a younger witch and a Fairy Queen challenge her in *Lords and Ladies*, Granny can't say, "No, I'd rather not, thanks." Part of the territory of being the best means accepting any challenge. This is Jason Ogg's position, as well (see chapter 14).

Pratchett goes into great detail about Granny in his Discworld fact books, so let's move on to Nanny Ogg. While Gytha (Nanny) Ogg may act as Granny's sidekick, she's not really an Avis to Granny's Hertz. After all, Nanny helps turn back time in *Wyrd Sisters*. She also delivers the offspring of the personification of Time and Wen the Eternally Surprised (*Thief of Time*). Anyone who is always there to help save the world is pretty powerful in our opinion. And she's as jolly as the Spirit of Christmas Present in Dickens's *A Christmas Carol*. In her home, her word is law. Just ask her daughters-in-law.

Tiffany, Magrat Garlick, and Agnes Nitt—young and upcoming witches (well, Magrat is a queen now)—don't exactly fit the *Charmed* school of young witches model, although they have the potential for just as much angst. The young witches are constantly engaged in the old-school versus new-school conflict. As you know, Magrat continually butts heads with Granny Weatherwax, who feels that Magrat's clothes and ideas of how to use magic are weird. Magrat's sort of a flower child/sucker for supernatural paraphernalia that Granny is quick to dismiss. And Tiffany and Agnes have moments, brought about through Granny's manipulation, which they live to regret. Yet Granny seems to see vast potential in Tiffany. And no wonder. Tiffany is possibly the most powerful of her peers, who include Petulia Gristle, Annagramma Hawkin, Lucy Warbeck, and Dimity Hubbub.

. . . Hardworking and Helpful.

Tiffany, the "big wee hag"—a moniker given to her by the Nac Mac Feegles in *The Wee Free Men*, *A Hat Full of Sky*, *Wintersmith*, and a fourth book Pratchett proposed writing, tentatively called *I Shall Wear Midnight* (as of this printing, that book has not yet been published)—is a hard worker, no question about that. She comes from a farming community of hard workers. She makes cheese, milks cows and goats, delivers babies, and apprentices herself to the witches of the land to do more of the same.

As Pratchett mentioned at a book signing in Naperville, Illinois, in October 2006, Tiffany's miniseries is based on words and hard work. Tiffany, Granny, Nanny, Petulia Gristle (the pig witch), and others exemplify this.

Okay, milking a cow or making cheese may not seem as impressive as calling down lightning or shooting fireballs at people. But somebody's gotta do it.

In all of the Lancre witch/Tiffany Aching miniseries, Discworld or some unfortunate individual needs saving from some threat: vampires (*Carpe Jugulum*), a "phantom" killer (*Maskerade*), an evil tyrant (*Wyrd Sisters*), a crazed fairy godmother (*Witches Abroad*), "Them" (*Equal Rites*), the Fairy Queen and her elves (*Lords and Ladies*, *The Wee Free Men*), the hiver (*A Hat Full of Sky*), or endless winter (*Wintersmith*). Then, like true fairy godmothers or like Glinda the Good (the Witch of the North in Oz), Granny, Nanny, Magrat, and Tiffany come to the rescue.

Not all of the Discworld witches are helpful. (Annagramma Hawkin, anyone?) There are more than a few bad apples, à la those in Oz, Earthsea, and other places.

. . . Followers of Tradition to a Degree.

As we mentioned in chapter 5, Granny and Nanny are firm believers in the rule of three, which was also enforced on the show *Charmed*. But some witches, like Lily Weatherwax, Granny's sister, follow tradition to the detriment of others.

Mercedes Lackey calls the storytelling traditions inherent in fairy tales "The Tradition" in her Five Hundred Kingdoms series, which begins with *The Fairy Godmother*, a story about a Cinderella type (Elena) who seeks to buck tradition and avoid a disastrous marriage by becoming a fairy godmother. (Thinking about *Witches Abroad* right now?) The Tradition—the magical force that propels heroes and heroines alike down a traditional path laid out in other fairy tales—wars against Elena's plans. Lily Weatherwax, had she been present, would've forced Elena toward her Cinderella destiny, no matter how ugly that destiny seemed. After all, that's what Lily does in *Witches Abroad*.

As we said in chapter 1, writers and compilers like the Brothers Grimm, Andrew Lang, Hans Christian Andersen, and others helped shape the tradition by the stories they included in their collections. But Pratchett tweaks tradition to fit his story.

. . . Odd.

In a series like Discworld, you've got to expect a few, well, oddities. How else can you explain a Mrs. Evadne Cake, a medium with precognition she can turn off and on, or a Eumenides Treason ("Myth Treason" to Tiffany) with her Boffo skulls and seeing-eye mouse (*Wintersmith*)? But every witch has an odd streak in a Pratchett-written series—even Magrat Garlick, who thinks she's normal, but . . . isn't. She's slightly "Luna Lovegood" (Harry Potter series; note that Magrat came first as a character)—the odd one even in an odd bunch. Or Agnes Nitt, the young witch with the marvelous singing voice and a split personality (Perdita—the thin witch inside the heavier witch). Or what about Granny, who is as ornery at times as Granny from the 1960s TV series *The Beverly Hillbillies?* Although they're odd, they're never boring.

These aren't your witches striving to blend in to avoid being burned at the stake. (Well, they probably want to avoid that.) Unlike Samantha Stephens, who wanted to get along with nosy Mrs. Kravitz and fit into the neighborhood, Discworld witches revel in their oddities. In fact, witches like Miss Treason deliberately try to fit the notion of the odd witch by going the extra mile—hence the mail-order skulls and stick-on warts. See? Odd.

. . . Noncacklers (Hopefully).

In Discworld, cackling is a sign of cracking, something akin to going to the Dark Side in the *Star Wars* series. No witch in her right mind (literally) would cackle. Black Aliss—the greatest witch, in Granny's opinion—cackled. Although she was the first to turn back time, she wound up over the edge.

Black Aliss, who went the way of the witch from Hansel and Gretel—shut up in an oven by two kids—is an allusion to Black Annis, the witch from the folklore of Leicestershire. A witch with a diet consisting of children is a sure sign of the cackler. That, and building gingerbread houses. Of course, a witch could go for the house-on-chicken-legs model—another sign of the cackler—à la Baba Yaga, the witch in Russian folktales. Mrs. Gogol, the voodoo witch in *Witches Abroad,* favored a hut on duck feet—a parody of Baba Yaga. That just shows you where Mrs. Gogol stood on the cackling front. (Crossing the border into Cackle Town.)

. . . Alone by Choice.

Ged's aunt in *A Wizard of Earthsea* lived alone—a product of the suspicions of others and the need for privacy when one practiced magic. Granny Weatherwax has her mountain cottage and soup for one. And although Nanny Ogg has a home with hot and cold running sons and daughters-in-laws popping in for visits, basically, it's just her and her cat, Greebo.

Witches tend to be loners, occasionally getting together with other witches to make up the rule of three or to train someone. Even someone in a family like Tiffany is still alone—that is, forced into a position of authority that makes her feel alone, as we learn in *Wintersmith*.

As Galadriel explained to Frodo in the film based on *The Fellowship of the Ring*, "You are a Ring-bearer, Frodo. To bear a Ring of Power is to be alone."[3] Bearing the mantle of power is to be alone.

In *Wyrd Sisters*, we're told that witches aren't managed by someone who considers herself "head witch." In other words, there is no archchancellor for witches. There's just an unofficial understanding that Granny Weatherwax is in charge. It's lonely at the top.

. . . Usually Not Wizards.

You might think that goes without saying, but in Discworld, there are some exceptions. We talked about Eskarina in other chapters. Mrs. Letice Earwig, Granny Weatherwax's rival in *Wintersmith*, uses wizard magic—behavior of which Granny disapproves as she explains in *Equal Rites*.

Is there a so-called "women's magic"? As we mentioned in chapter 4, wizards consider witches incapable of high magic and look disparagingly at the "womanly" art of hedge witchery. (They're only

---

[3] Posted at the IMDB site: http://imdb.com/title/tt0120737/quotes.

fooling themselves.) So in Discworld, the magic usage seems to be a point of division between the sexes. Yet someone like Idalia from the Obsidian Trilogy (Mercedes Lackey) is called a "mage" (a "wild-mage," to be exact), rather than a witch. She performs the same kind of magic that a male mage does and seems to be one of the best in the land. Hermione also performs the same magic that Harry or Ron does. But she's considered a witch. It's a matter of semantics.

. . . Not Religious.

Faith is the hallmark of a religion. If you don't believe, what's the point? Pratchett has said in more than one book that the witches aren't believers in the gods. (See, for example, page 15 of the paperback edition of *Witches Abroad*.) This is because they can see the gods and elementals at times and aren't very impressed by what they see, kind of like how we feel whenever we read stories from Greek mythology. For example, Tiffany sees Anoia—the goddess of things that get stuck in drawers—in *Wintersmith* and is less than awed. And she, of course, is wooed by the Wintersmith, whom she discovers has a major screw loose, but who at least is on the hot side when he takes on human flesh. Still, being a hottie does not automatically gain one worship and respect in the witches' book.

Witches see Death every now and then, especially since they're the ones who watch over the dead on the first night after death. Like the wizards, they know when they're going to die, which takes away some of Death's mystique.

While the witches' lack of faith in the gods might seem like a paradox—how can you not believe in something you can see?—it really isn't, if you think about having faith or trust in someone. You wouldn't put your trust in someone who has proven to be unfaithful or uncaring. And many of the gods and elementals of Discworld are untrustworthy, petty, vain, and just plain weird. The witches even see Death in "You're the Man keeping us down" terms.

Since the gods and personifications (more on them in chapter 9) behave so predictably—and illogically—at times, the witches feel they're the last resort for humanity. Remember in *Mort*, when Death says, "There's just me," in response to Mort's statement, "There is no justice"?[4] That's how the witches feel 24/7. Consider the fact that Tiffany has to save the people of the Chalk time and time again. And Granny and Nanny are always in the Save the World queue. A woman's work is never done.

. . . Shepherdesses.

Although Tiffany's grandmother (Sarah Aching) was considered a shepherdess by trade, rather than a witch, she not only watched her flock, she shepherded the land as well. Tiffany has inherited the instinct for shepherding—or safeguarding—the land and the lambs, especially the "strays" Wentworth and Roland de Chumsfanleigh (the baron's son), who are captured by the Fairy Queen in *The Wee Free Men*.

Granny, Nanny, and others have their own particular flocks—the people in the villages for whom they provide medicine or deliver babies and perform whatever task needs doing. This also includes shepherding their peers. When a witch looks as if she's ready to cackle, another witch has the obligation to check on her.

Another way a witch acts as a shepherdess is by finding other witches and keeping them from harm. That's the job of Miss Perspicacia Tick, the witch finder in *The Wee Free Men*. She's like a talent agent, in a way. She discovers Tiffany and later introduces her to Miss Level in *A Hat Full of Sky*. Miss Tick also is the writer of *Magavenatio Obtusis* (Witch Hunting for Dumb People), a book she slips into the town of Dogbend (page 39 of *Wintersmith*—the hardcover edition) to prevent the town from harming witches. This brings to mind yet another point. Witches are . . .

---

[4] *Mort* (New York: HarperTorch, 1987), 39.

. . . Teachers of One Another.

There is no Unseen University (see next chapter) for witches. Yes, we know that, in *The Wee Free Men*, Miss Tick tells Tiffany to open her eyes and see the school for witches. But she is speaking metaphorically, as Tiffany is quick to guess. Life is the great teacher witches depend upon. But mainly there's the community of witches · from which to learn.

Tiffany, Magrat, and Agnes all had the benefit of hanging with Granny and Nanny and learning from them or, in some cases, *in spite of* them. Tiffany's first teacher, however, was Miss Tick. In turn, Tiffany helps Annagramma in *Wintersmith* and encourages other young witches to do so when Annagramma gains Miss Treason's cottage.

⟋

Discworld might not have the shiny linoleum of suburbia embodied in *Charmed* or *Bewitched*. But it has what those shows don't have: a community of magic practitioners whose exploits will entertain you without fear of cancellation.

 ## Wise Women

I f you read fantasy or medieval fiction a lot, you've probably come across a wise woman or two. By this, we don't mean strictly female versions of King Solomon, although women bearing this title (wise woman) know a thing or two. We mean *witte wieven*, as they are called in Dutch folklore or "wise women"—the village herbalists and mystics others sometimes seek for prophecies or fortune telling.

(continued)

Sidebar (continued)

They're the ones to go to for potions or charms. Some might call them witches (specifically white witches) or hags or even the village "wisdom" as Nynaeve is called in *Eye of the World* by Robert Jordan.

With their knowledge of herbs, midwifery skills, and just plain common sense, Pratchett's witches seem to follow the wise woman tradition in folklore. They are like the powerful woman Princess Irene calls Grandmother in George MacDonald's *The Princess and the Goblin* and *The Princess and Curdie* and, of course, the wise woman in his novella *The Wise Woman*—a woman who lived alone and knew just what to do in order to tame a spoiled princess. (We can only imagine what Granny Weatherwax would've done with her!)

Being "the wise woman" isn't without hazards. In *Good Omens*, a book Pratchett coauthored with Neil Gaiman, a seventeenth-century witch, Agnes Nutter, who makes Nostradamus-like prophecies, is burned at the stake. While we may read the book and laugh, no one was laughing during the Salem witch trials back in 1692, when twenty people were put to death. Consider also the case of Bessie Dunlop, a midwife living in Dalry, Scotland, who was burned at the stake in 1576 after being charged with witchcraft. Although she was a real person, a number of stories associated with her life may be fact or fiction. One story is that, before she died, she was told to denounce her faith in God and admit that she served the devil. She did neither. A wise woman, indeed.

~

7

We're Off to See the Wizards

Wood and water, stock and stone I can master,
but there's a Wizard to manage here. . . .
—Treebeard in *Return of the King* (the movie)[1]

There's magic. . . . It don't take much intelligence,
otherwise wizards wouldn't be able to do it.
—Granny Weatherwax in *The Wee Free Men*[2]

WHO'S GOT THE POWER?

When was the first time you saw a magician? When you were a lit-tle kid, sitting wide-eyed with wonder while your older brother pulled a quarter out of your ear, thanks to his magic tricks book? When you were an older kid, sitting bored while the Great Lame-O the Magician, who had all the charisma of a soft-boiled egg, failed miserably at performing (and groused about his soul-destroying job)? Or was it just last year in Vegas, watching the latest magic debunker who explained how all the other magicians did their tricks?

Sooner or later, you discover that while Penn and Teller, David Blaine, David Copperfield, Houdini, the wizard in *The Wizard of*

---

[1] Posted at http://www.tk421.net/lotr/film/rotk/02.html.
[2] *The Wee Free Men* (New York: HarperTrophy, 2003), 357. (Like the old Magnum.)

Oz, or Borden and Angier—the rival wizards in Christopher Nolan's movie, *The Prestige*—are wizards at the sleight of hand, now-you-see-it-now-you-don't trick, they aren't . . . well . . . *real* wizards (Well, Angier had that weird Tesla-designed box. . . .)—the kind that lob fireballs at people and wear pointed hats.

Maybe you're thinking about Rincewind right about now. . . .

Many writers have written about wizards—no doubt inspired by the legends of Merlin (also known as Myrddin) the magician, King Arthur's teacher-wizard as rendered by Geoffrey of Monmouth and T. H. White (who favored the Merlyn spelling) in *The Once and Future King* and *The Book of Merlyn;* or Gandalf the Grey-turned-White wizard of *The Lord of the Rings* trilogy, J. R. R. Tolkien's baby. These are your über-wizards: powerful, self-sacrificing, wise, cranky old men—at least in appearance. (Well, they've been known to laugh every now and then.) Their powers go far beyond pulling a quarter out of someone's ear or making the Statue of Liberty "disappear." These are the kinds of wizards who put monarchs on thrones and help change the world.

Whether you call them wizards, sorcerers, male Aei Sedai (channelers), spell weavers, chanters, mages, magicians (a vast cut above Lame-O), thaumaturgists, dragon riders, or blacksmiths (see chapter 14), these power wielders come in all shapes and sizes these days. You could easily name several dozen without breaking a sweat. There are Harry Potter, Ron Weasley, Albus Dumbledore, the evil Lord Voldemort, and many others from the Harry Potter series. Pug conDoin (Milamber), Kulgan, Macros the Black, and other magicians populate Raymond Feist's Riftwar series. Ged/Sparrowhawk, the mage turned archmage; Ogion, his former master; and many others appear in Ursula LeGuin's Earthsea series. Then there are First Wizard Zeddicus Zu'l Zorander (Zedd) and his grandson Richard Rahl (a war wizard) in Terry Goodkind's Sword of Truth series; Rand al'Thor (the Dragon Reborn) and others of Robert Jordan's Wheel of Time series; the dapper Jonathan Strange and fussy little Mr. Norrell of Susanna Clarke's novel, *Jonathan Strange and Mr. Norrell*; Darrow, of Kate Constable's Chanters of Tremaris trilogy; the elemental wizards of Mercedes Lackey's Elemental Masters series and Kellen the Knight-Mage of the Obsidian Trilogy (written with James Mallory); Harry Dresden, the wizard detective created by Jim Butcher; dragon-riders Brom and Eragon in *Eragon*; the fake wizard turned real wizard Schmendrick in *The Last Unicorn* (Peter S. Beagle)—the list goes on and on and on.

In Discworld, there's a difference between wizards, magicians, conjurers, and thaumaturgists. Magicians are those who flunked out of Unseen University but at least they aren't conjurers or thaumaturgists—the lowest form of magic practitioner, a person lacking an education. Proper wizards earn their degrees from Unseen University.

In terms of wise, heroic wizards, on a scale of 1–10 (10 being the wisest/most heroic), many of Pratchett's denizens of Unseen University would probably rank a 2 at best, with Merlin, Gandalf, Ged, Dumbledore, and many of the others mentioned above solidly at the 10 spot. (Okay, maybe we'd give Ridcully and the Librarian a 5 or 6 for effort.) Pratchett's wizards are at the college don end of the spectrum—more apt to wield a knife and fork than a staff in action. It's not that they're powerless, they're just . . . well . . . hungry.

DISC-CLAIMER:
Plot spoilers ahead. Read at your own risk.

THE LOOK THAT SAYS "WIZZARD"

On a number of occasions, Granny Weatherwax and other witches mention that a witch's hat earns a witch respect. But what about the wizards? Is there a look that screams "wizard" (or in Rincewind's case—"wizzard")? When you think of the archetypal look of a wizard, perhaps you immediately think of Gandalf, Merlin, or the wizard in *The Sorcerer's Apprentice* (whose score, *L'apprenti sorcier*, a scherzo by Paul Dukas, was based on a story by Goethe) as animated in *Fantasia*. *The Sorcerer's Apprentice* wizard had your typical blue robe and the tall, pointed blue hat with moons and stars. Merlin also favored the tall, pointed hat and a robe with zodiac symbols, fur tippets, and owl droppings. A nice look for spring. Gandalf, not to be left out, wore a similar hat, a gray robe (until he became Gandalf the White), and a dashing silver scarf. Ooo-la-la. And of course there's the beard—white or gray—and the all-important staff—the medium through which power flows. (Wands are used in the Harry Potter series. Harry Dresden uses a wand and a staff.)

Pratchett's wizards are the equal of other wizards of fiction in fashion sense. They've got the beards, the pointed hats, the flowing robes, and the staffs. But Rincewind, a wizard wannabe, has a scraggly beard, a ragged robe, and a hat with the word "wizzard" on it. Not the kind of outfit that makes the best-dressed list or inspires confidence in Rincewind's abilities.

Evil wizards such as Abrim, the grand vizier in *Sourcery*, favor the turban-with-a-tiny-fez look set off with a thin moustache—a look Jafar rocked in Disney's *Aladdin* movies (*Aladdin*; *Return of Jafar*).

Another look that says "wizard" is the stuffed alligator, described by Quoth the Raven in *Soul Music*. Igneous Cutwell, a wizard with whom Death's one-time apprentice Mort has some dealings, also has one hanging from the ceiling of his shop. This brings to mind a story by L. Frank Baum called "The Stuffed Alligator," published in 1905. It concerns the capture, stuffing, and display of a young, disobedient alligator and how his mother rescues him through the aid of the Red-Eyed One, an alligator magician.

HEAD OF THE CLASS

Unseen University in Ankh-Morpork is to the Discworld series what Hogwarts is to the Harry Potter series; what the School of Wizardry on Roke is to the Earthsea series; what the City of Magicians on Kelewan and Pug's academy on Macros's island are to the Riftwar series; and what the Mage College of Armethalieh is to the Obsidian Trilogy—the place where magic is studied and taught. Hogwarts has its headmaster, the School of Wizardry on Roke its Arch-Mage, and Armethalieh its High Mage—the one who really runs the city. The three are considered the top wizards of their worlds. But in Unseen University, a place compared to the castle of Gormenghast (from the series written by Mervyn Peake), the archchancellor rules the roost.

The archchancellor supposedly is the leader of all of the wizards throughout Discworld, just as the Arch-Mage is the leader of all high mages in Armetheliah and was handpicked by the gods but elected by his fellow wizards. (Go figure.)

Who is like Mustrum Ridcully, who assumes the position in *Moving Pictures*? While not as kindly as Albus Dumbledore, he's big on charm. He's like *Fellowship of the Ring*'s Radagast in color (Ridcully the Brown), but unlike Radagast in that he yells at birds rather than befriends them, and hunts them with his hunting dragons. And he's like Saruman, but only in rank (the leader of the wizards). Bluff, blustering, and outdoorsy, Ridcully, a seventh-level wizard (out of eight levels), isn't the usual sort to hang around Unseen University. He attains the position for that simple fact. (The old archchancellor, Galder Weatherwax, an eighth-level wizard, disappears in *The Light Fantastic*.) He's also incredibly cheap, as he cheerfully withholds office supplies from the staff. And in his youth, he wanted to marry Granny Weatherwax!

Coin, a child sourcerer (an obvious wordplay on "sorcerer") in

Sourcery, briefly rules Unseen University and Ankh-Morpork, thanks to the plan of his crazy, vengeful father, Ipslore the Red. Since Coin is the eighth son of an eighth son of an eighth son, he is a "wizard squared," according to Pratchett, and therefore a source of magic, rather than just a practitioner of magic. Drum Billet, the old wizard in *Equal Rites*, expects Eskarina to be an eighth son of an eighth son. This is a parody of the seventh-son-of-the-seventh-son aspect of mythology. You know—the seventh son is the wizard, the hero, a healer, or has some other unusual fate in folktales. Seven is believed to be a special number. So why eight here? Eight is an extremely important number in Discworld. Consider the eight great spells; octarine, the color of magic and the eighth color of the rimbow (Discworld's version of a rainbow); the octograms wizards use—the list goes on and on.

A FEW GOOD . . . MEN?

Discworld has its share of eccentric wizards (almost a redundancy). We know many of the wizards of Unseen University by their titles, rather than their names. There's the Senior Wrangler, the Lecturer in Recent Runes, the Dean, the Chair of Indefinite Studies, Dean of Pentacles, and so on. But then there's Rincewind, who for a time has only one spell firmly anchored to his brain. He can't do magic to save his life.

And what of Unseen University's Librarian? Although he is currently an orangutan, he was once a human who was magically transformed into an orangutan. And no, he does not wear a pointed hat. With Pratchett committed to the fight to save orangutans, is there any wonder that the Librarian chose to remain an orangutan rather than return to being human?

It's only fitting that we again mention Eskarina, who invades the boys' club of wizardry by becoming Discworld's first female wizard. Of course, Granny Weatherwax could have had that honor, had she been allowed to attend Unseen University in her younger days.

THE STUDENT CENTER

It stands to reason that a place of learning has to have students. And a wizard is always in the process of learning. But they had to start somewhere. For many, the road from apprenticeship to mastery is unending. Maybe that's why many of Discworld's wizards are really old. Ponder Stibbons, a former graduate student-turned-head of Inadvisably Applied Magic, is one of the youngest wizards on staff. But there are students like Victor Tugelbend (*Moving Pictures*), who has the ability but lacks the drive to be a wizard, and Mr. Sideney (*Hogfather*), who lacks a moral compass and winds up in trouble for his part in the Hogfather escapade. They're about as far from true mastery as toast is from being an apple. Small wonder since the risk of death for wizards is far higher than for nonwizards.

Ged, Harry, Ron, Pug—we watch each on his road toward mastery. But does a wizard ever fully master his profession? Probably not. The wizards on Discworld keep learning one important lesson—how to stay alive.

A WIZARD'S JOB IS NEVER DONE

In *The Prestige*, the magicians always searched for the next trick—the one that would truly amaze an audience as well as catapult the magician to fame. Making the next discovery was their great work, like that of any scientist. But a wizard's great work seems to consist of putting the right person on the throne (a job for witches in Discworld), stopping evil wherever it may arise (as a knight would), and then fading away with the passage of time. Merlin, Ged, and

Gandalf accepted the fading aspect of life. Discworld wizards accept this insofar as they know when they're going to die. But as for putting the right person on the throne and other civic duties, well, they'd rather not get involved because doing so somehow always involves taxes. We can't blame them.

For some wizards, their great work is to find out what they're really made of. Schmendrick, in *The Last Unicorn*, didn't know he could work magic until he joined the unicorn's quest. And Harry Potter's soul-destroying life with the Dursleys proved to be the launching pad that gave Harry the resiliency he would later need in the fight against You-Know-Who. But what of Rincewind? Unlike self-doubting Schmendrick, he never comes to a place where he can work magic on his own. Yes, he works some in *Eric*—or at least seems to. But he was manipulated by a demon. And he works magic to a degree in *Sourcery*, but that's all due to the incredible amount of magic in the air because of the rule of sourcery. So, for Rincewind, his great work is remaining alive.

Some mundane tasks that a wizard handles might seem extraordinary to us. Wizards also are known for working the weather— stoking a breeze or blowing a cloud over the right place. Zedd, Ged, and many of the other mages of Earthsea were skilled weather workers. Even the wizards of Discworld accept this task as part of wizardry, but only act upon it when necessary. Teaching classes at Unseen University is another task they act upon only when necessary. But they are quick to lob a fireball at someone or something. They're trigger-happy.

For the wizard, words are of supreme importance—no matter what the task. Knowing the right words gives the wizard control. This is the lesson Brom taught Eragon in *Eragon*. This is what Ged learned in *A Wizard of Earthsea*. The Discworld wizards, too, are expected to have mastered the languages needed to cast spells— although they sometimes argue about those words.

MAGE WARS ROCK THE HOUSE

With all of that power, there are bound to be some egos and evil among wizardkind. Just about every world with wizards goes through mage wars, as writers like Robert Jordan, Terry Goodkind, J. K. Rowling, Mercedes Lackey, and others attest. If you read any of their series, you know that these wars are sometimes triggered by evil wizards (or those with seriously confused priorities) bent on world domination. A small band of plucky heroes unsure of their own powers is there to try to stop them, even if they wind up sacrificing their lives in the process. In the Harry Potter series, Harry, Ron, Hermione, Dumbledore, and other wizards are on the side of good against Voldemort and his Death Eaters. In *Debt of Bones*, it's Zedd versus the evil Panis Rahl and, in *Wizard's First Rule*, Zedd and Richard square off against Darken Rahl. In *The Farthest Shore*, Ged is pitted against Cob, a wizard who just happens to be dead. In the Obsidian Trilogy, the war is between the human and elf mages (not that there are many of the latter) on the one side and the evil Endarkened mages. Although mage wars can sometimes foster wars between humans and other beings, the emphasis in a mage war is on those who wield the power.

Sourcery describes the mage war in Discworld that results when the archchancellor's stolen hat is worn by the evil Abrim. Wizard egos get in the way of Ipslore and Abrim's twin quests for world domination. (More on the villain's quest in chapter 12.) Of course, Rincewind is in the thick of things (he usually is) and the world nearly ends—par for the course in Discworld and for the life of a wizard.

Top Gun

Who would win in a mage contest between the wizards of fiction? Take a look at the stats below.

MERLIN	PUG/MILAMBER	COIN THE SOURCERER
One of "the Old Ones" (the Gaels)[3] and the tutor of King Arthur. Can transform into any animal. He lives from backward to forward. He winds up imprisoned in a rock, however (*Le Morte d'Arthur*).	Has the power of two worlds—Midkemia and Kelewan; master of the lore of the eldar (elves); the equal in power to Macros the Black, who was considered the greatest wizard of all time.	Has unlimited power even though he's just a kid. He doesn't just use magic, he is a *source* of magic. No wizard on Discworld can beat him. This kid even took on the gods of Discworld.

---

[3] T. H. White, *The Once and Future King* (New York: G. P. Putnam's Sons, 1939, 1940, 1958), 221.

GANDALF (MITHRANDIR/ THE GREY PILGRIM/ OLÓRIN)	MUSTRUM RIDCULLY	GED (BEFORE THE FINAL EVENTS OF *THE FARTHEST SHORE*)	ALBUS PERCIVAL WULFRIC BRIAN DUMBLEDORE
Considered the wisest of the Istari, who came from over the sea. He's also one of the Maiar. The bearer of the ring of fire, he beat a balrog and later came back from the dead. He is the "servant of the Secret Fire, wielder of the flame of Anor."[4] Galadriel wanted him to head the White Council instead of Saruman. Saruman. Fought in the war of the ring that ended the reign of the dark lord, Sauron.	Reached the seventh out of eight levels. A hunting man, he is quick with a fireball or a crossbow bolt. He manages to avoid being killed in a place where assassination helps your career.	Considered the best wizard in Earthsea. He can transform into an animal. He defeated the shadow of himself; killed five dragons and possibly another when he was just a young man. Became a dragonlord as well. Later achieves Archmage status.	The world's most powerful wizard (according to the series). He's the one "He who Must Not Be Named" feared. He once was Chief Warlock of the Wizengamot and Supreme Mugwump of the International Confederation of Wizards. First Class, for Grand Sorcery.

---

[4] *The Fellowship of the Ring* by J. R. R. Tolkien (New York: Ballantine, 1955), 392.

In a contest of sheer power, it's hard to say who would win since all are considered the leaders of wizards. Coin has an edge simply because his powers are akin to the gods of Discworld and because he was able to trap the gods in a ball of thought. As Pratchett describes it, Coin's too powerful even to remain in Discworld. Yet he's human and probably could be killed, although we're not sure how.

Ridcully is the dark horse. There are advantages and disadvantages to his mage supremacy. *Advantages:* (1) He's difficult to kill. Ask anyone who wants his job as archchancellor. (2) He would probably fight dirty. (3) He became a seventh-level wizard at an early age. *Disadvantages:* (1) He'd probably rather spend his time hunting than perfecting his art. (2) He didn't attain the eighth level (probably out of self-preservation). (3) We're not entirely positive that he could beat any of the other wizards in the chart, especially the sourcerer (okay, we *know* he can't beat Coin). (4) We seriously doubt that he'd care, unless a fellow mage trespassed on Ridcully's property or took his Wow-Wow sauce.

Raymond Feist wrote a number of books on Pug, so you know how formidable an opponent he is. Could he beat Ridcully or Coin? Hmmm. The jury's still out, especially since Pug's powers are akin to the gods'. Since Tolkien and T. H. White focused on the horrors and sadness of war, rather than testosterone posturing among wizards, we can't know the full extent of the powers of Merlin or Gandalf. Merlin's part human and part, well, *other*, thanks to being the son of an incubus and a human. (There's no Hallmark card for that.) But Gandalf is Maiar—a spirit being like an angel, according to Tolkien's *The Silmarillion*. And as for Dumbledore, well, you know what happened to him in book 6.

8

~

The Reaper Man

*The Death of the Disc was a traditionalist who prided
himself on his personal service and spent most of the time
being depressed because this was not appreciated. He
would point out that no one feared death itself, just pain
and separation and oblivion, and that it was quite
unreasonable to take against someone just because he had
empty eye sockets and a quiet pride in his work.*[1]

*Dying is a very dull, dreary affair. And my advice to you is
to have nothing whatever to do with it.*
—W. Somerset Maugham[2]

A PERSONIFICATION TO REMEMBER

Many would agree with us that Death is one of the most loved characters of Pratchett's Discworld. The inevitable mortality of us
makes the idea of death scary, but we have a fascination with
Pratchett's quirky representation. This personification of death[3] is a
seven-foot-tall skeletal man dressed in a black robe, with a scythe,
who speaks in capital letters (more on this later). Readers are enam-

---

[1] *The Light Fantastic* (New York: HarperTorch, 1986), 104.
[2] Quoted at http://www.wisdomquotes.com/cat_death.html.
[3] A classic Western civilization physical embodiment of death with a unique personality.

ored with him, because of his endearing personality and his love of cats, among other things. He is the kind of guy you can sit down with and have tea, as he does with Miss Flitworth in *Reaper Man*. (Actually, we recall that being a quite uncomfortable situation.) Or you may want to play a game with him in his room of lifetimers with the guys (you know, War, Pestilence, and Famine—more on them in chapter 9). It is not uncommon to see Death at the gentlemen's club called Fidgett's. At times he is sympathetic, sentimental, and oftentimes he is humorous (not on purpose). After all, he is not the one who takes a person's life—just the one who picks up the dead.

Pratchett books are different from many other fantasy or science fiction stories in that he throws in enough death to make it clear that good doesn't always win. This creates the need for a character like Death because of the amount of souls in need of a pickup. He could have left it at that—you know, the clown[4] is hit over the head by the ferocious werewolf and dies from a brain aneurysm, then continue on with the story—but typically an appearance of the character Death is in order. And eventually everyone meets Death.

Death has been around on the Disc since the first book of the Discworld series in 1983: *The Color of Magic*. He makes his appearances in almost all Discworld books, with the exception of *Wee Free Men*, but the major Death-themed books are *Mort*, *Reaper Man*, *Soul Music*, *Hogfather*, and *Thief of Time*. Even though Death appears in earlier books, *Mort* is the one in which his character is truly developed.

In *Reaper Man*, it is explained that Death was created by belief, just as were all the gods of the Disc. "He evolved, as it were, along with life. As soon as a living thing was even dimly aware of the concept of suddenly becoming a non-living thing, there was Death. He was Death long before humans ever considered him; they only

---

[4] We are not referring to the Fools and Joculators Guild in this example, though their clownish makeup is worth being wary of.

added the shape and all the scythe and robe business to a personality that was already millions of years old."[5] He is one of the Four Horsemen of the Apocalypse. Death is not limited by time and space. He has no need to sleep, and knows everything[6]

OTHER PORTRAYALS OF DEATH

Humans have been fascinated and fearful of death since the beginning of time, well, the beginning of mankind. It is only natural that we have personified Death into a skeletal form holding a scythe; after all, the Romans personified Genius by depicting a man holding a cornucopia.

A medieval painting depicts Death as playing chess with a man (more on games with Death later). Death seems to be holding the chessboard on his lap, and both Death and the man appear to have smiles.

Martine Leavitt wrote the book *Keturah and Lord Death*, which portrays Death uniquely as a young man who is the collector of souls. He is in love with the girl Keturah, who persuades him to let her live for just one more day (this happens multiple times) by telling him stories but not revealing the end. She must search out a love superior to death, to be granted life. Keturah alone is able to see Death and therefore knows when someone near her is about to be collected by him.

Death Takes a Holiday is a romantic 1934 film about a personified Death who spends time on earth in hopes of understanding why humans fear him. He takes the form of a human named Prince Sirki. While taking a vacation from his job, he finds one who does not fear him and falls in love with her. While Death is on holiday, people

[5] *Reaper Man* (New York: HarperTorch, 1991), 123.
[6] Though he has trouble understanding things like plumbing, doorknobs, and music. His many attempts to play the violin have been in vain.

and other living things stop dying. *Meet Joe Black*, a 1998 loose re-make of *Death Takes a Holiday*, is similar in storyline, but was much less well received and twice as long.

In Neil Gaiman's Sandman graphic novels, Death is a gothic young female who finds humans interesting and enlightening. Ironi-cally, she is described as a joyful character, and she is able to cheer up her brother, Dream, in the first volume of the series (for more on that, see chapter 9). Neil Gaiman also has a portrayal of Death (Azrael) in the book *Good Omens*, which he co-wrote with Terry Pratchett.

BINKY, DEATH'S STEED

Since Death is one of the Horsemen of the Apocalypse, it is only ap-propriate that in Discworld he should have his own horse. Two horses shortly filled this order, but failed, due to too much limb repair (the skeletal steed) and too many fire hazards (the fiery steed torched the barn). Death then settled on a horse named Binky. His granddaughter, Susan, was so fond of Binky that he gave her a toy set of "My Little Binky" as a birthday present. Binky is a fantastic horse who walks on his own devised ground (he defies gravity; you may want to think of it as flying but it's not). Binky obliges Death by coming to him when-ever he snaps his fingers and makes sure a rider doesn't fall off when riding him. Binky is just as obedient to Susan as he is for Death.

Binky is cared for well at Death's Domain. He wears a silver har-ness. The blacksmith Jason Ogg, whom Death considers "superb" at his job, makes horseshoes for Binky. Jason Ogg is the oldest son of Nanny Ogg and the blacksmith of Lancre. (For more about Jason, see chapter 14.)

A FAMILY MAN

Death decides to start a family because he wants to know what it's like to be human. He adopts Ysabell as a baby, upon the death of her parents. Ysabell's daddy (Death) allows her to grow to be six-teen years old with the misconception that teenagers are easier to care for than young children are.[7] Housed in Death's Domain where there is no aging, Ysabell remains a teenager until she leaves. In *Mort*, Ysabell eventually falls in love with the main character. Mort and Ysabell marry and leave Death's home and become mor-tal once again. Upon leaving, the couple is given the titles of Duke and Duchess of Sto Helit. Little is said about their lives after that, but we do know that they have a daughter whom they name Susan. Susan, though not blood- (or bone-) related to Death, takes on his some of his characteristics (that is what happens when you have Death in the family). Mort and Ysabell die at the beginning of the book *Soul Music* in a coach accident.

DEATH'S GRANDDAUGHTER

Mary Poppins is a magical nanny who comes to care for the Banks children during a difficult time. She is a character in a series of children's books by P. L. Travers and also is the title of the Disney movie released in 1964. The reason we bring this up is that Prat-chett himself considers the character of Susan a "Gothic Mary Poppins" in *The Art of Discworld* book. One similarity is that even though Mary Poppins does magical things (such as having tea par-ties while floating in the air and jumping into chalk drawings on the sidewalk), she never admits that these things actually hap-pened. She also is sure to act very proper; in a way, that seems contrary to the actual situations she finds herself, and the Banks children, in. However, Susan, who as far as we know never tidied up a nursery using magic and song, is quite magical and tries very hard to be normal and proper. But, of course, the obvious similarity

---

[7] Upon experience of raising a teenager (at least partially) I am confident that there are some forms of humanity that Death will never understand.

is that she is in fact a nanny in *Hogfather* and spends much time during this employment beating up monsters with a metal poker.

As we mentioned before, Susan has inherited some characteristics from her grandfather Death. When she needs to, she can walk through walls (and objects), knows some things before they actually happen, and can find people. She has trouble remembering to do some normal human things, such as going to sleep and using doorknobs, just like dear old Granddad. Despite these similarities, she spends a lot of time trying to avoid Grandpa. Susan is mortal and does not like cats, unlike her grandfather.

Besides the nanny position, Susan has also been employed as a teacher. Her teaching techniques are unconventional but effective. It is not uncommon for her to take her class on field trips that involve not only long distances but also travel through time. Her other profession, though she tries to avoid it, is the ability to take over for Death. She is quite capable of doing Death's work when needed, complete with his voice.

EMPLOYMENT

It is certainly the job of Death to collect souls. He doesn't appear at all deaths, but makes sure everything is going okay. On special occasions, he collects the souls of ordinary people but, typically, his haul encompasses witches, wizards, and royalty. His job isn't morbid all the time; he brings good news upon death to some, such as no more dandruff.

Death has taken on multiple other jobs throughout the Discworld series, from a short-order cook (*Mort*) to an actor (*Wyrd Sisters*). Perhaps his most memorable job is as the Hogfather, in the book of the same title, when he tries to revive Discworldians' belief in the Santa Claus figure. He also has worked as a beggar, a farmer, and in the foreign legion as a soldier.

DEATH'S DOMAIN

It is quite apparent that one of Death's jobs is not, and will never be, interior decoration. Though he lacks imagination, Death does have the ability to copy things. Therefore, his Domain is decked out with very big rooms (they may seem unreasonably large), a bedroom suite, a library, and even a cat flap in the back door, which seems to have been installed in *Hogfather*. He finds no reason to lock the back door. Everything is dreary, in black and gray, with the exception of living things that include Albert (the manservant), daughter Ysabell (when young and alive), and many cats (which appear in *Hogfather*). The house appears small from the outside.

In the kitchen, you will usually find Albert frying up some type of food. It is a good thing that Ysabell, Albert, and Mort eat, because Death has no need to partake of food. Sometimes, Albert will deliver tea to Death in his quarters. Perhaps this is comfort food. Albert, although a wizard, also has been known to serve as the valet and gardener.

HOURGLASSES

Some of us are in daily contact with an hourglass—you know, the timekeeper with two (usually glass) bulbs that transfer some type of matter (typically sand) from the top section to the bottom one. Our daily encounter with this symbol, however, is no longer in physical form—it is in the form of a little icon on our computer screens and can cause a lot of frustration. Yes, the hourglass has become a modern symbol of consternation. How many times have you had to just stare at the hourglass on your screen and just wait and wait?[8]

---

[8] Typically, this happens during the most inconvenient times, such as when we are trying to show a coworker a really cool video clip before the boss walks in.

It wouldn't be right to discuss Death's home without addressing the hourglasses that are held within it. This includes the hidden room where the hourglasses of the gods are kept; Susan discovers this room in *Hogfather*. Hourglasses, at least those of humans, reflect how much life a person has left. Once the person dies, the hourglass disappears, and when a person is born, a new one appears. These hourglasses in Discworld, called lifetimers, are for the most part the classic glass and sand variety (Bill Gates is yet to have automated this process). A separate room is used to house the god hourglasses, which include those of the Hogfather, the Tooth Fairy, and other mythological characters that live in Discworld. (See chapter 9.) A lifetimer is displayed on the cover of *Mort* (of the HarperTorch edition that we have). In this book, Death turns Mort's lifetimer over to extend his life.

Hourglasses[9] are also known as sand glasses or sand timers. Hourglasses are items often used in fiction to represent time. Like a genie in a bottle, an hourglass was used in Disney's *Aladdin* where Jafar, the nemesis, traps Princess Jasmine inside. Of course, the hourglass used is much larger than our much-loved computer icon (it is hard to determine how large something is when animated). In the Harry Potter series, large hourglass-looking statues are used to keep score among the different magical houses at the Hogwarts School of Witchcraft and Wizardry. And maybe you remember the hourglass in *The Wizard of Oz*. You are led to believe they are similar to Pratchett's lifetimers, in that it is showing the time left in the life of the main character, Dorothy. In the end, that hourglass is used as a bomb.

Hourglasses have been symbols of our limited time on earth in various times and cultures. They have been used since the fourteenth century, but there is no evidence that they were used in ear-

---

[9] The parliament of Australia still uses an hourglass to time some proceedings.

lier times for real or symbolically. Some pirates were known to have pictures of hourglasses on their flags as a reminder of our mortality. In England, hourglasses were sometimes placed in coffins before burial. They have also been used as a timepiece on ships.

THE DEATH OF RATS

It is obvious that the character of Death is popular; just do an Internet search for "Pratchett's Death" and a whole slew of stuff comes up. While doing this, we came across a quiz that supposedly tells you which Death you are. One of us (Carrie) was crowned the Death of Rats, whatever that means.[10] Apparently, the quiz creators didn't consider her houseful of cats (two cats actually, but they seem to multiply). The Death of Rats comes into existence in *Reaper Man*, where Death is separated into many pieces (little deaths). The Death of Rats, a creation of this separation, does not want to go back into the form of Death. Death allows the Death of Rats to stay separate from him and finds him to be a companion of sorts.[11]

The Death of Rats has been known to collect the souls of rodents as well as those of rodentlike humans. For instance, in *Maskerade*, he collects Mr. Ponder who is immediately reincarnated into a rodent. He also has done various other errands for Death, such as delivering messages to Susan. He is approximately six inches tall and carries a small scythe, like his counterpart. He has been known to SQUEAK a good conversation that typically can be interpreted by reading the responses of those to whom he is speaking.

---

[10] Even though the very few questions asked in this quiz had nothing to do with rodents, there is a million-in-one chance that the quiz morphed into an all-knowing creature that knew that I had mice as pets in the past and probably would be the best person for the job.
[11] There was also a fly that did not enter back into the form of Death but has not been seen since.

WHAT'S WITH THE SCYTHE?

Apparently Father Time and the Grim Reaper are often connected or considered the same personification. It may be due to the fact that Death is often seen with a scythe, as is Father Time (Cronus, who was also the god of the harvest; for more about him, see chapter 9). This explains the scythe, which is a farming tool used for cutting grass and certain kinds of crops. It eventually succeeded the sickle in Europe in the 1500s. Scythes are still used, mostly in less developed countries, but have been replaced in much of the world by lawn mowers and motorized farming equipment. Another explanation for the scythe is that death is the "harvester of souls."[12] In *The Light Fantastic*, Death makes a point of explaining that he uses a scythe, whereas, in other worlds, the collections instrument for souls was upgraded to combine harvesters a long time ago.

Actually, while looking at a picture of a scythe, I (Carrie) realized that it vaguely resembles the machete my husband used to keep in his trunk. He claimed the machete was used for cutting grass also; he swears he saw it done this way in Jamaica (yeah, right). I don't recall Pratchett's Death cutting much grass, either, except that short period of time he worked for Miss Flitworth under the alias of Bill Door, in *Reaper Man*. You know, Good Old Bill, as the locals at the tavern referred to him after he purposely lost at pond (pool) and darts.

He spends a lot of time in *Reaper Man* trying to figure out how to make his scythe sharper.

CAPITAL LETTERS AND THE LANGUAGE OF DEATH

It seems appropriate that Death's words are represented in a unique way in the Discworld books. After all, he has no vocal cords to ac-

---

[12] Posted at http://en.wikipedia.org/wiki/Scythe.

tually make sound, being a skeleton and all. Death's words are all written in small capital letters. His talking is described in *Carpe Jugulum* as "an echo inside the head."[13] When he takes the place of the Hogfather in the book by the same name, the capital letters are no longer small. This must be due to a personality trait of extra confidence that he must portray as the Hogfather. Death is not real good with frivolous or everyday conversation. You would probably not ask him about the weather or make small talk with him about current events.

Capital letters, a.k.a. upper case or majuscule, would make no difference, for instance, in Chinese writing, where lowercase and uppercase letters are not distinguished. In English, capital letters have had meaning since around 1300. Other than signifying the beginning of a sentence or a name, capital letters are used at times to bring emphasis to a word or phrase. Capital letters are considered by some to be harder to read than lowercase letters and are sometimes used in legal documents to serve that very purpose. It has come to our attention very recently that writing in capital letters in e-mails can be a form of shouting—called "flaming"—at a person or group (offensive, we guess).

Due to the fact that Death knows all, he is therefore quite literate. His chosen form of writing is gothic script. For instance, in *Reaper Man*, he tries to teach a chicken named Cyril to "cock-a-doodle-doo" properly by writing it down on a board with a piece of chalk, and expects him to read it. Gothic script could be referring to the gothic alphabet, which we certainly would have difficulty reading, even though we aren't an illiterate chicken. The Gothic language is thought to have originally employed a runic alphabet known as the gothic runes. The gothic runes are thought to be the invention of the Goths who were dwellers of dunes (maybe these were decorated like Death's Domain). Runes were replaced with

---

[13] *Carpe Jugulum* (New York: HarperTorch, 1998), 15.

the gothic alphabet in the fourth century A.D. If we were referring to Death's writing style in font types, we probably would consider sans serif because it is considered gothic. Regular serif font is considered Roman. Serif fonts are considered easier to read than sans serif but typically the living don't read Death's notes. In *Hogfather*, it is mentioned that Death uses serifs in his handwriting when Susan finds a note in his handwriting.

DODGING DEATH: GAMES AND BOXES

Okay, time for an exercise that requires some imagination and a whole lot of insurance (on our part). Let's say you die. This is not a death threat; let's just say you do. Now, imagine that an Angel of Death appears to you. What do you do?[14] Many writers have toyed with the idea of wagering with Death by playing a game with him/her. The idea is if you win the game, then Death grants you another chance at life. This thought seems to date back to the Middle Ages; a medieval painting by Albertus Pictor depicts Death, as a skeleton, playing chess with a human man. In Pratchett's Discworld, it is not that Death can grant life; he is only able to give an extension.

The 1957 Swedish film *The Seventh Seal*, directed by Ingmar Bergman, has a medieval knight playing chess with Death. Death accepts the knight's wager of extended life if he wins against him in the game. During the movie, the knight reveals his game strategy to the local priest who turns out to be Death himself. The game buys the knight time to see his wife again and to help others during the threat of plague.

In the 1991 movie *Bill & Ted's Bogus Journey*, a sequel to the successful comedy *Bill & Ted's Excellent Adventure*, the main characters

---

[14] If you truly believe that you are going to meet a character like Pratchett's Death upon death, please do not write Terry Pratchett about this. In our opinion, Pratchett has stared blankly at too many walls.

successfully beat Death, played by William Sadler, at Battleship, Clue, electric football, and Twister, successfully, but Death keeps asking for a rematch.

In the Discworld series, there are multiple instances where Death is willing to wager death with a character by playing a game. In *Maskerade*, you find Granny Weatherwax playing against Death to keep a baby from dying.

A FEW THOUGHTS ABOUT CATS

If you saw the movie *Prince of Egypt*, an animated film about the Bible's Moses that was released in 1998 by Dreamworks, you have heard the song "Playing with the Big Boys." The sorcerers, who are trying to prove they are better than Moses and his God, use this song to summon gods. Now, you're wondering what this has to do with cats and, even more important, what this has to do with Death? Well, one of the gods that is called up is Bast. Bast was the Egyptian cat god and it was in ancient Egypt that cats were first taken in as pets. Now, we are not implying that Death worships cats, but he sure seems to like them a lot. In Pratchett's book *Sourcery*, Ipslore, in a contrary manner, asks Death, "[W]hat is there in this world that truly makes living worthwhile?" Death, after some thought replies, "CATS. . . . CATS ARE NICE."[15] In *The Last Hero*, Death confirms his affection for cats by saying, "I DON'T HOLD WITH CRUELTY TO CATS."[16] In *Hogfather*, Susan finds Death's domain full of living cats.

We, the authors of this book, collectively have a total of two cats. Which means that Linda has zero and I (Carrie) have two. We can understand why Death would like them so much. They are lovable and comforting, kind of like a bedtime cup of tea. It is quite

---

[15] *Sourcery* (New York: HarperTorch, 1988), 5.
[16] *The Last Hero*, illustrated by Paul Kidby (New York: HarperCollins, 2001), 67.

ironic that Death has such a love, if you will, for cats. After all, Death has no need to sleep, even though he made sure his bedroom has a bed, and cats can spend almost sixteen hours a day sleeping. It may be comforting to Death that cats can see him whether or not they are dead.

In conclusion, we would like to reiterate the importance of the personification of death in Pratchett's writings. Benjamin Franklin put it this way, "Certainty? In this world nothing is certain but death and taxes."[17]

---

[17] Quoted at http://www.brainyquote.com/quotes/quotes/b/benjaminfr151592.html.

9

~

A Powerful Personality

Old man trouble, I don't mind him
You won't find him 'round my door.[1]

IF YOU BELIEVE . . .

In beauty pageants, winning First Runner-up or Miss Congeniality
is a consolation prize. Look what it did for undercover FBI agent
Gracie Hart, played by Sandra Bullock in the movie of the latter
title. Although it proves that at least you have personality, everyone
would prefer to wear the crown.

In Discworld, if you can't be a god (Blind Io) but you're immortal, chances are you're the next runner-up—a personification of
something. (An "anthropomorphic personification" as Miss Tick explains in *Wintersmith*.[2]) Some might say you're still a god or, at
times, a royal pain.

The idea of personifying the seasons or other aspects of life

---

[1] Lyrics by Ira Gershwin from the song, "I Got Rhythm." Posted at http://www
.guntheranderson.com/v/data/igotrhyt.htm.
[2] *Wintersmith* (New York: HarperTempest, 2006), 174.

comes from mythology—a creative way of looking at the origin of all things. In the Discworld books, Pratchett often mentions how faith in their existence shapes these immortals. They are what they are because of what the people of Discworld believe.

Peter Pan once warned Wendy that every time someone expressed disbelief in a fairy, one died. In Discworld, particularly in such books as *Hogfather,* you can see the aftermath of this idea. When the plot to kill the Hogfather gets under way, the personifications people thought *should* exist but they needed more belief in them until they *could* exist used to believe in and which died out—the Verruca Gnome, the oh God of Hangovers, the Cheerful Fairy, the Eater of Socks, the Hair Loss Fairy, the God of Indigestion—gain existence once more, helped by a bathroom designed by Bloody Stupid Johnson.

Besides the ones above, who are the immortals of Discworld? We talked about Death in the last chapter. Let's move on to some of the other major elementals.

DISC-CLAIMER:
Plot spoilers ahead. Read at your own risk.

LET'S RIDE: JOINING THE HORSEY SET

Let's face it, if the four horsemen ride, well, the world is about to end. It's Armageddon and we don't mean the old Bruce Willis movie (although that *was* about a cataclysmic event signaling the end of the world). The four horsemen of the Apocalypse (five in Discworld, including Kaos) get a shout-out in chapter 6 of the Book of Revelation in the Bible and make a cameo in yet another sixth chapter, this one in an Old Testament book—Zechariah. In Revelation, they are the riders in white (Pestilence), red (War), black (Famine), and pale green (Death)—the anti–Easy Riders.

Nothing but a Pest

Pestilence is a plague or disease that can wipe out significant segments of a population. In the fourteenth, seventeenth, and eighteenth centuries, it was the black death (plague) that troubled several areas in Europe. In our day, the AIDS virus has killed millions.

But in Discworld, Pestilence is a whiny sort of guy who hangs out in hospitals. It's fitting that Death seeks out Pestilence first in *Thief of Time*, because he is first in the order of the riders listed in Revelation chapter 6. Being first doesn't make him the most powerful of the horsemen of the "Apocralypse" nor does it mean that he's the leader. He's just a herald of the end of the world.

War! Huh! What Is It Good For?

Aside from being the subject of an Edwin Starr song from 1970, the god of war in Greek mythology is Ares, the tempestuous and little-liked son of Zeus and Hera. (Yeah, we know. Kevin Smith played him in the *Xena: Warrior Princess* and *Hercules: The Legendary Journeys* series.) In Roman mythology, he is Mars—for which the Red Planet was named.

In Discworld, War is a henpecked husband married to a former Valkyrie. When you first see War, you can't help but think of a retiree who sits around reminiscing about the good old days. Yet he answers the call to action, when summoned in *Thief of Time*.

Famished

"When the Lamb opened the third seal, I heard the third living creature say, 'Come!' I looked, and there before me was a black horse!

Its rider was holding a pair of scales in his hand" (Revelation 6:5, New International Version). That's the description of the third rider—the one who measures the high cost of bread, a way of indicating its scarcity. You've read about the sad result of famine in various parts of the world due to drought and other natural disasters. And Ichabod Crane in Washington Irving's "The Legend of Sleepy Hollow" is described as a veritable poster child for famine. But in Discworld, Famine is a guy hanging out in a restaurant longing after mayonnaise (or salad cream, if you prefer). But he, too, joins in the battle for the universe in *Thief of Time*. What would the end of the world be without famine?

IT'S THE MOST WONDERFUL TIME OF THE YEAR: SEASONAL AND HOLIDAY PERSONIFICATIONS

It's About Time

Time isn't just something you mark or kill. In mythology, Time is actually a person—a personification of time. Every New Year's Eve, you hear about Father Time—the old man with the scythe (not the Grim Reaper) who gets ready to make way for the new kid on the block. But in Greek mythology, he is Chronos (also spelled Kronos and Cronus), a guy with a plethora of jobs on his résumé: the king of the Titans, the god of time, and the unhappy father of Zeus who made child abuse an art form. *Chronos* is the Latin form of the Greek word for "time." In Roman mythology, he is Saturn.

In Discworld, Time is a female—the mother of Lobsang Ludd whom Susan encounters in *Thief of Time*. (Maybe that's why Pratchett uses a capital letter in reference to Time in such books as *Reaper Man*.) You might call her "Mother Time," although she probably wouldn't answer to that.

Lobsang becomes the new kid on the block when he takes over for his mother as the personification of time in *Thief of Time*. Time for a change, we suppose.

In Hog Heaven

Back when you were a kid, maybe you believed in Santa. (Maybe you still do.) That's what kids usually do. We know that Santa Claus comes from the legends of Saint Nicholas—the bishop of Myra from the fourth century. The Hogfather is the Santa Claus/Father Christmas of Discworld, whose sleigh is pulled not by reindeer but by four boars (Gouger, Router, Tusker, and Snouter). For this spirit of Hogswatch, pork pies and sherry take the place of the cookies and milk kids leave out for Santa in our world. But many of their other trappings of the holiday are the same: the mistletoe, the sleigh, the stockings, the carol singers, the coal, etc. Makes you feel all warm inside, doesn't it?

A Winter Wonderland

Old Man Winter/Father Winter, the personification of winter, comes from Russian folklore. The Wintersmith is the personification of winter in Discworld. While a blacksmith forges metals, the Wintersmith forges snow and ice. Although the Wintersmith is as old as the hills, he appears to Tiffany Aching—his crush—as a young man.

Discworld also has a Jack Frost who personifies frost and has a fern fixation, apparently. While the Wintersmith pelts the world with Tiffany Aching–shaped snowflakes, Jack paints windows with fern patterns. But Jack Frost comes from Norse mythology and Russian folklore. You've probably seen him as a winter sprite—a mischievous creature in such movies as *Santa Clause 3* and obliquely in the 1996 *Jack Frost*, where he is a serial killer-turned-snowman who's "chillin . . . and killin'," according to the movie tagline. Talk about "Jack Frost nipping at your nose," as the song goes, not to mention your legs and other important appendages. (Thank you, Ben Pyykkonen, for your inspiration on that last line.)

Summer in the City

While the Summer Lady, the personification of summer, looks like Tiffany (thanks to some interference by Tiffany in an endless dance of the seasons), hers is a Pratchett makeover à la the Persephone story from Greek mythology (see chapter 1). Persephone was the daughter of Demeter, the goddess of the harvest. After Hades, lord of the Underworld, grabbed Persephone (without even *asking* for a date) and dragged her to the Underworld, Persephone's enforced stay caused Demeter to grieve and neglect the plants and trees—thus leading to the deadness of winter.

The Summer Lady is like Demeter in that she can cause plants to grow—which happens in the spring and summer. But she's also like Opora, the personification of the part of summer when fruit is at its peak. That season is August through September, according to Hesiod's *Theogony*.

YOU ARE WHAT YOU DO: HOW SOME PERSONIFICATIONS ARE DEFINED

"It's not who I am underneath . . . But what I do that defines me," declares Batman in Batman Begins.[3] Some of the other personifications in Discworld could say the same thing.

---

[3] From *Batman Begins: The Official Movie Guide*, by Claudia Kalindjian and the editors at DC Comics (New York: Time, Inc., 2005), 143. Script by Christopher Nolan and David S. Goyer. A fine guide and a fine time was had by all.

Sweet Dreams Are Made of Sand

Who is the Sandman? A being who puts people to sleep without boring them. If you read the classic graphic novels on the Sandman—*Preludes and Nocturnes* being one of them—written by Neil Gaiman (Pratchett's coauthor for *Good Omens*) and illustrated by Sam Kieth, Mike Dringenberg, and Malcolm Jones III, you might feel that that series provides the definitive portrayal of the Sandman. He is Dream—the personification of dreams a.k.a. Morpheus. (Morpheus in the *Matrix* movies had the opposite goal: to wake people up.) Dream, the younger brother of Death (a Goth-looking female), is one of the Endless—not the kind to hit people on the head with sandbags full of sand, like the Discworld Sandman does. Gaiman's Sandman is someone who could be summoned like the Death of Discworld—by an occult rite that traps him for several decades until he escapes.

Even if you haven't read Gaiman's graphic novels, you might know that Morpheus comes from Greek mythology. He's the most powerful of the gods of dreams (the Oneroi) and the son of Hypnos, the god of sleep. Ovid wrote about the family in *Metamorphoses*. Morpheus's brothers—Phobeter and Phantasos—also personify dreams.

Supposedly, the Sandman of mythology sprinkles dust in the eyes of children to make them fall asleep. "Ready for a visit from the Sandman, Rachel? Close your eyes." Well, that's what parents tell their kids. Wishful thinking. Speaking of wishful thinking, back in the 1950s a song called "Mr. Sandman," written by Pat Ballard, described some thoughts about the Sandman's job. It was popular in the United States and Great Britain.

Tooth Fairy

The Tooth Fairy has existed for ages, thanks to candy, stories told around Europe, and movies starring Kirstie Alley (*Toothless*). You know the racket—lose a baby tooth, gain money. Sweet. (Doesn't work if you pull out a permanent tooth.) But if you saw *The 10th Kingdom*—a fairy-tale miniseries on NBC in 2000 available on DVD (also a novel)—you know that the Tooth Fairy was a sadistic prison dentist. He didn't give money—only pain.

In Discworld, the Tooth Fairy isn't an imaginary figure who goes around leaving money under kids' pillows. Discworld's first bogeyman is the head Tooth Fairy, a job that passes to Banjo Lilywhite (see chapter 12) in *Hogfather*. The Tooth Fairy's tooth collection routes are parceled out like paper routes, and are managed by "tooth girls." That's why the Tooth Fairy is known in Discworld as Violet Bottler and various other names. But Tooth Fairy's headquarters is a castle full of small teeth—a castle formed from the beliefs of kids everywhere.

Discworld also has a Clinkerbell, who claims to be a troll Tooth Fairy in *Feet of Clay*. But that's another story.

The Soul Cake Duck

If you're looking for the Easter Bunny in Discworld, look no further than the Soul Cake Duck, who comes on Soul Cake Tuesday, rather than on a holiday like Easter. Soul Cake Tuesday signals the start of duck hunting season. On this day, children hunt for the chocolate eggs laid by the Soul Cake Duck. (In our world, we have the ones made by Cadbury or Hershey.)

We can't help wondering if the Soul Cake Duck inspired Puley the Pule Duck, who showed up in an episode of *The Adventures of Jimmy Neutron*.

THE FACES OF FEAR: NIGHTMARE PERSONIFICATIONS

Pixar's *Monsters, Inc.* showed some of the fears common to kids. Some personifications or creatures of the imagination are all about fears, some of which we never outgrow.

Old Man Trouble

Putting a name and a face to something you fear takes the edge off it. Trouble is the same way. Besides being a song by Stephen Sills and a line from a George Gershwin song from 1930 (just after the troublesome Stock Market Crash), Old Man Trouble is one of the odd gods of Discworld. You can gain a sense of his reputation in *Hogfather*, where he's described as "nasty." Isn't that just how trouble is?

The Scissor Man

The Scissor Man, who gets a mention in *Hogfather*, was a head-scratcher to us, even after Jasper Fforde, the writer of the Tuesday Next and Nursery Crime series, mentioned a Scissor-man in *The Fourth Bear*. Guess our moms forgot to tell us about him. In Fforde's book, the Scissor-man runs around with a giant pair of scissors and threatens to cut off the thumbs of a kid named Conrad. (There's no watchdog committee for behavior like that.) Sounds like something out of *Edward Scissorhands*—the 1990 movie directed by Tim Burton.

But the Scissor Man comes from a book by Heinrich Hoffman published in 1845 called *Der Struwwelpeter*—a book of "happy" nursery rhymes in the vein of Mother Goose-gone-Rambo. "Die Geschichte vom Daumenlutcher" ("The Story of the Thumb-Sucker") describes the fate of one Konrad—a thumb-sucker who failed to heed his mother's warning and wound up with both thumbs cut off by giant scissors wielded by a man known as "the tailor." The late Rod Serling, creator of *The Twilight Zone*, could not have come up with a more macabre tale—one sure to horrify parents and delight kids.

Discworld's Scissor Man isn't exactly a man, but a creature made of blades and with a stronger fear factor than "the tailor." This creature would be handy (or rather, "scissory") to have around the garment district of New York.

The Bogeyman

Did a parent ever warn you about the bogeyman? Most kids have been given a vague story about the bogeyman. The vaguer the story, the more frightening the imaginary creature. For some, he hides in the closet, like the monsters of *Monsters, Inc.*, waiting to jump out when the lights go off. For many, he hides under the bed—again, like some of the monsters of *Monsters, Inc.* For others, he might bear the face of the latest serial killer or, sadly, a hurtful relative.

In Discworld, there is more than one bogeyman. We talked about Discworld's first bogeyman earlier. But other bogeymen, for instance, Mr. Schleppel (*Reaper Man*), Shlimazel (*Hogfather*), and Shlitzen (*Feet of Clay*) exist, too. (Note the pattern of the bogeymen names.) Throwing a blanket over them creates in them a sense of "existential uncertainty," as Pratchett describes in *Feet of Clay* and *Hogfather*. In other words, they're not sure they exist. If only we could do that with bills.

∽

Imagine having the power to cause personifications to pop into existence. What would your fears or hopes bring into existence? Hopefully, you won't suffer the fate of Peachy, whose belief in the Scissor Man leads him to . . . the twilight zone.

~

It's a Small World After All

"Look, he's six inches high and lives in a mushroom,"
snarled Rincewind. "Of course he's a bloody gnome."[1]

A TINY BIT OF DISCWORLD

When Lemuel Gulliver, the sailor in Jonathan Swift's classic, *Gulliver's Travels*, was shipwrecked in Lilliput, he learned that the world was indeed small, for the land was filled with tiny people about six inches high (Lilliputians). Although normal-size back home, Gulliver was a giant to them.

Tiny people can also be found in Discworld. And we don't mean *really* teensy like Lucas, who was shrunk to ant size in *The Ant Bully*, or the kids or adults in *Honey, I Shrunk the Kids* and its sequels. We mean the four- to six-inch variety—possibly even a little smaller. They are the gnomes, Pictsies, fairies, and imps. Don't be a hater or an underestimater because they're small. If you were involved in a role-playing game and wanted some characters with power, you might do well to have some of these tiny titans on your side. Check out their stats.

---

[1] *The Light Fantastic* (New York: HarperTorch, 1986), 30.

GNOME ON THE RANGE

If you read Terry Brooks's Shannara series, you probably have a different take on gnomes than you would from *Gnomes* by Wil Huygen and illustrated by Rien Poortvliet, the Harry Potter series, *The Time-Life Encyclopedia of Things that Never Were*, or *Phantastes* (George MacDonald), or in old video games like *The Sims: Bustin' Out*, or if you checked out those found in gardens all across the world. In *Gnomes*, you find little old men about fifteen centimeters high (nearly six inches—the size of the Death of Rats, by the way) with long white beards and red pointed hats. (There are female gnomes as well. Unlike Discworld dwarfs, they don't have beards.) This is the concept of gnomes that many people have. Perhaps these are the creatures depicted in Tiffany's book, *The Goode Childe's Booke of Faerie Tales* (*The Wee Free Men*). But in the Shannara series, gnomes are bigger.

Gnomes aren't the same as leprechauns—the little green men of Irish folklore who supposedly know where gold is and often make shoes—or toy-making Christmas elves or the other kind of elves that make shoes also. Gnomes come from the folklore of a number of countries, including Germany, Switzerland, and France. Supposedly, they're helpful to humans, unlike some other fairy-tale folk (e.g., goblins and ogres). (In the Shannara series, they're anything but helpful, seeing as how they prefer to fraternize with the enemy of good.)

In Discworld, gnomes are about the same height as those described in *Gnomes*, judging by Wee Mad Arthur—the rat-catching precursor to the Nac Mac Feegle Buggy Swires—one of the City Watch's finest, who is described as "a mile high in pent-up aggression,"[2] the "Swires" mentioned in *The Light Fantastic*, who seem too

---

[2] *Men at Arms* (New York: HarperTorch, 1993), 52.

good-natured to be Buggy Swires, and the Glingleglingleglingle Fairy—a gnome in *Hogfather*.

Wee Mad Arthur is like a more cynical, tougher version of the Borrowers from Mary Norton's classic children's series of the same name. Instead of matchboxes and thimbles, he "borrows" rats he finds lying around. He may be small, but he's got skills.

And Buggy Swires . . . like Wee Mad Arthur, he's little but mean—not someone you'd want to cross if you're a perpetrator or an animal predator like a mountain lion.

In classic fairy tales, gnomes are bigger in size. They're more like dwarfs—the earth dwellers (which is what their name means in Latin) who guard a treasure hoard. (In the Harry Potter series, goblins perform this function at Gringott's Wizard Bank. There are garden gnomes in the series, however.) Think about Ruggedo the Nome ("gnome" without the *g*) King in *The Magic of Oz* and other Oz stories by L. Frank Baum. (Or not, if you wish.)

Pratchett included nomes (again without the *g*) in The Bromeliad—a series he wrote for kids. (*Truckers*, *Diggers*, and *Wings*.) In that series, which takes place in the late twentieth century, we first meet the nomes living in a store. In *Truckers*, a group of nomes find a group of garden gnomes on sale. The nomes aren't sure what to make of them. If they were like many people in the States, they would take the nomes and film them in various spots around the country. Don't ask us why. It's just done.

WHEN IT COMES TO BEING A NAC MAC FEEGLE, YOU CAN TAKE YOUR PICT

Irish playwright J. M. Barrie, author of *Peter Pan* and the subject of *Finding Neverland*, created Tinker Bell, a small, mischievous fairy "no longer than your hand,"[3] who scatters fairy dust everywhere.

---

[3] Quote from *Peter Pan* by J. M. Barrie (New York: Charles Scribner's Sons, 1911), 25.

You might also think of her as a pixie, but not like the Cornish pixies in *Harry Potter and the Chamber of Secrets* (who are stupid and mean) or the ones in the Artemis Fowl series by Eoin Colfer, where every fairy-tale creature tends to be on the tough side, due to the nature of the series. Because of Tinker Bell, Wendy and her brothers could fly.

As with everything else, Pratchett sets mythology on its ear. His pixies are Pictsies, a cross between pixies and Picts—tribal groups (possibly Aborigines or their descendants) living in northeastern Scotland before Scotland was . . . well, Scotland. The Picts were invaded by the Romans, the Gaels, and later, the Vikings. "Pict" means "painted" and probably refers to tattoos sported by some. (Bet you're thinking of *Braveheart* right now.) Although their history still remains somewhat shrouded in mystery, the Picts are known for their elaborately carved stones and brooches and their kings. If you happen to have read *The Bridei Chronicles* by Juliet Marillier, starting with *The Dark Mirror,* you read about the Picts and the kingdom of Fortriu, which only exists now as part of history.

According to Marillier's Web site, the Romans saw the Picts as "tiny, dark people who darted under stones for concealment."[4] Not exactly a PC description you'd want to add to a travel brochure. We can't help wondering whether this fanciful view inspired Pratchett in the creation of his Pictsies—the Nac Mac Feegles or the Wee Free Men. The Feegles have skin almost blue with tattoos, wear kilts, have red hair, and talk in a dialect reminiscent of Scottish. They're literally a family—a large family, since a kelda, the female leader of the clan, can have hundreds of children. They're like ants in a way, if ants could get drunk and liked to fight. But they mirror an ant's ability to lift objects far bigger and heavier than they are. And they can get in and out of impossible places.

---

[4] Quote from "History, conjecture and imagination: Author's notes on *The Bridei Chronicles*" posted at http://www.julietmarillier.com/Bridei%20historical%20notes.htm.

You can see echoes of the Picts' struggle for survival in the Feegles' battles with the invading Fairy Queen and her dromes (for more about them, see chapter 12 of this book) and grimhounds (see chapter 13) in *The Wee Free Men*, the hiver (*A Hat Full of Sky*), and the bogles (*Wintersmith*; we call them boggles or boggarts). Through it all, they seem to enjoy themselves. They're like the men of Rohan who sing in battle in *Return of the King* (the book). And why shouldn't the Feegles feel relaxed about the fight? They're dead, after all—or so they believe.

Everyone probably has their favorite Feegle. We're partial to Daft Wullie, "Big Man" Rob Anybody, and Not-as-Big-as-Medium-Sized-Jock-but-Bigger-than-Wee-Jock-Jock. At a book signing in Naperville, Illinois, in 2006, Pratchett confessed to a partiality for Daft Wullie, the brother of Rob Anybody—a name that's a job description, if anything. Maybe that's why Daft Wullie gets the best lines. The other Feegle names like Awf'ly Wee Billy Bigchin and Slightly Mad Angus are extremely descriptive as well. The female Feegles—the clan leaders—have normal names (Jeannie, Fion), and the most common sense, according to them.

It's fitting that the females are the leaders, since kings of the Picts supposedly succeeded to the throne based on their mothers' family line. Tiffany Aching is a temporary kelda after the death of the kelda in *The Wee Free Men*, until she surrenders the position by avoiding marrying Rob Anybody (to their mutual relief).

FEROCIOUS FAIRIES

Of course, Discworld has to have fairies as well. After all, the Fairy Queen has to have subjects. The fairies are the elves (see chapters 5 and 12). They're part of the Fairyland ambience. And they're not nice; they're annoying like mosquitoes and just as intent on blood. There must be something about having an address in Fairyland that causes a bad attitude.

Fairies have the ability to change their size, which is why we're mentioning them in this chapter. Although smaller than the Feegles, their cruel intent makes up for any height lack. The wasp-size ones with dragonfly wings that Tiffany and the Feegles encounter aren't your Tinker Bells, or the colorful and delightful, but mischievous flower fairies Anodos encounters in *Phantastes* (George MacDonald), or the human-size and hot fairies Finvarra and Midir in *The Hunter's Moon* (O. R. Melling), who also are mischievous. Discworld fairies are closer to the goblin-fairies who chase Anodos, and would make Brian Froud's *Bad Faeries* list for sure. Thankfully, they're defeated by poetry, just as the goblins were in George MacDonald's *The Princess and the Goblin*.

IMP-POSSIBLE

If you read *The Screwtape Letters* by C. S. Lewis, which features a correspondence between the demon Screwtape and his nephew, Wormwood; or Mercedes Lackey and James Mallory's Obsidian Trilogy (and plan to read the follow-up books to that series), you probably have a different concept of imps than those found in Discworld; *Princess Mononoke*—the groundbreaking 1999 movie by Hayao Miyazaki—or other anime features (e.g., *Howl's Moving Castle*—also by Miyazaki); or other fantasy books such as Jim Butcher's Dresden Files. In Discworld, imps are tolerated rather than feared or loathed. Although they're still considered demons, they're servants, like golems. They run the Dis-organizers and iconographs. How small are they? Small enough to fit in an organizer that fits in Vimes's pocket. Although many of them don't have names, some do (e.g., Sidney and Rodney—picture-painting imps).

Maybe the imp-in-the-box setup sounds familiar if you're into thermodynamics. Back in chapter 3, we talked about the second law of thermodynamics. To refresh your memory: "The total entropy of any isolated thermodynamic system tends to increase over time, approaching a maximum value."[5] Back in the day—1867 to be exact—a physicist named James Clerk Maxwell came up with a theory that apparently violated the second law of thermodynamics. Suppose, Maxwell says, there was a demon guarding a small trap-door between two connected boxes (box 1 and box 2) or a box divided in half (halves 1 and 2), both boxes or halves of which are filled with gas. If a molecule from box 1/half 1 moving faster than the ones in box 2/half 2 was allowed into box 2/half 2, well, the second law of thermodynamics would technically be broken. Why? Because the average speed and temperature of the molecules in the second box or half will have increased while decreasing in the first.

Imps even differ in concept from the dhlangs—the evil spirits Lobsang and Lu-Tze discuss in *Thief of Time*—the pure evil (an oxymoron if ever there was one) kind. But according to Susan Sto Helit, dhlangs are, as Pratchett describes, a "substition"—something people don't really believe in, unlike a superstition. But the dhlangs, we learn, are the Auditors. How fitting.

That concludes our little look at "Little" Discworld. If "It's a Small World After All" is running through your mind right now, well, don't blame us.

---

[5] Posted at http://en.wikipedia.org/wiki/Entropy.

I I

~

Home of the Brave

It, uh, seems to me that what you need is a hero.
—Hercules in the 1997 Disney movie *Hercules*, written and
codirected by Ron Clements

DISC-CLAIMER:
Plot spoilers ahead. Read at your own risk.

DO THE RIGHT THING?

You know the hero or heroine (especially a superhero or superheroine)
is about to enter the scene or perform a heroic deed just by the way the
music swells. You know—lots of clear, noble-sounding horns. *Dun-
dun-dun-dun!* Like the musical version of *Ta-da!* or *Voilà!* or *Eureka!*

The world of literature (including movies) has a heaping helping of heroes, heroes who fit the archetype described by Christopher Vogler as "someone who is willing to sacrifice his own needs on
behalf of others, like a shepherd who will sacrifice to protect and
serve his flock."[1] Risk and sacrifice are expected behaviors of the

---

[1] Christopher Vogler, *The Writer's Journey*, 2nd ed. (Studio City, CA: Michael Wiese Productions, 1988), 35.

HOME OF THE BRAVE

155

hero. It's part of the "Code"—but not the code referred to in *The Pirates of the Caribbean: Curse of the Black Pearl*. Pratchett refers to the Code in *The Last Hero*.

You remember those heroic moments long after you close the book or leave the movie theater: Sydney Carton's "far, far better" act of giving his life in place of Charles Darnay, the man who looks like him in Dickens's *A Tale of Two Cities*. Luke Skywalker taking the one-in-a-million shot to blow up the Death Star in *Star Wars: A New Hope*. Neo fully realizing that he is "the One" in the first *Matrix*. Trinity's amazing leap off a building and through a doorway in the same movie. Peter Parker saying, "Who am I? I'm Spider-Man," at the end of the first *Spider-Man* movie. Bruce Wayne as Batman gliding across the city at the end of *Batman Begins*. They're heroes larger than life, like the ultimate heroes from Greek mythology—Hercules/Herakles, Achilles, Jason, and Odysseus.

But what about Moist von Lipwig (*Going Postal*), Windle Poons (*Reaper Man*), or Roland de Chumsfanleigh (*Wintersmith*)? Or, for that matter, what about Adora Belle Dearheart, the chain-smoking golem advocate in *Going Postal* or Renata Flitworth, the elderly farm owner whom Death, as Bill Door, romances in *Reaper Man*? They don't look anything like your typical hero.

In Tolkien's *Lord of the Rings* trilogy, Terry Brooks's *The Sword of Shannara* (volume 1 of that series), and countless other epic fantasies, you meet an unlikely hero—the one you never expect to save the day. Discworld is full of the most unlikely savers of the day you'll ever find.

So, how do you spot the hero or heroine?

Follow the liver pills.

If you saw *Troy*, *Braveheart*, or *300*, you saw a bunch of buff, amazingly heroic types (and some wimps like Paris). But in *The*

Light Fantastic, up pops Cohen the Barbarian, who makes return visits in *Interesting Times* and *The Last Hero*, with his Silver Horde. Cohen is like Conan and Genghis Khan, with his conquering, take-no-prisoners panache. Cohen and Company have been heroes for many, many decades. They may be as old as the hills, but they're still bold enough to conquer an army and take on the gods of Discworld. And they seem to have no trouble finding willing women. Guess they're the geriatric James Bonds of their day.

With *The Last Hero*, we can't help thinking of *Cocoon*, the 1985 movie in which a group of retirees goes on a last adventure. But the Silver Horde, which includes Vena the Raven-Haired, are a little misguided in their efforts and have to be steered back by one of the true heroes of the story—Carrot. More on him later.

And then there's Windle Poons, the wizard who doesn't let his one hundred and thirtieth birthday or death stop him from becoming a hero. It's only fitting that his adventure take place in the same book (*Reaper Man*) as that of feisty Mrs. Flitworth, who risks her life to help the old Death defeat the new Death after the old Death (the one we know and love) is fired by the Auditors, who are living proof of the Peter Principle.

Even his fellow wizards discount Windle. After all, Windle is supposed to be dead. But as a zombie, Windle becomes an unlikely hero, one who has to help the other wizards and lead a ragtag group of "Fresh Starters"—Reg Shoe's support group for the undead—to victory against the parasitic life force threatening Ankh-Morpork. Helping save human lives is something you never expect a zombie to do.

Look for the uniform.

By this we don't mean the Watch. Yes, they're heroic. (Well, some of them are. We talked all about Vimes in chapter 2. We'll talk about Carrot and Angua in a minute.) But we're talking about the average joe like Maladict, Polly Perks, Igor, Lofty, Tonker, and the rest of the "men" of the Tenth Foot Light Infantry (the Ins-and-Outs) under the command of Sergeant Jackrum (*Monstrous Regiment*)—the kind who sacrifice their lives to run off to fight a war.

Polly is half-Fa Mulan, half-Rosalind (see chapter 5) in that she takes a man's name and garb to join the regiment (à la Mulan), but not his place (à la Rosalind, who impersonated a man, but did not assume the identity of someone else in the story). Instead, she joins up to search for her brother. As it turns out, there are a number of "Rosalinds" in the regiment. Unlike Joan of Arc, who saw war as a holy cause, Polly is a realist who doesn't really fight in the name of the god Nuggan or the Duchess—the semireligious figure of the book. She fights for the Duchess—the inn her family owns.

Look for the sword.

Although each member of the Watch carries a sword (standard equipment according to *Men at Arms*), not every member is a hero. A hero needs a sword. As Rob Anybody says in *Wintersmith*, "Who ever heard o' a Hero wi'oot a sword?"[2] You'll find a sword in many fantasy epics—Minneyar (Memory Year), Sorrow, and Thorn—three lost swords used to fight evil (Tad Williams); the famed sword of Jerle Shannara in the Shannara series; the Sword of Truth that only the Seeker of Truth can wield (Terry Goodkind); Narsil/Andúril in *Lord of the Rings*; Godric Gryffindor's sword (J. K. Rowling); and the grandfather of epic swords—Excalibur.

Captain Carrot fits the hidden king archetype because of his kingly bearing, parentage, and the heirloom sword he brings with him when he joins the Watch. We talked about that a bit in chapter 1. Now consider other hidden kings, such as Aragorn in *Lord of the Rings* and Arthur—men whose swords also have legacies.

---

[2] *Wintersmith* (New York: HarperTempest, 2006), 298. Obviously, we like *this* book.

Because Carrot follows the hero's code closer than the Silver Horde in *The Last Hero* (a title that always reminds us of *Last Action Hero*—the 1993 Arnold Schwarzenegger movie), he is able to save the day, along with Rincewind, the reluctant volunteer on the mission, and Leonard of Quirm.

Awkward, not-quite-a-man Roland, the son of the baron, takes up the sword in *Wintersmith*. (He's probably sixteen at this point.) We talked about him in chapter 1. He's the hero called in by Granny Weatherwax to help save the day. But since this is a Pratchett creation, the sword he wields to victory isn't the one he brings from home, but one from his vivid imagination—one that really works. Sort of like playing air guitar or *Guitar Hero*—only with a sword.

Never underestimate a woman.

Heroines aren't only found in the Lancre witch and Tiffany Aching books. There's Adora Belle Dearheart, golem advocate. Moist von Lipwig calls her "Spike," while her brother goes for the more affectionate "Killer." Sweet. She's not a Mary Jane Watson—tough, but in need of rescuing in every movie. She's more along the lines of a Rose Tyler (played by Billie Piper on the *Doctor Who* TV series), Princess Leia (Carrie Fisher) or Rachel, Katie Holmes's character in *Batman Begins*. Yes, these characters occasionally had to be rescued. But Rose had to rescue the Doctor occasionally and help save the world on practically every show. Rachel knew how to wield a Taser or a gun when a mugger threatened or Scarecrow and a vicious mob tried to harm a child. And Princess Leia had fighting skills. (The book series goes into her story more.)

Adora Belle's weapon of choice is a pair of well-sharpened stilettos, which she operates like Dirty Harry, the magnum-toting homicide detective (Harry Callahan) played by Clint Eastwood in the 1971 film of the same name, whose words she parodies in *Going Postal*.

Speaking of weapons, Conina is a weapon herself, thanks to the genes she inherited from her dad, Cohen the Barbarian. (Her mother was Bethan, a woman Cohen met in *The Light Fantastic*. She's no shrinking violet, either.) She's a warrior, able to handle weapons along the lines of a warrior like Shu Lien, Michelle Yeoh's character in *Crouching Tiger, Hidden Dragon*—the Oscar winner for best foreign language film in 2000—or Ziyi Zhang's character in the same movie— Jen, the vicious disciple of Jade Fox, a vengeful woman.

And then there's Lady Myria LeJean, the Auditor turned human, who fights against her own beings. She's also known as Unity. The concept of an enemy becoming an ally is one you see played out in books and movies. We can't help thinking of the Terminator who killed humans in the first movie, but sacrificed himself for the greater good in *Terminator 2*. Guess reprogramming helps. Also, there's something about tasting humanity for the first time, which causes some to see the light. The last unicorn, after becoming a human and experiencing human love in *The Last Unicorn*, found humanity difficult to give up. (But that doesn't mean she didn't give it up.)

But getting back to Lady LeJean, the pseudonym she takes upon taking on flesh, the human experience is simply too much to bear, as she discovers simply by eating chocolate. Maybe that's why she decides to go out with a bang as Thelma and Louise did in the 1991 movie that bears their names. Perhaps if a large vat of chocolate had been available, Thelma and Louise would've jumped into that instead of going off that cliff.

And how about that Sybil Ramkin Vimes—the richest woman in Ankh-Morpork? She's like socialite Veronica Vreeland in the old *Batman* animated series, in that she has a high social status and deeply cares about animals. Those animals just happen to be swamp dragons. But she's unlike Veronica, in that she's humble rather than bored and spoiled. She is there when the biggest dragon of all—the *draco nobilis*—attacks (*Guards! Guards!*). It's what brings Vimes and her together. (Some people prefer Internet dating services in their quest for a love connection.) And in *The Fifth Elephant*, she keeps her head when threatened by kidnappers, captured by werewolves, and bullied by politically minded dwarfs. It's hard to keep a good woman down.

Speaking of not keeping a good woman down, here we've gotta give props to Cheery Littlebottom, the dwarf who comes out of the closet, if you will, by admitting that she is a female. She's the Kay Scarpetta/Catherine Willows (Marg Helgenberger) of the Watch and tremblingly places herself in the danger zone when necessary.

Don't worry. We're not leaving out Angua, the werewolf on the Watch. She may look like a helpless female à la Conina and many other heroines in fantasy fiction (such as Kahlan Amnell in Terry Goodkind's Sword of Truth series). But she's not the type you'd want to meet in a dark alley or even a lighted one. And like Conina and Kahlan, she frightens most men. Like Vivian, the werewolf main character in *Blood and Chocolate*, she accepts without any existential arguments the fact that she is a werewolf, and can choose to avoid hunting humans, except in her capacity as a member of the Watch.

And there's Ludmilla, another werewolf and daughter of the medium Mrs. Cake, who with Windle Poons helps save the city in *Reaper Man*. Doreen Winkings is another comrade in the fight against the parasitic life force. While Ludmilla's existence as a werewolf is denied by her mother, Doreen is in denial about her own status. She insists that she's a vampire simply because she married one. Thankfully, there is such a thing as therapy.

Don't discount a kid.

In some Steven Spielberg films and Stephen King novels, kids and teens help save the day. That's par for the course in juvenile fiction and young adult fiction but is not usual in adult fiction. But in Discworld, you can take your pick among kid or teen rescuers. We've already talked about Tiffany Aching and Roland de Chumsfanleigh. There's also Nijel the Destroyer, the painfully thin hero wannabe who falls for Conina in *Sourcery*. Nijel may think being a hero is something you have to read about, but he tries like Keith and Malicia, who help defeat the rat king in *The Amazing Maurice and His Educated Rodents*. And then there are Coin and Lobsang, who act to destroy Discworld but then help save it once they're in their right minds. And who could forget Twyla and Gawain, Susan Sto Helit's charges who stand up to the menacing Teatime in *Hogfather*? Although they aren't full-fledged members of the hall of heroes, perhaps they will be someday, having had Susan as a nanny.

Many adults tend to underestimate or patronize kids, which Pratchett shows in a number of Discworld books. The wizards learn the hard way that underestimating Coin is the act of a fool. Lobsang also is measured and found wanting until his connection to the personification of Time is discovered. No one makes that mistake twice.

Aim for the assassin.

In *Day of the Jackal*, the 1971 novel by Frederick Forsyth, the assassin (the jackal) earned the grudging respect of the police detective who tracked him. In *The Fifth Elephant*, don't look for warm fuzzies between Vimes and Inigo Skimmer, an assassin and a member of the ambassadorial staff. Vimes only tolerates him. Yet, like Moist von Lipwig is for the Post Office in *Going Postal*, Inigo's the right man for the right job: to help school Vimes on Uberwald political protocol, as well as to safeguard Vimes and the others. Being an assassin certainly helps in an area as tough as Uberwald, especially if one has spy work to do. But like his namesake in William Goldman's *The Princess Bride* (Inigo Montoya the swordsman), he runs afoul of someone truly evil. Montoya had a better outcome.

Pay attention to Wordes.

No, that's not a typo. Journalist William de Worde—a man who shares Terry Pratchett's former profession—shows the power of the press to effect change. Oh, and annoy people as well, to which Commander Vimes and many others can attest. With the help of Gunilla Goodmountain, Sacharissa Crisplock (his "Girl Friday"), and black ribboner Otto Chriek, de Worde in *The Truth* exposes yet another nefarious plot aimed at deposing Vetinari—a plot with a *Man in the Iron Mask* twist. And like other journalists covering wars, de Worde heads for the hot spot—Borogravia in *Monstrous Regiment*. His reporting there helps expose the truth about the war.

De Worde is like crusading real-life journalists Bob Woodward and Carl Bernstein, who, in *All the President's Men,* wrote about their experiences covering the Watergate scandal during the 1970s, and fictional journalists such as Gray Grantham in *The Pelican Brief* (John Grisham) and the Lone Gunmen from *The X-Files* and the *Lone Gunmen* TV series, whose search for the truth helped save lives but also ended careers. Life's all about hard choices. Speaking of hard choices . . .

Trust a con man.

One of the most unlikely heroes of Discworld has to be Moist von Lipwig, who makes a living bilking others out of their hard-earned cash. (For shame!) But he's the perfect man to outcon the ultimate con artist Reacher Gilt, whose management of the Grand Trunk costs lives. (See next chapter for more on him.) Unlike the Joker, who smugly asked, "Who do you trust?," in the 1989 Tim Burton–directed *Batman,* when Moist says, "Trust me," you can't help doing so without fear of losing your shirt.

Countless graphic novels, books, and movies prove that we love a good hero story and sometimes even an antihero story. In Discworld, you can be sure to find both.

12

~

Who's Wanted and Why: The Villains, Stooges, and Thugs of Discworld

IN THE DISCWORLD SCHOOL OF VILLAINY

If you make the FBI's Ten Most Wanted Fugitives List, you know you've done something really wrong—something beyond simply being late with library books and DVDs or dumping your boyfriend or girlfriend without a good explanation (although that ranks right up there with kidnapping and terrorism in the opinions of some).

It should be of no surprise to anyone that international terrorists head the list, followed by kidnappers and murderers. But if a most-wanted list were made for sci-fi/fantasy or spy fiction villains and betrayers, it would include the usual suspects: Darth Vader. Darth Maul. Darken Rahl. (Hey, that rhymes.) Darth Sidious. He Who Must Not Be Named (Voldemort) and his Death Eaters. Chired Anigrel and the seriously twisted demon queen Savilla (Obsidian Trilogy). Smaug. The Borg. The Daleks and Cybermen (*Doctor Who*). The Vogons (*The Hitchhiker's Guide to the Galaxy*). Dracula. The Forsaken and Shai'tan. Sauron. Saruman. Orcs and trollocs and goblins (oh my!). The Joker. Venom. Ras Al Ghul. Dr. Doom. The White Witch of Narnia. Blofeld. Goldfinger. SPECTRE. Rosa Klebb. Gustav Graves. Le Chiffre. Prince Humperdinck. Count Rugen. Islington. Vandemar and Croup. King Galbatorix. Barry the evil mastermind (*My Super Ex-Girlfriend*). The sky's the limit for sci-fi/fantasy or spy fiction villains and betrayers.

Some villains in fiction are easily spotted, because they're the snarling, hysterical kind who burst into Snidley Whiplash laughter ("Nyeah-ha-ha" or "Ha-ha-ha-ha!") at the drop of a hat and croon over their plans to take over the world. (Boris Badenov, anyone?) Terry Pratchett even makes fun of that notion with the notes from the villain of *Maskerade*—the Opera Ghost (*Ahahahahaha! Ahahahaha! Ahahahaha! BEWARE!!!!! Yrs sincerely The Opera Ghost*[1]) and through comments made by Dark Lord Harry Dread and his posse, for whom villainy is a legitimate hazard of the hero's quest, one that Cohen the Barbarian and the Silver Horde accept.

Villains are what drive the hero(ine) to up and at 'em. The most memorable villains aren't prone to maniacal laughter or spittle-spewing diatribes. They get quietly biz-ay in their scheduled attempts to take over the world. After all, they don't believe they're being *villainous*. They do what they do because they believe they're *right*. It's all a matter of perspective.

In Discworld, Pratchett will sometimes throw a curve in regard to the villain. You might start off thinking that someone or something is evil (such as the dragon in *Guards! Guards!*) and wind up scratching your head at the end of the book. Much of the time, however, the villains are as plain as the nose on your face (unless you happen to be Voldemort in the movie version of *Goblet of Fire*, in which case you're lacking a nose of sorts).

Yes, the Discworld villains are a special breed—front-runners in what we call the Discworld School of Villainy—those who could

---

[1] *Maskerade* (New York: HarperTorch, 1995), 67.

teach other fictional villains a thing or two about villainy. Before we get into the enrollees, here's a handy list of prerequisites for any-one interested in villainy as a profession. You will need:

o A good plan or at least a compelling one, since good has nothing to do with it
o A will to succeed no matter what the cost
o An ego the size of Texas, Alaska, or the continent of Asia
o A secret weapon
o A broken moral compass

DISC-CLAIMERS:
Plot spoilers ahead. Read at your own risk. Please note also that even though Jeremy Clockson helped the Auditors to destroy Discworld, he can't be considered a villain, because he probably was not in his right mind at the time (more probably the left). Plus, since he is also Lobsang Ludd and helped save Discworld, one act cancels the other.

THE VILLAINS

Human Creeps

There's a whole slew of 'em: Deacon Vorbis the Omnian Exquis-itor (*Small Gods*); Carcer (*Night Watch*); Reacher Gilt (*Going Postal*); Lupine Wonse, a.k.a. the Grand Supreme Master of the Elucidated Brethren of the Ebon Night (*Guards! Guards!*); Captain Findthee Swing of the Unmentionables (*Night Watch*); Duke Felmet and the Duchess (*Wyrd Sisters*; see also chapter 5 of this book); Jonathan Teatime (*Hogfather*); Mr. Salzella the Opera Ghost (*Maskerade*); and even the genteel Lord de Worde (*The Truth*), just to name a few. They're like roaches or mice—they breed in just the right at-mosphere. They live and die by their code of beliefs. Those who dare to stand in their way don't stand for long.

Gilt-edged. With an eyepatch and a cockatoo on the shoulder, Reacher Gilt may look like a stereotypical pirate à la Long John Silver (*Treasure Island*), but he's never foolish or charmingly drunk like Captain Jack Sparrow in the *Pirates of the Caribbean* movies. He's more of a business pirate with the success of real-life early-nineteenth-century gentleman pirate Jean Lafitte; the panache of Captain James Hook (*Peter Pan*); and the ruthlessness of Gordon Gekko, the corporate raider in *Wall Street*, the 1987 movie starring Michael Douglas ("Greed is good"), or Captain Barbossa and the squid-faced Davy Jones in the *Pirates of the Caribbean* movies.

Con man Moist von Lipwig even admires the flimflam of Gilt, whose antics go beyond those of a con artist like Harold Hill in *The Music Man*. Gilt's not small-time like the guys who hustle people in three-card monte games. He's strictly a big-time gambler who fervently believes in "winner take all." That's the pirate's way.

The City Watch's Most Wanted. In the City Watch series, you find plenty of villains. After all, the job of a City watchperson is to catch criminals. And what better place to find a criminal than a big city like Ankh-Morpork? This is where you find your psychotic killers, such as Carcer (*Night Watch*), and your assassins, such as Edward d'Eath and Dr. Cruces (*Men at Arms*), whose purpose goes beyond the assassins' code.

Some criminals, like Dr. Cruces, sound so reasonable, you almost want to invite them to dinner to look at their brochures. ("Yes, I understand now why you're willing to kill anyone, including the Patrician, who stands in your way of putting the rightful king back on his throne. How can I donate to your cause?") But others, like the torturous, calipers-carrying Captain Findthee Swing (he of the rat's eyes), are more insidious, like Darth Sidious, the emperor in the *Star Wars* series of movies. Swing is like Toht, the Nazi torturer in *Raiders of the Lost Ark,* in that he tortures and maims because he loves to do it. And he hires people just like him to carry out some of his tasks—others bearing the uniform of authority. (For more on stooges and thugs, see "The Stooges and Thugs," page 172.) As with Wolfgang, death is a far better choice, in Vimes's opinion, than his continuing to walk the earth. You have to wonder what a good dose of Zoloft or even Thorazine would have accomplished in Swing's life.

Lupine Wonse is another villain with a get-rid-of-the-Patrician-and-get-the-rightful-king-on-the-throne agenda. He's of the maniacal laughter caliber of criminal, driven to the edge of madness by the noble dragon he summons.

Carcer, however, starts on the edge of insanity and keeps on going. He's a Jack the Ripper brand of serial killer—another person Vimes would rather see dead than alive. Vimes barely restrains himself from making that happen.

But among the most villainous in Ankh-Morpork—at least in Vimes's opinion—are the politicians—the ones on the right side of the law; the ones he can't prosecute, no matter how hard he tries. (Lords Rust, Downey, and Selachii—take note.) Many would agree.

Twisted Terrors. Jonathan Teatime, or Teh-ah-tim-eh as he prefers, the twisted assassin of *Hogfather,* has the same sort of joy the Swing displays in his work. Even Lord Downey, the head of the assassins and a man with "no actual morals,"[2] finds him repugnant. But that doesn't stop Downey from suggesting him as a possible assassin to do away with the Hogfather.

Deacon Vorbis, as we mentioned in chapter 4, exudes a kind of rational evil. He doesn't get hysterical or foam at the mouth. Watch the master at work. Vorbis calmly places the tortoise god Om on his back in the hot sun so that Om will die. Later, he hands someone a harpoon to kill a porpoise. Now *that's* evil. But to Brutha, the

---

[2] *Hogfather* (New York: HarperTorch, 1996), 16.

hapless devotee of Om, Vorbis is villainous because he has no real belief in Om. That is Vorbis's downfall.

And what of Lord de Worde in *The Truth*? What a guy. Like Dr. Cruces and other villains, he plots to replace Vetinari. He belongs to the same Icy Fathers League as Lycaelon Tavadon, in Mercedes Lackey's Obsidian Trilogy, or Darth Vader—someone who could betray his son at the drop of a hat and not consider anything wrong with that. Worde also is just as prone to look down on the "lesser races" as is Tavadon. Don't look for any speeches from either of them on Father's or Friendship Day.

Nonhuman or Undead Creeps

The Auditors of the Universe. They may be just gray cloaks (until they take on human flesh, as they do in *Thief of Time*), but the Auditors are a plague on humanity. Orderliness in the universe is their passion. Unfortunately, humans are too disorderly, in their opinion. And Death is a continual nuisance to them.

The Auditors are petty bureaucrats, with their penchant for rules and having things done their way. (Perhaps you're thinking of the DMV or some other civic office right now.) They are the "rat king" (see next section) of the universe with their collective mind-speak and avoidance of the first person. Think Big Brother (*1984* by George Orwell) is bad? They watch the human drama, not unlike the black-robed Auditor in Samuel Beckett's play *Not I*. They're so lacking in imagination that the only names they can come up with after taking on flesh are those of colors (Mr. White, Mr. Orange).

When they're not trying to replace Death (*Reaper Man*), destroy Discworld (*Thief of Time*), or arrange for the elimination of the Hogfather and other personifications (*Hogfather*), we're not exactly sure what the Auditors do. Sweep stars, maybe? Tidy drawers?

The Undead and Fairyland Creeps. Angua's brother, Wolfgang (*The Fifth Elephant*), is in good company with the de Magpyr family of vampires (*Carpe Jugulum*), the Dragon King of Arms (an old vampire in *Feet of Clay*), the Fairy Queen (*The Wee Free Men; Lords and Ladies*), and Mr. Slant, the zombie lawyer. In most cases, they're respectable but villainous. They're the kind who send others to do their dirty work. (Well, Wolfgang does his own dirty work.)

Slant works for such human creeps as Reacher Gilt, Lord de Worde, and Lord Downey. You can usually find him weaseling people out of trouble or hiring such thugs as Mr. Pin and Mr. Tulip (see "The Stooges and Thugs," page 172). He's like a walking episode of *Law and Order* (insert the subtitle of your favorite spinoff), where the criminals sometimes go scot-free.

While Angua's von Uberwald clan (the baron and baroness) enjoys the power and prestige of the werewolf in Uberwald, Wolfgang thinks only of being at the top of the food chain. Even a vampire like Lady Margolotta—who has some Godfather tendencies, in Vimes's estimation—considers him to be a monster. Ironic, isn't it? He's like the worst of the Bond villains—completely mental.

Back in Ankh-Morpork, the Dragon King of Arms is not only a snob, but a meddler in politics. In *Feet of Clay*, he's content to work in the shadows, putting the person of his choice on the throne of Ankh-Morpork, in the vein of Dr. Cruces and the guild leaders. He has an ancient malevolence on par with many of the vampires in Anne Rice's Vampire Chronicles and the Volturi in Stephenie Meyer's *New Moon*. That's why he's considered the real villain, rather than the murdering golem. After all, the golem is an ignorant pawn made by other golems. But the Dragon King of Arms just screams "megalomaniac." And anyone who tries to kill Vimes is just wrong in our book. (For more on the Dragon King of Arms, read chapter 15.)

The Fairy Queen, like other treacherous queens in literature, especially the queen in the Snow White fairy tale and the Evil Queen of *The 10th Kingdom,* wants a world to control—the default wish list of the villain as well as that of the Brain of *Pinky and the Brain*—and has many elves to do her bidding. She's beautiful. She's deadly. She's undoubtedly insane. But she's pitiable, as Tiffany Aching discovers in *The Wee Free Men.* After all, isn't she just wookin' pa nub?

Creepy Animals and Insects. Many fantasy series (Anne McCaffrey's Pern series, Christopher Paolini's Inheritance series, a number of series by Mercedes Lackey) feature the bond between a human and a dragon. For the most part, this is a good thing. Not so in Discworld. The summoned noble dragon of *Guards! Guards!* acts the part of the wily, but vicious dragon—more on the Smaug end of the spectrum than on the lovable Saphira (*Eragon*), Ancaladar (*To Light a Candle*), or Ruth (*The White Dragon*) end. After all, quite a few deaths take place at her "hands" and she has a hoard like Smaug. Also, she has a mental link with Wonse and twists his strings like a maniacal puppet master. But then there's the matter of her culinary needs—the usual diet of the marauding dragons. Hint: Lady Sybil Ramkin fits the profile. (In contrast, Ancaladar eats cattle.) Yet all of that changes when the dragon meets little Errol. She wanders off like a lovesick puppy—like the dragon in the first *Shrek.*

And let us not forget Spider, the rat king of the rat catchers in Pratchett's Carnegie Medal–winning book, *The Amazing Maurice and His Educated Rodents.* Spider is really eight rats operating with one mind, thanks to their tails being tied together. Humans are the target of Spider's wrath. (We get no respect.)

The idea of creating rat kings by tying rats together by the tail didn't originate with Pratchett. There are folktales based on attempts by humans to join rats together. And a museum (Mauritianum) in Altenburg, Thuringia, Germany, has the actual mummified remains of a rat king. (Ugh.)

Speaking of small, vicious animals, who could forget Big Fido, a small white poodle who just happens to be the crazed leader of dogs in *Men at Arms*? (You might be thinking of *All Dogs Go to Heaven* right about now. Or maybe that's just us.) He tries to off Angua and Gaspode—the talking mongrel. Big Fido believes dogs are superior to all animals (sort of like master-race thinking). It is only a matter of time before he amasses a following large enough to take over the city. Unfortunately, his time runs out.

Evil Entities. The Summoning Dark in *Thud!* and the hiver in *A Hat Full of Sky* are the "rat kings" of the supernatural world—a conglomerate of minds acting as one mind. These entities are considered villainous, since they tend to take over the minds of people—like the wizard Sensibility Bustle and Vimes. But the hiver seems, well, pitiable almost with its plaintive request to die. Still, no one thinks, *Wow, it would be great if the hiver would stop by for a long visit.* Even Jeannie, the kelda who is jealous of Tiffany, pities Tiffany when the hiver gets on her trail.

The Summoning Dark, on the other hand, is a demonic entity made up of the desire for revenge. It flourishes in the heightened atmosphere of Koom Valley as it tries to use Vimes in its quest to destroy. It's like something out of *The Exorcist* franchise of movies. Nasty. Approach with caution.

And then there are the entities that are named by indefinite pronouns, such as Them (*Equal Rites*) and Others (*Moving Pictures*). Like the Fairy Queen and her elves, their mission (and they've decided to accept it) is to take over the world. Them, a.k.a. the Shadow creatures, come from the Dungeon Dimension as do the Others (a.k.a. Things). There goes the neighborhood. . . .

Magical Human Creeps

There's nothing worse than a villain with magical powers. Think: Voldemort. That's why an Ipslore the Red, who nearly succeeds in destroying the Disc, is a particular nuisance even after he's dead, thanks to having his essence in the staff given to Coin. He's like a demonic spirit who possesses a person and uses him or her as a puppet. And the evil vizier Abrim causes a mage war that doesn't help, either. As Pratchett mentions in *Pyramids*, "There is no such thing as a good Grand Vizier. A predilection to cackle and plot is apparently part of the job."[3] So Abrim is just doing his part to carry on the tradition.

But consider the case of Lilith de Tempscire (a.k.a. Lily Weatherwax), the fairy godmother and Granny's "good" sister in *Witches Abroad*. Is Lily Weatherwax evil? Well, she makes harmful choices and resorts to murder. She also tries to force the Cinderella of the story—Ella—to marry a frog, all for the sake of a happy ending. She's not tragically misunderstood as Elphaba, the so-called Wicked Witch of the West (a tweaked character of L. Frank Baum) is, in Gregory Maguire's *Wicked*. And on par with villains everywhere, she believes that she's the "good one"—the one whose actions are for the sake of humanity.

Lilith is an allusion to Lilith, the mythical first wife of Adam, mentioned in *The Lion, the Witch and the Wardrobe* by C. S. Lewis. In that book Lilith is the White Witch, Jadis. There's a reference to Lilith in *The Alphabet of Ben-Sira*.

THE STOOGES AND THUGS

Isn't it funny how there's always a stooge for hire whenever a megalomaniac seeks to take over the world? Unlike the Three

---

[3] *Pyramids* (New York: HarperTorch, 1989), 144.

Stooges from the old TV show (and countless movies—okay, they really can be counted), these stooges are usually tireless wreckers of humanity or just out for the money, like the pirates of the *Black Pearl*. But the ways of stooges make for entertaining reading.

Don't you wonder what goes through the stooge's mind when the plan comes up?

Megalomaniac: I'm going to use this virus to kill billions of people. You will assist me.
Stooge: Cool!
Megalomaniac: We'll *all* perish! Every single one of us! Even you! Ha-ha-ha-ha!
Stooge: Yeah! Woo hoo!

Obviously a screw is loose somewhere. You don't have to have intelligence to be a criminal stooge. Having brawn and a willingness to hurt others are two good prerequisites. That's why Teatime uses Chickenwire, Banjo Lilywhite, Medium Dave Lilywhite, Peachy, and Catseye to help carry out the plan to off the Hogfather. (When we think of Banjo and Medium Dave, we can't help thinking of the counting song "Green Grow the Rushes, O," which has the lines "Two, two, the lily-white boys,/Clothèd all in green, Ho."[4])

Although he doesn't fit the stooge mold (i.e., unintelligent), student-wizard Sideney helps with the Hogfather plan, to make extra money. But those who follow Dark Lord Harry Dread (*The Last Hero*)—namely, such henchmen as Slime, Armpit, Butcher, Gak, and a troll that continually says, "Dat's me"—do.

For Lupine Wonse, there are the Elucidated Brethren of the Ebon Night, who include Brother Fingers, Brother Doorkeeper, Brother Plasterer, and others. For Lily Weatherwax, there's the Duc, who's

---

[4] Quoted at http://en.wikipedia.org/wiki/Green_grow_the_rushes,_O.

really a frog, and the snake women, who are really snakes, to help her carry out her nefarious plans. (For more about the Duc and the snake women, see chapter 13.)

Even if the stooges have some intelligence (like the board members of the Grand Trunk Company in *Going Postal*), the villain has to be able to outthink them and even dispose of them when they become a nuisance. He or she wouldn't be a villain if he/she was sentimental, even about a stooge.

Greed, misplaced nationalism, or religious ideals is also a motivator for the stooge. That's why in *The Fifth Elephant*, we find that Dee, the king's "ideas taster," is used by the werewolves, rather than the originator of the plan. That's why Deacon Cusp helps Deacon Vorbis.

Another sort of stooge can be found in *The Wee Free Men*—the dromes. They are the dreamweavers, and we don't mean the 1975 song by Gary Wright nor do we mean the Dreamweavers of Trudi Canavan's *Priestess of the White*—although Canavan's dreamweavers can send dreams. They're golems of a sort—gray, walking gingerbread men much larger than the tiny gingerbread man of the *Shrek* movies (but smaller than the big gingerbread man in *Shrek 2*) and certainly malevolent. Dromes are akin to Morpheus (see chapter 9), in that they provide dreams. But the Feegles compare dromes to spiders for their ability to weave dreams like webs to trap their next meal. In a way, they're like big, bloated Shelob in *The Two Towers* and the other giant spiders in *The Hobbit*.

As for your thugs, well, there's Chrysophrase, the extortionist troll thug (Coalface is the right-hand stooge of Chrysophrase). Although Chrysophrase is an employer and a club owner akin to a mob boss, he's still a thug. Who else but a thug would try to bribe Vimes (see *Thud!*)?

And who could forget the "fun-loving," elves in *Lords and Ladies*—the full-size models—or the wasp-size ones (see chapter 10)? These aren't your happy Keebler elves, who sing and make cookies, or the beautiful, wise *Lord of the Rings* or Obsidian Trilogy elves. Like

Teatime, these elves are predatory and vicious, the kind who smile as they kill like the werewolves who like to play "the game" in *The Fifth Elephant*. They love to hunt others for sport—a plot element seen in other stories as well.

And then there are the thugs for hire: art appreciator Mr. Tulip and the brains of the outfit—Mr. Pin in *The Truth*—figure heavily in the plot to get rid of Vetinari (plot #6,000; everyone tries to get rid of Vetinari or Vimes). You can't help but think of Mr. Wint and Mr. Kidd, the polite thugs in *Diamonds Are Forever*. And of course, there's Mr. Gryle, the banshee thug employed by Reacher Gilt in *Going Postal*.

And let us not forget the thugs in uniform—corrupt watchmen, a term that's almost a redundancy in Ankh-Morpork. There's Captain "Mayonnaise" Quirke (*Men at Arms*, *Night Watch*), Sergeant Knock (*Night Watch*), and the rest of Captain Swing's sadistic Unmentionables—the SS of Ankh-Morpork.

Like the villains, thugs and stooges usually come to a bad end unless they agree to betray their bosses, in which case they probably will come to an end anyway . . . just like this chapter.

13

~

Les Animaux

Animal minds are simple, and therefore sharp. . . .
The whole panoply of the universe has been neatly
expressed to them as things to (a) mate with, (b) eat,
(c) run away from, and (d) rocks.
—*Equal Rites*[1]

Maybe we won't catch you ordering *Charlotte's Web* or any other cute animal story (*Flicka* or *Lassie*, anyone?) through Netflix. Maybe *Animal Farm*, George Orwell's searing indictment of Russian-style communism, or Brian Jacques's Redwall series with its *Lord of the Rings*–epic style of animals is more your speed. You know—where animals behave as people and even wield a sword and other weapons.

While a series like Artemis Fowl may be "*Die Hard* with fairies" (according to its author), *Animal Farm* is *Doctor Zhivago* with animals. So, what is Discworld? We consider it *Les Misérables* with animals. *Les Animaux*, if you will.

---

[1] *Equal Rites* (New York: HarperTorch, 1987), 77.

GIVE US YOUR POOR, YOUR TIRED, AND YOUR WRETCHED

Victor Hugo's classic story of poverty and redemption might seem like a far cry from the daily life of a talking dog named Gaspode or an extremely smelly, old wirehaired terrier named Wuffles—the pride and joy of Lord Vetinari. But think of Gaspode as Jean Valjean, the beleaguered hero of *Les Misérables,* whose crime of stealing bread to feed his family nets him the unwavering persecution of Inspector Javert. Think of Wuffles as Gavroche, the kid who rats out Javert. (Remember, Wuffles is the one who exposes Charlie as the fake Vetinari, thus helping foil the plan of Mr. Tulip and Mr. Pin.)

Think of Gavin, the wolf who runs with a pack of wolves in *The Fifth Elephant,* as Eponine Thénardier, a young girl in love with Marius Pontmercy, a revolutionary, and dies to save him. We thought of Eponine because of the love triangle. If you saw the play *Les Mis,* you know that Marius loves Cosette, Jean Valjean's daughter. Well, there's the Angua-Carrot-Gavin triangle. What Gavin's relationship is to Angua before she arrives in Ankh-Morpork, we can only guess. (And we try not to think too deeply about that.)

Consider also, the tragic life of Chubby, the stolen dragon in *Men at Arms* who . . . well . . . explodes. Can't you see echoes of the ill-used Fantine who tragically dies in *Les Mis?*

Now think of Dangerous Beans, Peaches, and especially Darktan of *The Amazing Maurice and His Educated Rodents* as the students at the barrier fighting in the revolution. Darktan, of course, is Enjolras—the leader of the student rebels. Can't you just hear the music swelling? ("Do You Hear the People Sing?")

WE'RE FULL OF HOT AIR

Okay. Maybe we're full of hot air and you would prefer us to get to stuff like *Pet Sematary*, the 1983 Stephen King book turned into a movie, where buried pets and people come back to life and turn evil. (All right, all right. Maybe you didn't see that one.) Greebo, Nanny Ogg's pet cat, would probably have a starring role. Or how about Amazonian strawberry poison dart frogs? They're not in Discworld. We're just mentioning them because we think they're cool.

Maybe you won't think a comparison to *Les Mis* so far-fetched if you recall the barricades built all over Ankh-Morpork in *Night Watch* and the songs the flag-waving rebels sing, an allusion to the song of the rebel students in *Les Mis*—"Do You Hear the People Sing?"

But we digress. Getting back to Pratchett's Animal Kingdom, the closest animal you'll find to the heroic Lassie (the famous collie) or Rin Tin Tin (a series of trained German shepherds who acted in the movies during the 1920s and 1930s—a time when maybe your grandmother wasn't even alive) ideal is a dog named Laddie the Wonder Dog in *Moving Pictures*. He's like Lassie and Rin Tin Tin except he was almost designed by Nature to be in moving pictures—he even barks photogenically! But while he helps save the day (Good boy!), he has an almost pathological need to be affirmed.

In Discworld, you won't find a load of heroic animals that seem as if they're self-cleaning. Instead, you find animals full of hot, smelly air, such as the swamp dragons at the Ankh-Morpork Sunshine Sanctuary for Sick Dragons started by Sybil Ramkin Vimes. Pratchett talks all about swamp dragons in *The Last Hero* and other places, so we won't go into that much. What we can tell you is that they're not like the dragons you find in the Pern series by Anne McCaffrey (and Todd McCaffrey, her coauthor son), the Dragon Jousters series by Mercedes Lackey, the Inheritance series by Christopher Paolini, or any of the hundreds of other series with dragons.

And Gaspode is sort of an anti-Lassie—tough talking and street-wise; not a puppet of "the Man" like Laddie. (If Joe Pesci could play a dog, he could probably play Gaspode.) Oh, sure, he helps save the day in *Men at Arms*, *The Truth*, *Moving Pictures*, and *The Fifth Elephant*. And he's briefly known as Gaspode the Wonder Dog in *Moving Pictures*. But you've probably never seen Lassie as filthy as Gaspode. And Lassie, alas, only barks, no matter how many times Timmy asks, "What is it, girl?" (And the gender thing is another issue.)

And then there's the matter of Wuffles—a sixteen-year-old dog who likes to bite people. Not exactly Rin Tin Tin. Yet Wuffles is a beloved pet just as Greebo is and Gaspode was briefly. But in Disc-world, pets are no more "owned" than people are—at least the smart ones aren't.

Of Rats and Men

Martin and his father, Luke (guess Luke can't use the Darth Vader line, "Luke, I am your father"), are your epic-style heroes of Redwall. No question about that. You don't get a name like Martin the Warrior or Luke the Warrior for knitting sweaters. They're part of the tradition of heroic mice, one you find in the Newbery award–winning book, *Mrs. Frisby and the Rats of NIMH* by Robert C. O'Brien and *The Rescuers* by Margery Sharp. And then there are rats like Ripfang, the pirate, who are the opposite—nasty, mean— the manner of many rats in fiction. (Many, but not all.)

Discworld is rat, rather than mice, country. There are the Death of Rats (see chapter 8), Dangerous Beans, Darktan, and Hamnpork. (And there's the ratlike Nobby.) They're in the Justin sphere of heroic animals, Justin being the kindly, heroic rat in *Mrs. Frisby and the Rats of NIMH*. They're proof that the most unlikely being (e.g., hobbits) can save the day.

Like the rats of NIMH, the Discworld rats suddenly discover that they're cleverer than others of their species, thanks to eating garbage at Unseen University (also the site of Gaspode's change). The NIMH rats gained their intelligence through being experimented upon. Maurice gained his through, well, eating a magically enhanced rat. You are what you eat.

Running with the Wolves

Down through the ages, wolves have gotten the shaft in literature, what with Aesop's fables, Maugrim in *The Lion, the Witch, and the Wardrobe*, and all. Pratchett only partially rectifies that with his inclusion of wolves and werewolves. Some are good, like Lupine the "mostly" wolf werewolf in *Reaper Man*. Some are bad—werewolf-movie bad. We talked about them in chapter 4. These aren't your "gender-confused" wolves à la the *Shrek* movies.

Gavin—all wolf, not a werewolf—is the typical alpha male—reeking of "competent power," as Pratchett describes in *The Fifth Elephant*. (As opposed to the wolf Eats Wrong Meat, who probably just reeks.) The wolves of Gavin's pack in *The Fifth Elephant* have a social order akin to that of the wolves that raised Mowgli in *The Jungle Book* by Rudyard Kipling, or the wolves in Jean Craighead George's award-winning series about an Inuit girl who lives with a pack of wolves. Although the Discworld wolves probably wouldn't raise a human child, they're willing to tolerate humans and even snack on them, as Angua warns Carrot in *The Fifth Elephant* when he threatens to underestimate them. They're very intelligent animals and even have a system of passing on information that's just as effective as the clacks.

Cats "You" Later

Whether or not you're a cat lover, you can find plenty of cats in fantasy—at least in kids' fantasy; for example, Erin Hunter's Warriors series featuring warring factions of cats.

In Discworld, you'll find cats with a Pratchett twist. In the

Carnegie medal–winning book *The Amazing Maurice and His Educated Rodents*, Maurice is a street-smart cat with a plan. He's the Discworld version of Thomas O'Malley, the alley cat in Disney's *The Aristocats*. Maurice could probably out-con Moist von Lipwig, who is a con artist supreme. He subscribes to the talking animal school of which Gaspode is a charter member, thanks to the influence of Unseen University (and on Maurice's part, a judicious diet of rats).

In many fiction stories, cats are the province of witches. Some are used as familiars. Nanny's battle-scarred cat Greebo is a little too familiar. He's not like Hermione's cat Crookshanks in the Harry Potter series, being of a pillaging personality. But even he gets a comeuppance when Granny gains a kitten (You) in *Wintersmith*.

Even Death has a soft spot for cats, as we mentioned in chapter 8. But it's doubtful that even he would like Ratbag, the family cat of the Achings. We're introduced to Ratbag in *The Wee Free Men*. He belongs to the nasty pet cats school of which Si and Am, the sinuous Siamese cats owned (if a cat can be owned) by Aunt Sarah in *Lady and the Tramp*, are members. (Even Greebo, as nefarious as he seems, is more lovable.)

Sisterhood of the Snakes

What fictional wild kingdom could be complete without snakes? But like the wolves, snakes have a bad rep, thanks to a certain snake in the Garden of Eden. In the Harry Potter series, you know that Voldemort, who can talk to snakes, has a huge snake named Nagini. And, of course, there's the python Kaa in Rudyard Kipling's *The Jungle Book*. Even though Kaa helps rescue Mowgli at one point (mainly so he can have a few monkeys for a snack), he's still viewed as sneaky. Not content with just one snake, Kipling adds three more— Nag and Nagaina, two nasty cobras, and Karait, another poisonous snake, all of which encounter the mongoose Rikki-Tikki-Tavi (in the short story of the same name in *The Jungle Book*).

In Discworld you find the "iridescent women"[2] also known as the Sisters in *Witches Abroad*. Granny Weatherwax spots them as the snakes they really are. You might call them a Sisterhood of the Snakes, like the *Brotherhood of the Wolf*. With the pair of them, we couldn't help thinking of Si and Am, who created havoc in their household. But unlike those cats, these sisters meet the "mongoose" that is Magrat, who goes all "Rikki-Tikki-Tavi" on them (if you'll pardon our Rudyard Kipling).

A talking snake makes an appearance in *Sourcery*, when Rincewind is cast into a snake pit—usually the fate of fantasy heroes, even would-be ones like Rincewind. (Think of the snake pit into which Indiana Jones falls in *Raiders of the Lost Ark*.) And lastly, there's a rumor that Vetinari has a snake pit in which prisoners are thrown. But that's-s-s probably just a rumor.

Hungry, Hungry Hippos

If you saw *Fantasia* (the first one, from 1940), you know that Disney's "Dance of the Hours" (composed by Amilcare Ponchielli) featured dancing hippos. Très chic. In Discworld, hippos play an important part as well, thanks to Roderick and Keith (*Feet of Clay*) —heraldic hippos of Ankh-Morpork who also appear on a stamp (*Going Postal*). Only in Discworld. . . . And to think some people prefer lions or dragons on their coats of arms.

Quoth the Raven, Nevermore

The *Corvidae* species of birds, of which ravens and crows figure prominently, are seldom birds people in stories want to have around. Isn't it always the evil wizards who have a crow hanging from their shoulders or use crows to do their bidding (Saruman)? Even in Edgar

---

[2] *Witches Abroad* (New York: HarperTorch, 1991), 199.

Allan Poe's most famous poem, the raven is a figure of mystery. But Pratchett, as usual, takes even an archetypal harbinger of doom and has fun with it. Quoth does come with death, since he is the self-proclaimed mouthpiece and noble steed of the Death of Rats and seems fixated on eyeballs. But at least he works for the heroes (the Death of Rats, Susan).

If you happen to read *The Name of the Wind* by Patrick Rothfuss, you read of another Quoth—Kvothe to be exact. But he isn't a raven.

The Dogs of War

By this we mean the grimhounds from *The Wee Free Men*, rather than the 1981 flick directed by John Irvin (based on the book by Frederick Forsyth). This makes the huge phosphorous-dusted hound in *The Hound of the Baskervilles* (Arthur Conan Doyle) look like something out of *Scooby-Doo*. Come to think of it, that hound business was a precursor to the unmaskings in *Scooby-Doo*. But we digress. . . . Getting back to the grimhounds, maybe in your mind you picture the most vicious dog you can ever imagine—massive, snarling, a super-size junkyard dog with a hangover. The grimhounds have a resemblance to the hound in Doyle's masterwork, with their "eyes of fire,"[3] massive build, and black fur. But the ghostly grimhounds' flaming eyes are the real thing, unlike those of the hound in Doyle's book. And their orange eyebrows? To die for.

The grimhounds are so fearsome, they get an honorable mention in *Going Postal* as one of the items you shouldn't ask about. Don't believe us? Look at chapter 2 of that book.

---

[3] *The Wee Free Men* (New York: HarperTrophy, 2003), 131.

Amped-up Amphibians

In many fairy tales, frogs or toads talk and turn out to be princes or some other titled person in disguise. There's "The Frog Prince" (major clue there) of *Grimm's Complete Fairy Tales*, "The Princess and the Frog" in *The Door in the Hedge* (Robin McKinley), and Gogu the faithful frog friend (guess what he really is?) in *Wildwood Dancing* (Juliet Marillier). Unlike the master of Toad Hall in *The Wind in the Willows*, the toad in *The Wee Free Men* wasn't always a toad. He isn't a prince, however—he's a lawyer. Well, we won't touch that one. You can insert your own joke. But another amphibian hits the royalty circuit—the frog Duc of *Witches Abroad*. Too bad he's a pawn of Lily Weatherwax and meets up with a zombie on a quest for revenge.

Staggering About

The hunting of the white stag has been the key to an adventure in or out of Faerie in many a story. Think of the ethereal White Stag the Pevensies discover in *The Lion, the Witch and the Wardrobe*, which leads them out of Narnia. Pwyll, son of Dyyed, a prince in one of the stories of the *Mabinogion*, tries to steal a stag from Arawn, a King of Annwvyn—one of the kings of the Otherworld—and winds up having to serve him as punishment for his impertinence. Robin McKinley carries on the tradition in her short story "The Hunting of the Hind," in *The Door in the Hedge*, by showing a hunt that nearly kills a prince.

The stag Tiffany sees in *The Wee Free Men* isn't graceful or ethereal. It's a wild animal that happens to be part of the nightmarish, wintry landscape of Fairyland like the Bumblebee women (the big women with the little wings). It's also a signal to Tiffany that she's not in Kansas anymore.

Unintelligent Unicorns

We'll end this chapter with unicorns. Picture a unicorn running blithely through a forest or sniffing buttercups. That's their usual posture in books. Pratchett and Mercedes Lackey (well, in her 500 Kingdoms series, at least) have a similar idea in that the unicorns of their worlds are rather unintelligent, vapid even. In *Lords and Ladies*, the unicorn is a wild beast that can't talk and doesn't seem to want to heal anything, but instead kills like a cornered animal. This is contrary to the way unicorns are usually portrayed in fantasy—you know, as majestic, magical talking beasts dripping with wisdom, which kill only when threatened by evil beings. They would prefer to heal, rather than kill. Like elves, they're piercingly beautiful and mysterious. Think of the female unicorn—you know, the unnamed one (except when she's given a fake name—Lady Amalthea) who searched for other unicorns in *The Last Unicorn* by Peter S. Beagle (the novel and screenplay) or the one foolish Princess Lily dares to touch to the detriment of the world in *Legend*, the old Tom Cruise movie from 1985. But in Discworld, you don't want to get too close to one. And you can't, unless you're like Granny Weatherwax and certainly not Nanny Ogg. (And the answer to that riddle is . . .)

In Obsidian Trilogy, the unicorns Shalkan and Calmeren have cloven hooves and a deerlike appearance, as does the unicorn in *The Last Unicorn*. What we know about the unicorn in *Lords and Ladies* is that he is huge and heavy like a horse, rather than deerlike.

Hmm. Maybe we can make a case for *The Sound of Music*, instead of *Les Mis*. You know how the *Sound of Music* song goes, "Do—a deer?" Picture the unicorn. . . .

Okay. Maybe not.

Part Three

Power, Police, and Paraphernalia: The Way Things Work in Discworld

〜

14

It's Magic

Oh ho, ho, it's magic, you know
Never believe it's not so.[1]

EIGHT WONDERS OF DISCWORLD

There were seven wonders of the ancient world: the Great Pyramid in Giza, the Temple of Artemis, the Statue of Zeus (Olympia), the Hanging Gardens in Babylon, the Mausoleum of Maussollos, the Colossus of Rhodes, and the Lighthouse/Pharos of Alexandria. They were monoliths to human ingenuity. Yet only one exists today—the Great Pyramid.

Imagine what it was like to see those wonders. Seeing anything amazing always begs the question, "How'd they do that?"

A place like Discworld is beyond one of the wonders of the world, because it is magical and magic is the very stuff of the Disc—part of the fabric of daily life. And isn't magic the reason why we read fantasy—the wonder of it all? So let's take a sightseeing tour of Discworld to see the eight magic wonders of that world. Why only eight?

---

[1] From the song "Magic," recorded by Pilot in 1975. Lyrics by David Paton and Bill Lyall were posted at http://www.superseventies.com/sl_magic.html and at http://www.davidpaton.com/index.shtml. An oldie but goodie.

As we said before, eight is an important number in Discworld. Better bring a camera. You don't want to miss these shots.

DISC-CLAIMER:

Plot spoilers ahead. Read at your own risk. Although we picked the following, you may have a different idea of the magic wonders of Discworld. Also, their order does not indicate order of importance.

I. The Chalk

The Chalk? you may balk. You may have expected us to say something like Fairyland, the Fairy Queen's realm, since Tiffany Aching takes a journey through it in *The Wee Free Men*. But Fairyland is part of the Otherworld, which tries to intrude upon Tiffany's world in *The Wee Free Men*. We'll get to that in a minute. Meanwhile, we picked the Chalk because at first glance it might seem like an ordinary region akin to a quaint English farming community. But consider the fact that Miss Tick talked about the impossibility of growing a witch on chalk. However, the Chalk not only produced Tiffany, but Sarah Aching (Granny Aching) as well.

In "Cult Classic," an essay in *Meditations on Middle-Earth*, Pratchett remarked that the land was very much a character in *The Lord of the Rings*. He could tell that by the loving details Tolkien added to make the setting prominent. In *The Wee Free Men*, Pratchett takes that aspect a step further by making the Chalk actually rise up against the Fairy Queen. Like we said, the Chalk is a magical wonder.

2. The Dancers

We're probably back in your good graces with this selection. The Dancers, a ring of stones up in the Ramtops, figure heavily in *Lords and Ladies*. It's like Stonehenge in Wiltshire, England, or the

Ring of Brodgar in Orkney, Scotland—the kind of Neolithic tri-lithons in existence for thousands of years; a place where stories start and mysteries abound. You can find stone formations like this all around the United Kingdom. Legends are built around such places.

We can't help thinking of Celtic mythology, particularly the *Mabinogion*—the myths of Wales—which contains stories like "Pwyll son of Dyyed," "Branwen the daughter of Llyr," "Manawyddan the son of Llyr," and "Math the son of Mathonwy." In these stories, white stags run about, hunted by Welsh kings, and magical wars happen. You know, the usual Otherworld happenings.

In Discworld, the Dancers are a gateway to Fairyland, which is a nightmare place, as *The Wee Free Men* clearly shows. (We have to wonder if the Dancers are the trilithons Tiffany sees at a distance from the Feegles' mound in *The Wee Free Men*.)

Trilithons such as the Dancers are also "weather computers" op-erated by druids in the days before Doppler radar, as we learn in *Lords and Ladies* and *The Light Fantastic*. Belafon, the druid and "computer hardware consultant"[2] in *The Light Fantastic*, operates a piece of rock "software." This is fitting, since the real-life Druids were known to frequent stone circles.

3. Holy Wood

Holy Wood is the Hollywood of Discworld captured in *Moving Pictures*, where movie magic happens literally. But like most of the seven wonders of the ancient world, this is a place you can't visit any-more. It's buried under tons of rubble, like Pompeii in the aftermath of Mount Vesuvius's eruption in A.D. 79 or the fall of the mythical cities of Atlantis or Númenor in Tolkien's trilogy. Like most places with a thin line between reality and the "twilight zone" of Faerie (the fairy world), what you see is sometimes difficult to believe.

---

[2] *The Light Fantastic* (New York: HarperTorch, 1986), 60.

This background look at the Discworld "clicks" is all about the silent movie era, which began just before the turn of the last century and lost steam in 1929. During this era, such actresses as Theda Bara, Clara Bow, and Mary Pickford, and actors such as Douglas Fairbanks Jr., Charlie Chaplin, and Buster Keaton reigned supreme. But since *Moving Pictures* is an homage, you can find allusions to several different movie genres as well as to silent and "talkie" movies, such as *Gone with the Wind* (Pratchett's *Blown Away*), *Lassie, Conan the Barbarian* (Pratchett's *Cohen the Barbarian*), *The Gold Rush* (Pratchett's *The Golde Rushe*), *The Gold Diggers of 1933* (Pratchett's *The Golde Diggers of 1457*), *The Third Man* (Pratchett's *The Third Gnome*), *The Fog, Attack of the 50 Ft. Woman, King Kong, Valley of the Dolls* (Pratchett's *Valley of the Trolls*), *Snow White and the Seven Dwarfs*, and others.

But beyond the movie magic is the horror of the Chaos-causing "Others" who want to take over Holy Wood and the world. See, that's what happens when the line between reality and the nightmarish Otherworld is crossed by the unwary (*The Grudge/Grudge 2* or any other horror film). Sadly, many places around the Disc are gateways to the Dungeon Dimension.

The Others are not to be confused with the Chaos-causing "Them" of *Equal Rites*—another group out to take over the world or even the Chaos-causing "Them" that Nanny Ogg uses as a euphemism for the Lords and Ladies (the elves) in *Lords and Ladies*.

4. Jason Ogg's Smithy

A much happier place is Jason Ogg's smithy. Jason Ogg is part of the legion of fairy-tale blacksmith/farriers. Amazing things can happen at a blacksmith's forge. In *Smith of Wooton Major*, by J. R. R. Tolkien, a boy who swallows a fairy star tucked away in a slice of cake later becomes a blacksmith of incredible skill and a traveler in the land of Faery. In *Spindle's End* by Robin McKinley, Narl is the fairy prince turned blacksmith—nearly a physical impossibility since fairies can't stand the touch of iron. The Brothers Grimm included some stories involving blacksmiths, namely "The Three Brothers," in which one brother, a blacksmith/farrier, is so skilled at his trade, he can shoe horses even while they were running. In "The Master-Smith,"[3] a folktale from one of the collections of Peter Christen Asbjørnsen and Jørgen Moe (see chapter 1), a blacksmith makes a deal like the one Jabez Stone (a character in "The Devil and Daniel Webster") makes with the devil (who is sometimes known as Death in some versions of the tale) to become the best blacksmith (and farrier) of all. Although he can't duplicate the wonders he sees a stranger perform at the forge, he is given three wishes from the stranger (who is possibly God and travels with Saint Peter) to help him trick the devil, and keeps his soul.

As Pratchett mentions in *Equal Rites*, "Any halfway competent blacksmith has more than a nodding acquaintance with magic, or at least likes to think he has."[4] Jason Ogg may not be the magic practitioner that wizards are or his mother, Gytha Ogg, is. But, as we learn in *Lords and Ladies*, he can shoe anything—magic in itself. Unlike the master-smith of that story, Jason doesn't try to trick Death. He instead keeps to the code of being the best at anything. And being the best means you have to keep working at the trade of which you're the best.

5. Fourecks

Remember *The Lost World* by Arthur Conan Doyle (and the movie)—the South American country where dinosaurs still walked the Earth in a pre–*Jurassic Park* way? (Not to be confused with *The Lost World* by Michael Crichton, where dinosaurs still walk the

---

[3] You can check out the story, which is posted at http://oaks.nvg.org/lg4ra2.html.
[4] *Equal Rites* (New York: HarperTorch, 1987), 3.

Earth in a post–*Jurassic Park* way.) And how about *The Island of Dr. Moreau* by Jules Verne—where a mad scientist goes gene-splicing crazy by making animal–human hybrids? And then there's *Lost Horizon* by James Hilton (and the movie) where two men find a Tibetan lamasery—Shangri-La—after crash landing in the Himalayas. And last but not least, there's the ultimate castaway story: *Robinson Crusoe* by Daniel Defoe, which inspired the movie *Cast Away* with Tom Hanks and a volleyball named Wilson.

Fourecks, the so-called "last continent" of Discworld, is a lost world in transition, part Shangri-La, part *Crocodile Dundee* (G'day, mate), part *Island of Dr. Moreau* and *Robinson Crusoe* with a touch of Aztec history and *South Pacific*, thanks to wizard and housekeeper castaways from Ankh-Morpork. Mrs. Whitlow can't seem to wash those men right out of her hair, but goes for island wear with a flair. The minor god encountered by the wizards is the Dr. Moreau who makes creatures that evolve. Alas, the wizards' utopia crumbles at the first sign of an argument and danger. But there are no T. rexes, sadly, or lamaseries—just a version of Unseen University (BU instead of UU). It's not Shangri-La, but it's home.

6. The Library of Unseen University

If you checked out those *Librarian* movies on cable (*The Librarian: Quest for the Spear*; *The Librarian: Return to King Solomon's Mines*), you saw a librarian in a more active state than those at your local branch, thus proving that a library can hold wonders beyond those in books.

The library at Unseen University is one of the most magical and dangerous places on the Disc, thanks to L-space and such magical books as *The Summoning of Dragons* by Tubal de Malachite, which is a point of contention in *Guards! Guards!* and *Necrotelicomnicon*— an evil book by Achmed the Mad, a Klatchian Necromancer.

Supposedly, every book ever written or yet to be written appears in this library. (We wonder if this book is there.) In L-space, creatures such as the Kickstool crabs and the Thesaurus loiter. The Librarian is the steward of this realm and one who handles the books like a lion tamer.

We can't help thinking of Merlin in *The Sword in the Stone*, with his magical library of books, again some of which hadn't yet been written. The Beast in Robin McKinley's novel *Beauty*, a retelling of the Beauty and the Beast story, has a similar impossible library.

7. The Post Office of Ankh-Morpork

A post office isn't exactly what you would call a place of magic, not in our world anyway, where years seem to pass while you wait in line and the check's always in the mail. (Maybe that *is* magic.) But magic happens at the Post Office of Ankh-Morpork. And we're not just talking about the sorting engine created by Bloody Stupid Johnson (see chapter 19). We mean the mystical link between the Postmaster, Moist von Lipwig, and the mail. He can hear the letters speak. (But "can he hear the letters sing" à la *Les Mis*?)

Moist von Lipwig is no Henry Chinaski, the disgruntled postal clerk in *Post Office*, an autobiographical novel by German writer Charles Bukowski; yet they share the same desire to get out of Dodge. But Pratchett adds a touch of mythology with Moist's Hermes-like gold getup, not to mention the visions Moist sees of the Post Office of the past. Kind of reminds us of the ghosts Jack Torrance saw in the Overlook Hotel in *The Shining*, the 1977 novel by Stephen King, which came out in film form in 1980 and as a miniseries in 1997. Of course, Jack *was* going crazy when he saw the ghosts, and wound up trying to kill his family. But it brings up a point about atmosphere. Just as being in the hotel changed Jack for the worse, the Post Office helps change Moist for the better. Now, that's magic.

8. The Pyramid of Djelibeybi

You don't have to hop on a plane and head to Egypt to visit a great pyramid—not if you read *Pyramids*. It's fitting that one of the magical wonders of Discworld is also a pyramid—the Great Pyramid that Teppic feels coerced to have built for his late father. (Not to be confused with the Great Pyramid of Tsort, which is an allusion to the Great Pyramid at Giza.) Teppic's pyramid is the pyramid to end all pyramids—and to end the world, while it's at it.

Constructing a pyramid back in ancient times normally required thousands of workers and many years to complete. Case in point, the pyramid at Giza might have taken a workforce of possibly 100,000–300,000 people ten to twenty years to build. (Historians aren't really sure about the numbers.) But the pyramid for King Teppicymon XXVII is assigned to be completed in three months with just a fraction of that workforce. How is that even possible? "Pyramid energy," Euclidean geometry, and temporal displacement—the perks of a world of magic. And this pyramid can do what the pyramid at Giza can do—make a whole country disappear without the aid of a volcano.

⌣

There you have it—the eight great magical wonders of Discworld. And no travel arrangements were necessary. Perhaps these wonders will stick around longer than the Colossus of Rhodes.

A Few Words About Footnotes

Another magical wonder of Discworld are the tiny notes you find at the bottom of many of the Discworld novels. If you've slogged through a high school or college research paper, perhaps you thought you'd die if you had to write another footnote, let alone look at one. Footnotes are not usually the most interesting items on a printed page.[5] But the footnotes strewn throughout the Discworld novels are among the funniest footnotes you can find in books. If you miss them, you miss key information and vital backstory.

Pratchett's not the only author who has fun with footnotes. Jasper Fforde, the writer of the Tuesday Next and Nursery Crime series, goes wild with his. Sometimes characters converse through his footnotes! Susanna Clarke, the writer of *Jonathan Strange and Mr. Norrell*, also uses footnotes to help tell the story of the history of magic in England.

But getting back to Discworld, where else but in the footnotes can you find the hysterical story of Glod (*Witches Abroad*), the philosophy of Ly Tin Wheedle (*Mort*), or the résumé of Mrs. Marietta Cosmopolite (a former seamstress, but not a "seamstress," if you know what we mean) as *Moving Pictures* describes? But then, you probably already knew that.

---

[5] Well, this one isn't bad.

15

A Hierarchy of Power

Power at a point. That's what Tacticus said.
And here it's the one right on the end of Ahmed's crossbow.
—Vimes to Lord Rust in *Jingo*[1]

Power. People die for it, vie for it, lie for it. Books are written about it: *How to Win Friends and Influence People*—the Dale Carnegie classic. *The 48 Laws of Power* (Robert Greene). *Power vs. Force: The Hidden Determinants of Human Behavior* (David R. Hawkins). *Get Anyone to Do Anything: Never Feel Powerless Again* (David J. Lieberman). We use PowerPoint on our PowerBooks and take power walks and naps.

If you're a student of history, you're well aware that back in the sixteenth century, philosopher and statesman Niccolò di Bernardo dei Machiavelli wrote a treatise on power called *The Prince*.[2] One doesn't have to be a prince to be a mover and a shaker in a town. We looked for ways his advice seemed to be played out or ignored in Discworld.

---

[1] *Jingo* (New York: HarperTorch, 1997), 387.
[2] All quotes from *The Prince* were taken from text downloaded from http://www.constitution.org/mac/prince.txt. Rendered into HTML by Jon Roland of the Constitution Society. See also, *The Prince*, translated by W. K. Marriott (New York: Dutton/Everyman's Library edition, 1958).

DISC-CLAIMER:
Plot spoilers ahead. Read at your own risk.

ANKH-MORPORK

A prince ought to inspire fear in such a way that, if he does not win love, he avoids hatred; because he can endure very well being feared whilst he is not hated.

—From *The Prince*, chapter XVII "Concerning Cruelty and Clemency, and Whether It Is Better to Be Loved than Feared."

The View from Vetinari's Desk

Ankh-Morpork—the New York, London, or Shanghai of Discworld—is the largest city on the Disc. It is the City that Works—a nickname Chicago bears in our world. (Get it? Chicago Bears? We're still trying on the puns.) It is a city where Patricians seldom come in names other than Vetinari. Oh sure, there have been Patricians before Lord Havelock Vetinari came to power (Crazy Lord Snapcase, a.k.a. Psychoneurotic Snapcase; Giggling Lord Smince). But now that he has the position, he's managed to hold on to the reigns of power pretty tightly, even after several assassination or impeachment attempts by nobles and guild leaders such as Lords Downey (head of the assassins), Selachii, and Rust. But Vetinari's the one who established the guild system in the first place, with its thieves, assassins, alchemists, beggars, clockmakers, "seamstresses," and so on. And his training as an assassin makes him a leader almost impossible to get rid of. Just what the doctor ordered for Ankh-Morpork.

Vetinari is the Denethor of Ankh-Morpork, a steward who does not sit on the throne of the city. Not that he would want to anyway, since it is wood covered in gold foil, as he reveals to Carrot in *Men at Arms*. Although he is not loved, he inspires fear the Machiavellian way. Any genuine despot would do the same thing. His life seems to reflect a principle found in chapter VIII of *The Prince*: "A prince ought to live amongst his people in such a way that no unexpected circumstances, whether of good or evil, shall make him change."

The way he handles Moist von Lipwig, the con man-turned-Postmaster in *Going Postal*—by dangling freedom in front of him and taking it away—seems to reflect a chapter 5 principle: "He who becomes master of a city accustomed to freedom and does not destroy it, may expect to be destroyed by it." In other words, you can allow freedom, but only so far as you can control it. Vetinari keeps Moist and Vimes on a long leash, but a leash nevertheless.

Capable Carrot

Carrot Ironfoundersson, Captain of the City Watch and Vimes's right-hand man (or right-hand dwarf, according to Carrot), might be that long-awaited king and thus the most powerful man in the city, but he refuses to be other than a watchman for the time being. Yet he has the charisma to unite people, as Vimes and Angua notice several times. He lives out the chapter VIII principle—the one about not changing. But how about chapter XVII, the one we mentioned earlier concerning the inspiration of fear or love? In that same chapter, Machiavelli remarks: "Upon this a question arises: whether it be better to be loved than feared or feared than loved? It may be answered that one should wish to be both, but, because it is difficult to unite them in one person."[3] Carrot somehow manages to inspire both.

---

[3] *The Prince*, translated by W. K. Marriott, 92.

Vimes Invested

Vimes, as the duke of Ankh-Morpork, is the second most powerful man in the city, to the chagrin of the nobility. His rank is that of a knight with the title "Sir" like Paul McCartney, Elton John, Sean Connery, and . . . but, sorry, not Terry Pratchett (he is an Officer of the Order of the British Empire, however). Vimes chafes at being known as "Vetinari's terrier." But he knows which way the power wind blows. And it usually blows Vetinari's way.

Within any power structure, a clear chain of command is helpful. So the chain of command in Ankh-Morpork would go like this:

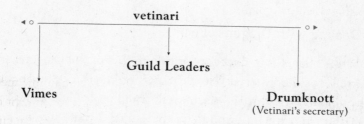

But if you add the Watch, which Commander Vimes heads, the chain goes like this: (*See diagram on the following page.*)

In *Feet of Clay*, Vimes describes himself as an advocate of the people. He seems to live by a principle found in chapter IX ("Concerning a Civil Principality") of *The Prince*: "[O]ne cannot by fair dealing, and without injury to others, satisfy the nobles, but you can satisfy the people, for their object is more righteous than that of the nobles, the latter wishing to oppress, whilst the former only desire not to be oppressed."[4] While Vimes does not ignore the faults of the people, he at least knows that, like sheep, they need a shepherd.

---

[4] Ibid., 52.

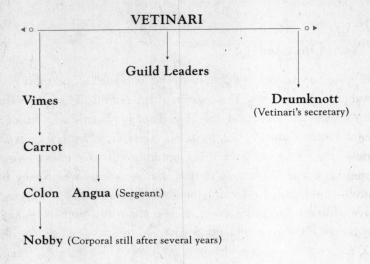

Dealing with Dragons

Vimes's belief is in direct opposition to that of the Dragon King of Arms, who hopes to put a noble puppet on the throne and be the power behind the throne. Machiavelli could probably take lessons from the Dragon King, who plays the political game like a chess grand master. Don't like the pieces you have? Substitute new ones— those who will do your bidding. The Dragon King's "chess board" consist of the books of family heritage, which he uses to his advantage. This fits with Machiavelli's suggestion that a prince study the art of war, described in chapter 14 of *The Prince*. With all wars, even those fought behind closed doors rather than on the battlefield, strategy counts.

The actions of the noble dragon of *Guards! Guards!* however, seem to embody a principle found in chapter VIII ("Concerning Those Who Have Obtained a Principality by Wickedness"): "[I]n seizing a state, the usurper ought to examine closely into all those injuries which it is necessary for him to inflict, and to do them all at one stroke so as not to have to repeat them daily."[5] She's also a firm advocate of crushing freedom, as Lupine Wonse learned the hard way.

Moist Makes the Most of Matters

And now on to that other branch of civil service: the Post Office. Due to his crimes, Moist von Lipwig has the reins of power firmly thrust into his hands by Vetinari. It is either that or be executed. By the end of *Going Postal,* he's not only the Postmaster, but also the head of the Grand Trunk—the clacks company. Since we'll have to wait and see how he does as the head of both (perhaps *Making Money,* the next installment of his story published in October 2007, explains that), we can only suggest this advice from *The Prince,* taken from chapter VI ("Concerning New Principalities Which Are Acquired by One's Own Arms and Ability"): "A wise man ought always to follow the paths beaten by great men, and to imitate those who have been supreme, so that if his ability does not equal theirs, at least it will savour of it."

By the way, the Post Office hierarchy goes like this (Moist's perspective):

But from Miss Maccalariat's perspective, it goes like this:

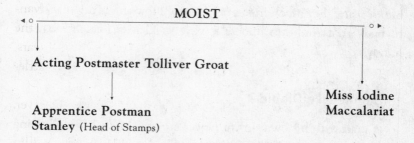

MOIST

Acting Postmaster Tolliver Groat

Apprentice Postman Stanley (Head of Stamps)

Miss Iodine Maccalariat

[5] Ibid., 48.

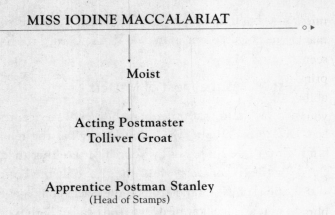

Get Rid of Ridcully?

We talked about Mustrum Ridcully, the archchancellor of Unseen University, in chapter 7. Ridcully is yet another leader who has maintained power for quite some time, despite attempts to murder him—murder being the way to gain another level in wizarding circles. The position of archchancellor of old embodied a principle of Machiavelli from chapter VII of *The Prince* ("Concerning New Principalities Which Are Acquired Either by the Arms of Others or by Good Fortune"): "Those who solely by good fortune become princes from being private citizens have little trouble in rising, but much in keeping atop." How true. Ridcully seems to buck that tradition. Guess it pays to keep a loaded crossbow handy.

Dabble Like Dibbler?

A man with his own sort of power around Ankh-Morpork (and other places it seems) is Cut-Me-Own-Throat Dibbler—the persistent purveyor of the sausage-in-a-buns that a person eats to his detriment. He is also an agent to some as well as a former movie mogul, having taken over from Thomas Silverfish in *Moving Pic-*

tures. You know what happens to that career and the groups he manages in *Soul Music*. Is he a success? A failure? Although he may seem "to follow the paths beaten by great men"—the chapter VI principle we mentioned earlier—no one would say that Dibbler's abilities savor of greatness. They savor of someone trying to rip you off.

Keeping Company with Chrysophrase

Speaking of ripping people off, there's thug "prince" Chrysophrase, who wears a suit and engages in such activities as money lending at 300-percent interest (the mark of a loan shark) and extortion. He is chairman of the Silicon Anti-Defamation League—the troll watchdog committee. No one can deny that Chrysophrase has power. Whether you love or hate him, he's a true Machiavellian devotée, one who lives out the chapter VIII principle we mentioned earlier ("A prince ought to live amongst his people in such a way that no unexpected circumstances, whether of good or evil, shall make him change") and others. Unlike Dibbler, he is a "success" in Ankh-Morpork—an accepted hazard of life in a corrupt city.

Shine On

Mr. Shine claims to be "the indisputable king of the trolls,"[6] as we learn in *Thud!* But instead of being a rock like shale, Mr. Shine is a diamond, but more than a "diamond in the rough"—the description for Aladdin in the movie *Aladdin*. Diamond trolls become kings. Cream rises to the top, apparently. But war follows in the wake of the rise of the diamond troll.

A good chess player studies his or her opponent and learns to anticipate the opponent's moves. Mr. Shine studies the dwarfs—the

---

[6] *Thud!* (New York: HarperTorch, 2005), 217.

enemies of the trolls. How does he do this? By playing the strategy game Thud. This fits with Machiavelli's notion that "to exercise the intellect the prince should read histories, and study there the actions of illustrious men, to see how they have borne themselves in war" (chapter XIV: "That Which Concerns a Prince on the Subject of the Art of War").

LANCRE

Kings and Barons and Witches, Oh My

With Lancre being a principality, the king is where the buck stops. Verence II, the former fool, is the king of Lancre as of *Wyrd Sisters*, with Magrat as his queen in *Lords and Ladies*. Their word is law (unless some vampires happen to take over the castle, as in *Carpe Jugulum*). But the real power in Lancre, even with vampires around, belongs to the witches, especially to Granny Weatherwax (see chapter 6), the top witch in Lancre, a title her close friend and associate Nanny Ogg does not dispute. So any king worth his salt would get the witches on his side, as the second Verence does in *Wyrd Sisters*. (This is a lesson Duke Felmet fails.)

The witches, like the wizards, adhere to the "a cat can look at a king" principle. While they may call him "Your Majesty," they still do as they please, except when someone foolishly tries to lock them in a dungeon.

Granny is a textbook example of the Machiavellian principle concerning being feared rather than loved. Having a witch's hat is the key to power, as Granny reminds Tiffany Aching as well as any reader of any book Granny happens to be in.

According to *Lords and Ladies*, the chain of command in Lancre goes like this:

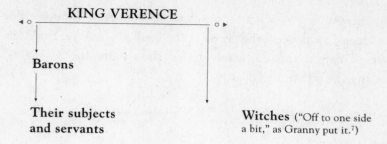

KING VERENCE

Barons

Their subjects
and servants

Witches ("Off to one side
a bit," as Granny put it.[7])

But we think the chain of command goes like this even if
witches claim not to meddle:

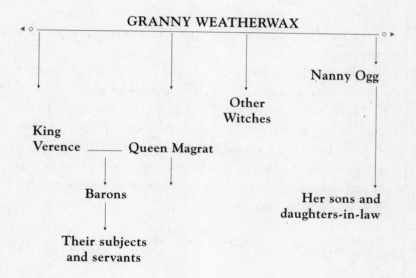

GRANNY WEATHERWAX

Nanny Ogg

Other
Witches

King
Verence ——— Queen Magrat

Her sons and
daughters-in-law

Barons

Their subjects
and servants

THE CHALK

In Tiffany's farming community, the Chalk, the baron is supposedly
top man under the king. But the real power belongs to Granny
Aching, which still continues after her death. Even the baron seeks

---

[7] *Lords and Ladies* (New York: HarperTorch, 1992), 156.

Granny Aching for wisdom. Now that's power. And Tiffany is able to access that power—the power of the land—in *The Wee Free Men*. With Tiffany as the only witch around, she assumes the reins of authority, upon Granny's death.

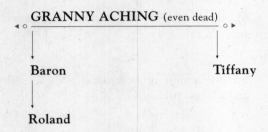

So in *The Wee Free Men*, the chain of command is something like this:

In *Wintersmith*, we learn that in the baron's home, Roland's aunts (Danuta and Araminta) rule with an iron fist while the baron is ill, thus adhering to the curtailing of freedom principle in *The Prince*. They are not successful at cowing Roland, who is a reader of books by tactical titan General Tacticus and knows all of the secret passages in his home. Again, we'll have to wait and see how Roland shapes up as a leader. Thanks to his hero training, courtesy of the Feegles, we think he'll do just fine.

UBERWALD

> *Those who unexpectedly become princes are men of so much ability that they know they have to be prepared at once to hold that which fortune has thrown into their laps, and that those foundations, which others have laid before they became princes, they must lay afterwards.*
>
> —From *The Prince*, chapter VII, "Concerning New Principalities Which Are Acquired Either by the Arms of Others or by Good Fortune"

Uberwald is *the* place for politickin' and power-grabbin', as Pratchett reveals in *The Fifth Elephant*. Different factions—vampires, werewolves, and dwarfs—scramble up the totem pole of power. In Shmaltzberg, the newly crowned Low King, Rhys Rhysson, exudes more political savvy than a popular favorite, Albrecht Albrechtson (an allusion to Alberich in the Ring Cycle—see the end of chapter 5). Judging by the way he (and that pronoun is debatable by the end of the book) handles Dee and Albrechtson, he embodies to a degree the principle from *The Prince*'s chapter VII quoted earlier, even though his election to the throne is not unexpected.

The first task the Low King takes to establish a good foundation is to establish the authenticity of the Scone of Stone, the scone upon which all Low Kings sit when crowned. Although the scone was made in Ankh-Morpork, Rhysson manipulates his political rival into authenticating the scone. A good move.

The true queen of Machiavellian principles in Uberwald is Lady Margolotta, the vampire who is the Dragon King and Vetinari's equal in political genius. As she explains to Vimes, "Politics is more interesting than blood."[8] Her shenanigans are like chess moves in a way, as she moves one piece here (Wolfgang) and another there (Vimes), but never puts herself—the queen—in check.

When we first meet her in *The Fifth Elephant*, she's studying *Twurps' Peerage*—the who's who of Ankh-Morpork—to find out who Vetinari might send as a delegate. This is the same chapter XIV *Prince* principle that Mr. Shine and the Dragon King's tactics show.

DJELIBEYBI AND BOROGRAVIA

The prince . . . ought to make himself the head and defender of his powerful neighbours, and to weaken the more powerful

---

[8] *The Fifth Elephant* (New York: HarperTorch, 2000), 347.

amongst them, taking care that no foreigner as powerful as
himself shall, by any accident, get a footing there.

—From *The Prince*, chapter 3,
"Concerning Mixed Principalities"

Therefore, one who becomes a prince through the favour of the
people ought to keep them friendly, and this he can easily do
seeing they only ask not to be oppressed by him.

—From *The Prince*, chapter 9,
"Concerning a Civil Principality"

In Djelibeybi in Klatch, a pharaohlike king rules in the manner of
Egyptian pharoahs in our world. In *Pyramids*, Teppic (actually Ptep-
pic) ascends to the throne after the death of his father. Before abdi-
cating the throne in favor of his half-sister Ptraci, he even has a
dream like the pharaoh of the Bible—a dream of seven fat cows and
seven thin ones (Genesis 41:17–24)—a dream that seems to come
with the job of being the king. With the kingdom squarely between
Ephebe and Tsort, Djelibeybi is in a perfect spot to influence the
political arena of either country. But as Teppic learns, the first
Machiavellian principle described in this section is firmly in place
within the foreign policy of Djelibeybi. In short, keep each country
happy and believing you support them, but keep them out of your
land.

During his travels, Teppic learns about the Ephebian culture:
that they have an elected Tyrant as a leader and are a democracy (or
"mocracy" as Teppic describes it), rather than a monarchy—an idea
he hopes does not catch on.

Both principles above can be seen in *Monstrous Regiment*, in
Borogravia to be exact, a duchy like Luxembourg ruled by a duke
and duchess or, rather, the Duchess who is believed dead. Borogravia is a country usually at war with its neighbors. During the war
with Zlobenia, Vimes, as the duke of Ankh-Morpork, winds up in

Borogravia (sent by Vetinari) to "bring things to a 'satisfactory' conclusion"[9] after the Borogravians destroy several clacks towers. That's Ankh-Morpork's way of sticking its fingers in every political pie as well as demonstrating the first principle above (act supportive, but make sure no one gets into power that you can't control). If that means keeping out Prince Heinrich, the ruler of Zlobenia, well, so be it.

Vimes's attempts to assess the political climate and end the hostilities involve curtailing Borogravia's "freedom" to continue the war with Zlobenia. But after meeting Polly Perks and her regiment, Vimes learns what Prince Heinrich fails to learn: to ask the people what they want.

According to Machiavelli, a principality is composed of two groups: the nobles and the people. A ruler who governs by the will of the nobles winds up alienating the people. A usurper attempting to take over an area would do well to avoid alienating the people. Prince Heinrich, take note.

OTHER HELPFUL POWER PRINCIPLES

To rise in the political sphere, it helps to be an assassin. Vetinari and Teppic both trained as assassins. In Discworld, being an assassin is a profession for a gentleman, particularly an upwardly mobile gentleman. It certainly helps Teppic kill off a pyramid. And it usually helps one move up the wizard ladder.

The view is great from behind the scenes. Carrot, like Lady Margolotta, knows how to act behind the scenes. Carrot gains Vimes's social standing (duke, commander) and has thus far eluded the grasp of those who would force him to ascend to the throne of

---

[9] *Monstrous Regiment* (New York: HarperCollins, 2003), 18.

Ankh-Morpork. Lady Margolotta, as we've already mentioned, is adept at moving pawns.

Never count on werewolves to get ahead. Dee tries to play the game of politics and loses badly, having been duped by werewolves. (Isn't that always the way?) Even Angua knows that werewolves cannot always be trusted.

Never cross Vetinari or Mustrum Ridcully. They have a strange way of not dying. Ridcully, usually armed to the teeth even when going to bed, foils all would-be assassins. And Vetinari is almost immortal in the way that he refuses to die.

Avoid scheming against your employer. Mort, Death's onetime apprentice, tries by sparing the life of a princess and thus making "ripples in reality"[10] as everyone in Discworld winds up doing. Alas, that is not the way to get ahead in a job. He winds up dueling with Death. By the same token, Lupine Wonse, Vetinari's secretary in *Guards! Guards!*, is less than loyal to his boss when he schemes to depose Vetinari and put a stooge king on the throne. Wonse winds up DOA.

Albert, the wizard who would prefer to be immortal than die a wizard on earth, learns the true value of getting ahead: suck up to Death.

Never borrow money from Chrysophrase or hire Cut-Me-Own-Throat Dibbler. In fact, you're better off not talking to either of them.

---

[10] *Mort* (New York: HarperTorch, 1987), 229.

≈

16

Why the Watch Works

*A constable was empowered to apprehend "all loose,
idle and disorderly Persons whom he shall find disturbing
the public Peace, or whom he shall have just
Cause to suspect of any evil Designs."*
—The Metropolitan Police Act of 1829[1]

TEN O'CLOCK AND ALL'S WELL?

If you've read the City Watch miniseries (*Guards! Guards!*, *Men at Arms*, *Feet of Clay*, *Jingo*, *The Fifth Element*, *Night Watch*, *Thud!*) within the Discworld series, maybe you consider the watchmen the few, the proud, but ultimately, the inept—a far cry from the forensics experts of *CSI* (and its thousands of spin-offs) or other law enforcement agents in *Law and Order* (another show with multiple spin-offs). But that's not so far from reality, particularly in England and Australia in the seventeenth, eighteenth, and nineteenth centuries!

Before 1674, depending on where you were—within the sprawling metropolis of London or the country—you would probably find the same amateur, unskilled form of peacekeeping taking place since the Middle Ages. But after 1674, the duty of keeping the peace fell

---

[1] Posted at http://en.wikipedia.org/wiki/Police.

upon the shoulders of the justice of the peace—the magistrates. In country settings, this was probably the largest landowner in the area. Justices were part of a larger Commission of Peace body. But untrained constables did the legwork of keeping the peace. After all, there was no police force as such with rules in place. And the constables were men from the area who rotated the duty.

The justice of the peace had the authority to hold a trial and carry out a judgment. Depending on the offense, the sentenced person might be whipped, placed in the stocks, or fined. Needless to say, justice wasn't always served.

In London, justices weren't the wealthy landowners. They were the tradesmen—also known as "trading justices"—who received a fee every time a criminal was brought before them. So, some "administered justice," as often as possible—sometimes by inventing reasons to have people brought before them.

Also, in many of the parishes of London, watchmen were on patrol from 9:00 P.M. until sunrise. Some parishes also hired thief takers—bounty hunters like Stephanie Plum of Janet Evanovich's series—some of whom were thieves themselves (unlike Stephanie Plum)! Before the passing of the Watch Acts, watchmen were selected from the homeowners in the area and served for a year. They could question individuals out on the streets at that hour ("Up to no good? Push off home, you!"), but couldn't do much about stopping crime. Also, they were part-timers. They rotated with men who, like them, had other employment. And there's something about not getting paid that puts a damper on one's enthusiasm.

Constables, during the daytime, had more authority to question and detain minor criminals. But, alas, they were few and could do little to deter major criminals—like those of the Carcer (*Night Watch*) variety.

When Charles I allowed for watchmen to be hired, the low salary kept away more qualified applicants. Many watchmen were poor or poorly chosen. Picture a frail, elderly man holding a stick and a lantern. There's something about the sight that doesn't ensure confidence in the justice system. Unfortunately, many also were corrupt (like Quirke or Sergeant Knock in *Night Watch*) and unskilled. (Bet you're thinking of Fred Colon and Nobby Nobbs right about now. . . .)

So, two brothers (half brothers really)—Henry and John Fielding—set out to set up a system of policing the city and its environs. Their dream began because Henry Fielding decided not to be the kind of trading justice he observed. Instead, thanks to his training as a journalist and a lawyer, he wanted to reform the office of magistrate and the laws concerning the poor. Having set up his magistrate's office at Bow Street, Henry also established a criminal law journal in the mid-eighteenth century. So, in a way, he was like William de Worde, the journalist in *The Truth* and *Monstrous Regiment*. Henry's journal later became known as the *Police Gazette*.

The advent of the Bow Street Runners—thief takers used by Henry and later John, who were rewarded due to the criminals they apprehended—helped in the later establishment of a regular police force. But during their lifetimes, the brothers could not get the government to agree on the necessity of having a regularly employed police force. John's plan for expanding the role of the Bow Street Runners was continually thwarted.

THE POLICE: EVERY BREATH YOU TAKE . . . I'LL BE WATCHING YOU

In the nineteenth century, the Watch Acts (particularly, the Metropolitan Police Act of 1829) were passed, allowing a tax to be levied to hire full-time watchmen. Sadly, it took the deaths of eleven people and the injury of five hundred (the Peterloo massacre of 1819), after an altercation between soldiers and unarmed civilians at a protest rally, for the government to see the need for a better-trained peacekeeping unit. These were London's first police officers—a group which Sir Robert Peel, the home secretary at the time (the Vetinari of his day), helped set up. Richard Mayne and Charles Rowan, the first joint police commissioners in the formation of the police, are predecessors in a way of Commander Sam Vimes and Carrot Ironfoundersson. Ex-soldier Rowan (the Vimes), who was older than Mayne and had military training, was considered slightly more senior in rank. Mayne, like Carrot, had a strong sense of civic duty as well as knowledge of the law.

No longer would these peacekeepers be called watchmen. They would be patrolmen. But they earned a nickname as well—bobbies, after Sir Robert Peel. The first police—a group of about three thousand—wore uniforms and patrolled like Ankh-Morpork's watchmen.

At the time this book is published, Vimes's counterpart in the Metropolitan Police Service is Sir Ian Blair, a man who rose in the ranks just like Vimes, from constable to commissioner.

EQUAL OPPORTUNITY EMPLOYMENT

In *Men at Arms*, Vimes is forced to bend with the times by hiring practices represented by significant segments of the population (e.g., a werewolf, a dwarf, a gnome, and a troll—most of whom moved up the promotion ladder faster than Nobby). However, as you know, Vimes draws the line at hiring vampires until forced to do so in *Thud!* when Sally (Salacia Deloresista Amanita Trigestatra Zeldana Malifee . . . von Humpeding—vampires have incredibly long names) comes on the scene.

The City Watch hiring practices mirror the Race Relations Act 1976 and the Sex Discrimination Act 1975 in Great Britain (acts of Parliament), as well as such U.S. laws as Title VII of the Civil Rights Act of 1964 and its subsequent amendments and Title 42. Read for yourself:

British Law
Part II: Discrimination in the Employment Field
Discrimination by employers . . .
(1) It is unlawful for a person, in relation to employment by him at an establishment in Great Britain, to discriminate against another—
(a) in the arrangements he makes for the purpose of determining who should be offered that employment; or
(b) in the terms on which he offers him that employment; or
(c) by refusing or deliberately omitting to offer him that employment.
Race Relations Act 1976, 1976 CHAPTER 74[2]

U. S. Law
SEC. 2000e-2. [Section 703]
(a) It shall be an unlawful employment practice for an employer—
(1) to fail or refuse to hire or to discharge any individual, or otherwise to discriminate against any individual with respect to his compensation, terms, conditions, or privileges of employment, because of such individual's race, color, religion, sex, or national origin; or
(2) to limit, segregate, or classify his employees or applicants for employment in any way which would deprive or tend to deprive any individual of employment opportunities or otherwise adversely affect his status as an employee, because of such individual's race, color, religion, sex, or national origin.
Title VII of the Civil Rights Act of 1964 (Pub. L. 88–352) (Title VII)[3]

In Britain, the Race Relations Acts were passed starting in 1965. But further revisions were needed, making necessary the Race Rela-

---

[2] Posted at http://www.johnantell.co.uk/RRA1976B.htm.
[3] Title VII of the Civil Rights Act of 1964 (Pub. L. 88–352) posted at http://www.eeoc.gov/policy/vii.html.

tions Acts of 1968, 1976, and the Race Relations (Amendment) Act 2000. Third time's the charm, apparently.

Lately, however, with affirmative action under fire in the United States, reverse discrimination cases have had their day in court in some states, with demands for the end of quota-hiring systems, especially in regard to promotions on the force. It will be interesting to see whether the hiring quotas will come under fire in Discworld as well.

In the meantime, the Watch keeps on ticking.

Ripped from the Headlines?

If you watch the original *Law and Order* and its trillions of spin-offs, you know that their cases are "ripped from today's headlines." In other words, they mirror many real-life cases.

While the news hasn't featured any golem or werewolf killings (at least to our knowledge), there have been real-life criminals who could have served as inspiration for the criminals the Watch tries to apprehend. For instance, such serial killers as Jack the Ripper, Ted Bundy, and John Wayne Gacy were the "bogeymen" who haunted police just as double-murderer Carcer has haunted the Watch.

Although there have been serial killers who killed more people, Jack the Ripper remains larger than life because he was never caught or identified, unlike Carcer. He (and police aren't entirely sure that only one person was involved) operated in Whitechapel in 1888, killing five prostitutes (possibly more; again, the police aren't sure of the number) in a grisly way that gained him his nick-name.

These real-life killers helped spawn such twisted fictional serial killers as "Buffalo Bill" of *The Silence of the Lambs* by Thomas Harris (the book; the 1991 movie screenplay was by Ted Tally).

17

Time Waits for No One

GOT THE TIME?

If you were in, say, Armethalieh in Mercedes Lackey/James Mallory's Obsidian Trilogy series, you'd measure time by bells ("See you in half a bell, dude"), specific days (Light's Day), or by wars and epochs (the time of Great Queen Vielissiar Farcarinon; the Great War). In other fantasy series, time is regulated in a similar way (the Third age of Middle-earth and the calendar according to the "Shire-reckoning" of Tolkien's *Lord of the Rings*).

In our world, we measure time by ages and eras (Ice Age, Napoleonic era, Victorian era), the Gregorian calendar (rather than the Julian calendar named after Julius Caesar), B.C.–A.D. demarcations (thanks to Venerable Bede, an eighth-century monk scholar who first used A.D.), and by how long we have to wait in line at Starbucks or the grocery store ("That took ages!").

In Discworld, there's a hodgepodge of ways to measure time.

Calendars and Almanacs

Societies of our world have differing calendars (Gregorian, Hindu, Chinese, Japanese) in which the names of months or even the number of days in a month vary. But in a place like Discworld, where centuries and years are marked by animals, food items, or inexplicable terms (the Century of the Fruitbat, the Year of the Intimidating Porpoise, Century of the Anchovy, the Year of the Impromptu Stoat, Third Ning of the Shaving of the Goat), and the months have such names as Grune, Ick, Spune, and Offle, you've got to expect some weirdness.

The naming of years and centuries in Discworld reminds us of the Chinese calendar, a calendar with a sixty-year cycle based on the moon phases, the sun, and conjunctions of planets. As you know, in China the years follow a cycle of animal names (year of the dragon, year of the ox). You've probably seen a chart of them on a placemat wherever you go for dim sum. And although some of us born in years like the year of the rat could wish that the year bore the name of a cooler animal (such as the year of the tiger), it certainly beats being born in the Year of the Impromptu Stoat.

Terms like the Third Ning, although made-up, remind us of the different dynasties in the history of China—part of the era/epoch-based way of measuring time.

You probably know a year in Discworld can last for eight hundred days and runs through eight seasons, rather than the usual four. (If you don't know, you do now.) Imagine what you'd do with all of that time. Take two summer vacations?

Almanacs also record the moon phases. *Poor Richard's Almanack,* developed by Benjamin Franklin, lists the times of sun and moon risings and planetary configurations. In Discworld (especially the Chalk and the Ramtops), an annual almanac called the *Almanack And*

Book Of Dayes (*Equal Rites*, *Lords and Ladies*, *The Wee Free Men*) is used to gauge the weather and serves as bathroom tissue. Quite handy.

Holidays and Special Days

Our holidays and special days tell us a lot about who we are as a people and what we believe in. We celebrate Hanukkah, Christmas, Kwanzaa, Martin Luther King Day, Kasmir Pulaski Day (a Chicago holiday), New Year's, Groundhog Day, Valentine's Day, and hold events like Oktoberfest and elections. In Discworld, they also celebrate New Year's, along with such holidays as Hogswatch, Soul Cake Tuesday, and Fat Lunchtime—like Fat Tuesday in our world. And then there are Troll New Year, Chase Whiskers Day, and Sektoberfest, a two-week event involving a beer festival, like Oktoberfest. Pratchett describes these and other holidays in *Terry Pratchett's Discworld Collector's Edition 2005 Calendar* and *Discworld's Ankh-Morpork City Watch Diary*.

In Discworld, certain rituals help mark the seasons, holidays, and such special occasions as weddings. There's the Morris dance, which comes from the traditions of the British Isles. In our world, the Morris is danced at the beginning of spring and summer. It's been around since at least the fifteenth century. Seven dancers, usually male, wear white clothes, bells, and clogs. In *Wintersmith*, the usual Morris dance occurs in May, to usher in the summer; and in *Reaper Man*, it ushers in the spring. As we mentioned in chapter 5, Jason Ogg and Lancre Morris men gather to dance for the king's wedding on Midsummer's Eve. But then there's the Dark Morris—a Pratchett creation. Danced without bells, it ushers in the winter in *Wintersmith*.

The Time of Your Life

Another way of measuring time is by the lifetimer—the hour-glass that measures a life. Death carries one for each person he visits who is about to die. The lifetimer is a symbol of the mortality of man. As the Romans would say, *"Memento mori"*—"Remember that you are mortal." This is reminiscent of the grim reminder of mortality in Genesis 3:19, "For dust you are and to dust you will return" (New International Version). But the lifetimer used by Wen the Eternally Surprised (for more on him, keep reading) in *Thief of Time* grants time to the person to whom it is given.

The Discworld Time Lords: The Monks of History

If you're a fan of the *Doctor Who* TV series, one that has been around since the 1960s, you know that the Doctor is a Time Lord from Gallifrey—someone able to travel back and forth through time. He's the last of his kind. So, why'd we bring him up? Because of the Monks of History in Discworld. They are time lords, in a way—the ones who monitor and shape time. Their existence is top secret. But the people of Discworld feel the effects of their constant vigilance. (Maybe you're thinking of the Men in Black right about now . . .)

In the creation of the Monks of History, you can find a hint of Eastern religions. There's the great Lu-Tze the Sweeper, a follower of the Way of Mrs. Marietta Cosmopolite and master of déjà fu—using time as a weapon, rather than, say, kung fu. Lu-Tze, who appears in *Night Watch*, *Thief of Time*, and *Small Gods*, reminds us of Zen master Lao-tzu, writer of *Tao Te Ching*, and blind Master Po, the Shaolin monk who trained Kwai Chang Caine in the 1970s TV series *Kung Fu*.

Other members of the order include Marco Soto—the monk who finds promising novice Lobsang Ludd; the Master of Novices; the Abbot (with his "circular aging," a phrase meaning reincarnation); chief acolyte Rinpo; and Qu, a monk inventor/weapons master like Q in the James Bond series.

Instead of a TARDIS (the Doctor's police box/time travel machine—a sentient machine the initials of which stand for "Time and Relative Dimension(s) in Space"), a time machine à la H. G. Wells, or a souped-up DeLorean used by Dr. Emmett Brown in *Back to the Future*, the monks' mode of time travel is the portable procrastinator, which slices time. (More on them in chapter 19.) As they slice, the monks get to Zimmerman Valley, a time-slicing state that can't simply be calculated by a velocity formula like:

$$\text{Average Velocity} = \frac{\Delta \text{position}}{\text{time}} = \frac{\text{displacement}}{\text{time}}$$

With Zimmerman, we can't help thinking of a cross between Silicon Valley and Dean Zimmerman, a Rutgers professor who wrote a paper with the heading "Defending an 'A-theory' of Time," which we saw on the Internet. Undoubtedly a coincidence.

Perhaps it's only fitting that Wen the Eternally Surprised, founder of the Monks of History, and the personification of Time are the parents of Lobsang Ludd. It takes time to make time.

On the monastery grounds, you find the Mandala, sands showing the currents of time. This concept didn't originate with Pratchett. According to Hindu beliefs, the Mandala is a sand graph of the universe, one used for purposes of contemplation. We would prefer to contemplate a box of Thin Mints and a stretch of white sand in Jamaica. But that's just us. (For more on the Mandala, see chapter 19.)

18

But Is It . . . Art?

STATE OF THE ART

Years ago (okay, I will admit it was during the early 1980s; yes, I'm that old) during my senior year at Northwestern, I [Linda] took a drawing class taught by late Chicago artist Ed Paschke, one of the professors at NU. In between sessions involving sketching unclothed models—sessions I giggled through—our class took a tour of some of the north side art galleries in Chicago. In one gallery, a young man proudly exhibited his sculpture (I'm not sure what else to call it) to his adoring public, one of whom apparently was his patroness, a tiny elderly woman in a fur coat who looked as if she dripped money.

His sculpture consisted of a paint roller standing in a paint tray. He'd set the roller on fire. Why, I don't know. For the effect, maybe? While it burned merrily, his patroness beamed. I could only gawk and wonder, *Is that . . . art?* He seemed to think so. I wondered how much his patroness had shelled out for him to create that . . . thing, or how much (if anything) he would charge for it. Judging by a nearby wall filled with other pieces of . . . art consisting of three large sticks nailed together in varying criss-cross shapes and bearing price tags in the hundreds of dollars, I would guess a great deal of money.

The question *But is it art?* comes up a lot in the Discworld novels. After all, numerous art pieces adorn the museum that is Discworld. Mr. Tulip, one of the thugs hired by the zombie lawyer, Mr. Slant, on behalf of Lord de Worde (for more about them, see chapter 12) provides a lesson in Discworld art appreciation in *The Truth*. I've taken some of his advice, and that of other art connoisseurs to heart, to explore the state of the arts in Discworld.

Check out the brush strokes. I've never been to the Musée du Louvre—the home of some of the most well-known pieces of art in the world, so I have to rely on the witness of others, not to mention a viewing of *The Da Vinci Code*. During a trip to Paris in the mid-1990s, my older brother Chris and sister-in-law Lisa stood in a really long line at the Louvre to see Leonardo's *Mona Lisa*. They told me they were impressed by the sheer age of the painting. (They didn't bring back a T-shirt, though.)

The *Mona Ogg*, painted by Leonard of Quirm, is, of course, a parody of the *Mona Lisa*, with artist/engineer Leonard acting as the Leonardo da Vinci of Discworld. If you've seen the cover of *The Art of the Discworld*, you've seen the *Mona Ogg*, which supposedly was inspired by a young Nanny Ogg. But *Woman Holding Ferret* by Leonard of Quirm is an allusion to Leonardo's *Lady with an Ermine*, painted in 1485. (Speaking of Leonardo, *The Koom Valley Codex* mentioned in *Thud!* is an allusion to *The Da Vinci Code*.)

Theme-wise, *Three Large Pink Women and One Piece of Gauze* by Caravati (an allusion to Italian Baroque artist Michelangelo Merisi da Caravaggio perhaps?) reminds me of the ballerina pictures by Impressionist painter/sculptor Edgar Degas, including *Three Ballet*

Dancers, One with Dark Crimson Waist, and *Three Dancers in Violet Tutus.* Of course, Caravaggio was known for paintings with such simple descriptive names as *Boy Bitten by a Lizard* and *Boy with a Basket of Fruit.* Charming.

The Battle of Ar-Gash by Blitzt (like *blitz*) seems to be a parody of Leonardo da Vinci's *Battle of Anghiari* (1503–6). *The Battle of Koom Valley* by Methodia Rascal, a huge painting that hangs in the Royal Art Museum in Ankh-Morpork in *Thud!,* is reminiscent either of of paintings by Jan Matejko, a nineteenth-century Polish painter known for battle scenes such as the *Battle of Grunwald,* or an eighteenth-century American artist John Trumbull who, like Matejko, was known for military figures and battle scenes, including the *Battle of Trenton,* the *Battle of Princeton, The Surrender of Cornwallis at Yorktown,* or *The Death of General Warren at the Battle of Bunker Hill.* Trumbull worked during the time of the American Revolution and later.

Waggon Stuck in River by Sir Robert Cuspidor reminds me of the *Haywain* triptych by Hieronymus Bosch in 1500–15. Whether it was actually inspired by Bosch's work is anybody's guess.

Man with Big Fig Leaf by Mauvaise reminds me of the fig-leaf controversy surrounding works by the famed Italian Renaissance master Michelangelo di Lodovico Buonarroti Simoni (Michelangelo to his friends). Daniele Ricciarelli (a.k.a. Daniele da Volterra), a painter and sculptor, painted a fig leaf over a certain part of the male anatomy in Michelangelo's fresco *The Last Judgment* during a time when nudity in paintings was considered a no-no.

Watch out for fakes. In the 1966 movie *How to Steal a Million,* starring Audrey Hepburn, Peter O'Toole, and Charles Boyer, Audrey played Nicole, the beleaguered daughter of an art forger (Charles Bonnet, played by Hugh Griffith) who paints like van Gogh and had a father who sculpted in the style of Benvenuto Cellini—the sixteenth-century sculptor/painter known for his

Perseus sculpture and his *Diana of Fontainebleau* bronze figure. The conflict begins when Charles sells his "Cellini" *Venus*—which was made by his father—to a museum, claiming to be an art collector. Audrey convinces O'Toole's character—Simon Dermott—to help her break into the museum to steal it, to avoid having her father revealed as a forger.

The Cellini of Discworld might be Scolpini—a sculptor mentioned during Mr. Tulip's art discussion in *The Truth*. We don't actually see Scolpini's work, but we're told how to spot a real one and the fact that anyone could steal the piece Tulip views. Shades of the plot to *How to Steal a Million*.

Remember the Chicago art gallery pieces mentioned earlier— the twigs and the paint roller? In *Thud!* two pieces by Daniellarina Pouter brought back memories for me: *Don't Talk to Me About Mondays*, which looks like a pile of rags, and *Freedom*—a stake with a nail in it. Beauty is indeed in the eye of the beholder.

Pay attention. Leonardo da Vinci's studies on the perception of the human eye and the effects of light changed the way that painters viewed their craft. He paid attention to the design of the human body and took into account what the eye really sees: how much color close up and at a distance; how the form/shape of the eye (with all of its parts) affects its overall function, particularly in gauging the proportions of an object. This helps a painter correctly depict limbs on people in paintings. Foreshortening happens when the artist doesn't take into account what his or her eye is really seeing.

We can't really see a painting like *Three Large Pink Women and One Piece of Gauze* unless an artist like Paul Kidby draws it, so it's hard to gauge whether the artist, like Leonardo da Vinci, is a student of the eye's form and function. *Thief of Time* does reveal that *The Battle of Ar-Gash* by Blitzt features a striking use of light. Perhaps Leonardo would have been pleased.

What's music to some is only so much noise to others. Let's turn now to the world of music—an art form as varied in Discworld as it is in our world. Classical—Doinov's Prelude in G is mentioned in *Maskerade*, and *Überwald Winter*, an opera the Wintersmith loves, in *Wintersmith*; pop—"music with rocks in" is described in *Soul Music*. There's ethnic music—"Gold, Gold, Gold," a dwarf refrain (*Feet of Clay*); and bawdy comic songs—"The Hedgehog Song." And then there are the songs with a patriotic twist, such as "Carry Me Away from Old Ankh-Morpork," "I Fear I'm Going Back to Ankh-Morpork," and "We Can Rule You Wholesale"—the Ankh-Morpork civic anthem. Music to stir your soul and conscience.

Everyone in Discworld has an opinion about music. In *Soul Music*, which details the musical career of Imp y Celyn—a.k.a. Buddy Holly (an obvious allusion)—the question is whether music with rocks in is a legitimate form of expression. (According to the Guild of Musicians, the answer is no, unless they can profit by it.) Well, it is an issue that causes a lot of trouble for Discworldians. This subject has been long debated, since the early days of rock, back when the real Buddy Holly was alive, and continues even today with regard to rap.

And of course, Granny has an opinion every time Nanny tries to sing "The Hedgehog Song." (See *Witches Abroad*.) Is it art? Is "The Hokey Pokey"? It all depends on what you like.

The same argument can be made for the Discworld series. Some may balk at the parodies and puns. "But is it art?" they ask. If you're reading this book, we think you know the answer to that question already.

19

Terry Pratchett:
Titan of Technomancy

Together, my lord Sauron, we shall rule this Middle-earth.
The old world will burn in the fires of industry.
Forests will fall. A new order will rise. We will drive the
machine of war with the sword and the spear
and the iron fist of the orc.
—Saruman in *The Two Towers*[1]

GADGETS AND WIDGETS

Buzz through a novel by Michael Crichton, Tom Clancy, or Clive
Cussler and you'll usually find enough gizmos to run or destroy a small
planet. These are your techno-thriller writers. But would you place
Terry Pratchett in that group? You would if you read the Discworld
novels closely enough. They're all about the gadgets.

Technology shows the advancement of a civilization. Some
would argue that it also shows its imminent destruction and sepa-
rates the haves from the have-nots. Whatever the case may be,
technology reveals where we are at as a society.

---

[1] Posted at http://www.imdb.com/title/tt0167261/quotes. Good site for quotes in case you
haven't memorized the dialogue.

So, what about Discworld? Who would've thought that a world without computers or TV, and with watchmen patrolling with bells, would have any kind of technology? But it does. There's enough technology to almost rival a Tom Clancy or Michael Crichton novel. No, we're not drunk. Think of *The Flintstones*, the Hanna-Barbera cartoon series of the 1960s, which featured a prehistoric setting but technology akin to the 1960s—hence the car run "through the courtesy of Fred's two feet" as the closing song of each episode goes. In Discworld, technology is what Pratchett calls *technomancy*.

First, let's look at some of the inventors.

Inventors

Many of us take for granted the labor-saving devices we have, such as the computer, the DVD, the microwave, Ginsu knives, or that thing you throw in the microwave that helps you hang and cook bacon. (You know. That thing.) But they all came from the brain of someone—sometimes the kid just down the street or in your own home, the one who dreams of winning the science fair. Henry Ford, Benjamin Franklin, Mary Phelps Jacob, George Washington Carver, Sara Goode, Thomas Alva Edison, Leonardo da Vinci, and many others left a legacy of innovation. Discworld has several inventors, the most well known of which are Leonard of Quirm and Bergholt Stuttley (Bloody Stupid) Johnson. Judging by Johnson's inventions, his nickname seems apt.

Leonard of Quirm. Leonard da Quirm or Leonard of Quirm is the Leonardo da Vinci of Discworld. Naturally. He's a gentle genius with an amazing knack for inventing killing machines, including the gonne (*Men at Arms*) and flying machines, such as a flapping-wing-flying-device (*Men at Arms*) reminiscent of the ones Leonardo da Vinci (see sidebar on page 237) and Daedalus (the artist/inventor from Greek mythology) invented. Alas, he's terrible at naming them. He's so dangerous, he has to be locked up in the Patrician's Palace for the good of humanity.

Bergholt Stuttley (Bloody Stupid) Johnson. Johnson, an inventor and landscape gardener, parodies Lancelot (Capability) Brown, the renowned eighteenth-century British landscape gardener whose parks decorated England. Although Johnson doesn't actually appear in any of the Discworld books, being dead and all, his legacy is described. He has a kind of genius, too—a genius for errors. In other words, he's IN-capable. (Ha, ha!) His inventions, for instance the sorting engine in *Going Postal*, turn out flawed but still brilliant in other ways. Although this machine was designed to sort mail, it winds up affecting the space-time continuum. Not something you'd want at your local post office—or maybe you would.

Okay, with that said, let's get on with the stuff.

Communication Pieces

The clacks. Whenever they're not queuing up at the Post Office, sending pigeons, or consulting Mrs. Cake's crystal ball, the Discworldians send messages to one another via the clacks—a variation on the telegraph and also the semaphore (optical telegraph) network, which has been in place in our world for, oh, a couple hundred years, especially in France, thanks to semaphore stations set up by French engineer Claude Chappe back in the late eighteenth century.

If you read *Going Postal*, you know that Adora Belle Dearheart's father, Robert, is the one who helps develop the clacks and the Grand Trunk. Unfortunately, he is rooked out of the company by embezzlers and Reacher Gilt. (More on Gilt in chapter 12.)

The clacks system also involves c-mail like the Internet's e-mail. How? We're not sure. It just does.

Speaking tubes. In the *Hogfather*, Lord Downey makes use of a speaking tube. In this phoneless era, this is undoubtedly the receiver/microphone to an intercom such as those of the late nineteenth century—the kind used to communicate from one room to the next—cutting-edge technology back in the day. (You can see these in use sometimes in old TV shows.) Sometimes you had to blow into them (or at least people thought you had to) for sound to carry through. Even today, with technology so much more advanced, you still see people blowing into microphones and asking, "Is this thing on?"

Dis-organizers/PDAs and Iconographs. Vimes has a number of organizers, or Dis-organizers as they are referred to, Dis being an allusion to the name of a city in Dante's *Divine Comedy*. Unlike the organizers before PDAs such as Palm Pilots and BlackBerry products came on the scene, Vimes's Dis-organizers are powered by tiny imps. (More about them in chapter 10.) He starts off with the fifteen-function imp-powered Dis-organizer—a gift from Sybil (*Feet of Clay*). In *Thud!* Vimes gets the Dis-Organizer Mark Five, the Gooseberry™— another imp-powered product. We don't have to tell you that this is an allusion to the BlackBerry and iPod/iTunes (Pratchett's iHUM™). But we did.

As for the iconographs—the magic cameras of Discworld that Pratchett made up—the imps run them as if they were computer chips. Like iconography, which involves the painting of religious icons, the iconograph involves recording images by painting instead of recording them on film. If you've seen *The Flintstones*, you know this is the way of many of that series' labor-saving devices. Wilma's camera might simply be a bird painstakingly pecking a picture on a small piece of marble.

Timepieces

As we mentioned in chapter 17, the monks of history use procrastinators. These devices store and release time. Many are stationary, but some are portable. They differ from the time machine used by the Time Traveller in H. G. Wells's 1895 novel *The Time Machine*, or the DeLorean, the 1980s car that runs on plutonium in the *Back to the Future* trilogy, in that you can't program it to go to a specific time or place and appear there instantly. Using portable procrastinators enables Lobsang and Lu-Tze to travel around Ankh-Morpork once time had stopped. Handy when you want to avoid traffic.

Another innovative timepiece is the great glass clock Jeremy Clockson builds in *Thief of Time*. It uses crystals and the cosmic quantum tick (Newton's tick of the universe) to measure time. But because it also destroys the universe (you see now why Jeremy has an Igor working for him), we can't see the marketable value of such a timepiece. A Rolex is preferable.

Qu, the inventing monk who is an allusion to the Q of the James Bond series, talks about yet another timepiece—an exploding Mandala. The Mandala—"colored chaos" as Pratchett refers to it in *Thief of Time*[2]—is a roomful of sand, but not one in which you'd set a toddler to play. These are the sands of the universe according to Hindu beliefs—thus far more potent than the sands of

---

[2] *Thief of Time* (New York: HarperTorch, 2001), 55.

the timekeepers Death uses. Exploding Mandala is exploding sand—sort of like having time blow up in your face.

Other Magical Items

The wizards have their hands in the technological stew with the omniscope (*Going Postal*)—a magical mirror—and Hex, a "thinking" machine Ponder Stibbons monitors, which controls thaumarhythms. With Hex, we can't help thinking of the old-fashioned computers of the 1950s and 1960s—the ones that used to take up a whole room and spit out keypunch cards. Gone are those days, since the invention of the personal computer. He also reminds us of K9, the robot dog who was a rolling fount of information in the *Doctor Who* series.

The magic mirror is a staple of fairy tales. Consider the "mirror, mirror on the wall" of "Snow White and the Seven Dwarfs" and new tales such as *Fairest* by Gail Carson Levine. Lily Weatherwax uses mirror magic in *Witches Abroad*, just as the Evil Queen did in *The 10th Kingdom*.

WEAPONS AND WARFARE

If you saw any of the *Lord of the Rings* movies, you saw some of the weapons or machinery ancient civilizations might have used in times of war (the trebuchet, bows and arrows, the crossbow, the battering ram, the sword). Fancy.

If you're a Clancy aficionado, you're used to major machines of war, such as tanks, guns, fancy ammo, chilling chemical weapons, and nukes aplenty. Well, a whole arsenal of weapons is mentioned throughout the Discworld series, especially in the City Watch books. After all, the watchpeople come armed with a truncheon, sword, and a crossbow.

Many of the weapons used by the Watch were developed by

Burleigh and Strongintheam. Of course, when we read about Burleigh and Strongintheam, we thought immediately of Smith & Wesson, the famous U.S. gun manufacturing company founded by Horace Smith and Daniel Wesson back in 1852. Burleigh and Strongintheam make the Discworld weapons of choice—crossbows such as the ominous Streetsweeper or the Shureshotte Five mentioned in *Jingo*. If Dirty Harry, the magnum-carrying police officer popularized in the 1970s by Clint Eastwood, existed in this series, he would probably carry either one of those or the Locksley Reflex 7 crossbow (reminiscent of Robin Hood's name—the Earl of Locksley), also mentioned in *Jingo*.

On an armory visit in *Men at Arms* (a very appropriate title), Nobby Nobbs finds several "toys," which include the glaive, a siege crossbow, and a morningstar. If you're up on medieval weapons, you know that a glaive is a pole weapon—a blade with a single edge attached to a pole. A morningstar is a macelike club with spikes. Handy for crowd control. The "'Meteor' Automated Throwing Star Hurler" is, of course, an allusion to the throwing stars or *hira shuriken* that ninjas use—thin-bladed metal stars.

We already mentioned the gonne—Leonard of Quirm's weapon of destruction. There are other weapons: the clong-clong, dakka, the pika, and the uppsi of the Dojo of the Tenth Djim mentioned in *Thief of Time*. The clong-clong could be *nunchaku* or nunchucks—the two sticks chained or roped together. The pika could either be an allusion to the pike—the spearlike medieval weapon—or one like the feathered spear wielded by Shu Lien in *Crouching Tiger, Hidden Dragon*. The uppsi could be a throwing star, while the dakka stick could be a tonfa—a wooden shaft about two feet long with a handle. Usually a person wielding the tonfa has a pair. Or they could all be made up by Pratchett. He does that, y'know.

Of course, chocolate proves to be the best weapon of all, one used against the seemingly invincible Auditors in *Thief of Time*. It also beats depression, too. It may not be high tech, but it gets our vote for best weapon.

The Inventive Mind of Leonardo da Vinci

The constituent parts of nature are finite, but the works that the eye commands of the hands are infinite.

—Leonardo da Vinci[3]

It pays to have keen observation. While Leonardo is known for lacking a university education, he made up for it by an irrepressible curiosity. Could a man fly like Daedalus and Icarus? Sure. All you need is the right design and a grip on aerodynamics. Thus Leonardo created a hang glider of sorts that hundreds of years later was built and flown. He called it an *uccello*—a great bird.

He also had a grasp of engineering and the value of a good pulley system. They would've loved him at Home Depot. Like his Discworld namesake, Leonardo had a few weapons and other war toys in his creative arsenal, namely the tank, a giant crossbow, and the steam-powered cannon, as well as an apparatus for breathing underwater. Many of these were created under the patronage of the Duke of Urbino. Ironically, Leonardo was against war.

Yet others are also credited in the history of the cannon and the creation of gunpowder before the tenth century. Some form of gun-powder, or at least saltpeter, was in use in China, along with the

---

[3] From *Leonardo* by Martin Kemp (Oxford: Oxford University Press, 2004), 113.

precursor to the cannon. Exactly who came up with the ultimate formula for gunpowder is debatable. Thirteenth-century Franciscan friar and philosopher Roger Bacon, whose genius Leonardo admired, had a recipe. And a German monk named Berthold Schwarz may also have invented a type of cannon. Still, you have to give props to the maestro of the Renaissance—Leonardo da Vinci.

20

In the Real World

Maybe by now you're wondering just as we are what would happen if the Discworld characters were suddenly sucked into the vortex of reality/game show TV in our world (with Terry Pratchett's approval, of course)? Which characters would last on *Survivor* or *Survivorman*? *Amazing Race*? *American Idol*? *Project Runway*? *The Bachelor*? *The Apprentice*? *Are You Smarter than a Fifth Grader*? DIY shows like the ones you see on HGTV or TLC? Based on the books of the Discworld series, we can only guess.

First, the contestants . . .

SURVIVAL OF THE FITTEST

You already know about *Survivor*—the CBS show that drops ordinary people like us on remote locations and leaves them to . . . survive. And you probably watch *Survivorman*—the Science Channel's ultimate Robinson Crusoe experience with its one-guy-no-camera-crew approach—too.

Due to their against-all-odds survival on Fourecks (or XXXX if you prefer) in *The Last Continent*, Mustrum Ridcully, the profs of Unseen University (the Dean, the Senior Wrangler, the Lecturer in Recent Runes, etc.) and their refined housekeeper, Mrs. Whitlow, would make a formidable team on *Survivor*. We'll call them Team UU, since we don't know the Survivor site (we don't make those up) and can't think of a clever tribal name to go with an island location we don't know. The wizards have the benefit of magic. Mrs. Whitlow . . . has the benefit of being Mrs. Whitlow. Unfortunately, the wizards tend to argue, so we would expect any alliances to end by the second week. As the weeks progress, we expect Team UU to whittle down to Ridcully and Mrs. Whitlow for sure, due to Ridcully's tenacious grasp on life. And since Ridcully is a gentleman and a little afraid of Mrs. Whitlow, we expect Mrs. Whitlow to be the lone survivor of that team.

Meanwhile, Rincewind and the Luggage (Team Coward) would make powerful allies. And since the Luggage, that sapient pearwood box of menace, could swallow the other contestants one by one, they would be unstoppable! Yeah! But Rincewind has a tendency to leave the Luggage behind. So, there goes that alliance before it even gets off the ground.

Vimes and Colon (Blue Team) would make an excellent team due to their ability to survive murderous werewolves and golems in *The Fifth Elephant* and *Feet of Clay*, respectively. But since both are family men, expect neither to show up at the *Survivor* drop site— not if Sybil Vimes and Colon's wife have anything to say on the subject.

The team to beat is Rincewind, Conina, and Nijel (Team Wunderkind), based on their team-up in *Sourcery*, in which they survive the mage war. With a deadly weapon like Conina, the daughter of Cohen the Barbarian, there's no way they could lose, unless the Luggage is involved and it's ticked off by someone. But since Conina and Nijel don't enter the Dungeon Dimension and

Rincewind does, we wouldn't expect them to out-survive Rince-wind.

Of course, the nature of a TV show like *Survivor* means that only one person can survive. That means we're down to Mrs. Whitlow and Rincewind for the final match. Since Rincewind has survived everything that Pratchett has thrown at him, well, he's the evident favorite, one who would out-survive even Mrs. Whitlow.

Because of his involuntary survival skills, we could see Rincewind acing *Survivorman* as well. Again, we're not drunk. Rincewind could give Les Stroud a run for his money. Because he makes the trip to Fourecks as well as survive in the Dungeon Dimension and other extremely hostile environments, we would back Rincewind to win, hands down. Of course, in a hand-to-hand combat, Les Stroud could beat Rincewind easily. So could Greebo, Nanny Ogg's villainous cat. But Rincewind is the original Survivorman.

A Race Against Time

The Amazing Race pits team after team on a race across designated locations around the world, with embarrassing side games thrown in involving plowing, pulling, or carrying large or slippery objects for our viewing pleasure. We don't have to tell you who would be an incredible match-up for that show. Okay, you convinced us. We'll tell. Our dream teams: Rincewind, Two-flower, and the Luggage (team 1); Granny, Nanny, and Magrat (team 2); and Nobby Nobbs, Sergeant Colon, Lord Vetinari, and Leonard of Quirm (team 3).

Since Twoflower has an amazing ability to find danger everywhere as we learn in *The Color of Magic*, *The Light Fantastic*, and *Interesting Times*, this would be a race not only against time but for survival as well. But we can almost predict that his team would be locked in a Turkish prison somewhere and would be eliminated within the first twenty-four hours.

Leonard of Quirm, Nobby, Colon, and Lord Vetinari travel to Al Khali, a city in Klatch, in Leonard's Going-Under-the-Water-Safely Device, otherwise known as a submarine (*Jingo*). Because they play nicely together in that city, they would make a great team. But since Nobby and Colon usually try to avoid dangerous travel, we would expect their team to be eliminated early on, especially since Vetinari is too busy running Ankh-Morpork and Leonard is virtually a prisoner.

Because Granny, Nanny, and Magrat are able to successfully turn back time in *Wyrd Sisters*, we would expect them to win this game easily. Plus, they've got those handy broomsticks to travel on.

Fit for Fashion?

Bravo's *Project Runway* provides a would-be fashion designer a chance to hit the big time. Although we're not 100 percent positive, we wonder if someone like Magrat Garlick, who is known for her interesting fashion sense, would be a good contestant. Although Granny Weatherwax and Nanny Ogg routinely mock her outfits, Magrat still soldiers on.

For their work in dressing Magrat in *Witches Abroad*, we also would nominate Nanny Ogg and Granny Weatherwax as contestants. After all, they have magic at their disposal, although Granny probably wouldn't use it. And Granny's got that withering stare that's just perfect for sessions with haughty judges. But since neither really cares deeply about fashion, well, we would expect a few stern lectures from the industry judges on fashion à la that of Miranda Priestly (Meryl Streep) to Andy Sachs (Anne Hathaway) in the 2006 film *The Devil Wears Prada*.

We'd also nominate the fifth-level wizard Spelter in *Sourcery*, who rigs up a fake archchancellor hat with lace and Ankhstones for Coin. Quite fetching.

A Star Is Born

We would kill to see someone like Agnes Nitt, Nanny Ogg, Sybil Vimes, or any of the Nac Mac Feegles on *American Idol*. Agnes sings arias in *Maskerade* and has an amazing voice. But is she the pop star that everyone is looking for? Probably not, as *Maskerade* proves when Christine is chosen for the "visible" lead in the operas, instead of Agnes. Well, Agnes could still sing the songs while the other contestants lip-synched.

Nanny Ogg, who is fond of songs like "The Hedgehog Song," would be a favorite because of her cheerful personality. But she'd get voted off within minutes by Simon, Randy, and Paula. Ditto Sybil. She can sing "The Ransom Song" from the opera *Bloodaxe and Iron-hammer* (*The Fifth Elephant*). But does that have a beat America wants to dance to? More than likely, no.

The Feegles would provide many moments of entertainment early on, being fond of singing while inebriated. But we're fairly certain that, at the last moment, Christine would make an appearance and place far higher than anyone else in Discworld, even if she's not listed as a contestant.

An Apt Apprentice

Since the witches of Discworld have the apprentice thing down pat, getting on a show like *The Apprentice* is a natural segue. And since most of the witches are industrious, they might stick around for a while. However, in the category of "plays nicely with others" (okay, there is no category on the show like that; we would call this "being a team player"), many of the witches would not pass muster since they barely tolerate each other. Still, with magic at their disposal (if magic traveled through the vortex as well), no one would dare tell any of them, "You're fired!"

Instead of Donald Trump, Martha Stewart, or any other celebrity boss, who is better than Granny Weatherwax to take over the reins? In *Wintersmith*, Granny Weatherwax is the one consulted when the question of who will get Miss Treason's cottage arises. And since Granny Weatherwax is the unofficial witch in charge, if she were a contestant on *The Apprentice*, she would run the show in no time flat, anyway.

Equally Eligible

Who but Carrot Ironfoundersson would interest an audience (well, a female audience) on a show like *The Bachelor*? Some of the female officers of the Watch (Angua and Sally) would agree. And maybe William de Worde or Moist von Lipwig (*Going Postal*) could generate some interest. But perhaps Sacharissa Cripslock and Adora Belle Dearheart would object. (Carrot would probably object to being on such a show as well.)

We're pretty sure who *wouldn't* make the contestant cut. None of the wizards of Unseen University have the interest to be on this type of show, unless it was *The Bachelorette* and Mrs. Whitlow was the star. And as far as the other watchmen are concerned (Nobby, Detritus, etc.), well, there's always next year. . . .

As for bachelorette shows like *The Bachelorette* or *I Love New York* (insert your own nickname equivalent for the Ankh-Morpork bachelorette of your choice), we suspect guys would choose such characters as Sally, Angua, Conina, Adora Belle, Sacharissa, Sally, Tawneee (Nobby's girlfriend in *Thud!*), and others for reasons known only to them.

Smarter than the Average Kid?

The Jeff Foxworthy–hosted *Are You Smarter than a Fifth Grader?* boasts questions taken from first to fifth grade textbooks and makes fools out of adults. Seeing as how the average fifth grader has to have a breadth of knowledge that many Ph.D. candidates might have had a hundred years ago, we can only suspect that a Renaissance man like Leonard of Quirm or Ponder Stibbons, the smartest of the Unseen University profs, would survive only a few questions before being embarrassed by the average kid.

A friend of ours who recently received a doctorate claimed that she didn't know some of the answers to the questions asked on one show. See what we mean?

Denizens of DIY

If you have a hankering for Home Depot, you probably are a DIYer and hit HGTV or TLC pretty heavily. These channels are rife with DIY shows where homeowners watch in horror or stupefied resignation as designers "improve" their homes. (Okay, not all DIY shows are like this.) See, these shows are perfect for Leonard of Quirm, Bloody Stupid Johnson, or Coin, the young sourcerer of *Sourcery*. Coin's ability to create things is unparalleled. Remember how he shows the other wizards the Garden of Maligree, the last sourcerer? And remember his redecorating scheme for Unseen University? (Knock down walls. Change the ceilings and flooring. Give the building a new glass and marble look. Get rid of the library.) A decorating scheme that bold and controversial is "good TV," especially if you are a fan of certain designers on *Trading Spaces*.

That's why Bloody Stupid Johnson, with his amazing flair for getting things wrong, would be the DIY king of any network, if he were actually "alive" in Discworld and not just a series of posthumous anecdotes.

As for Leonard, well, no door would be closed to a man of his talents. Not only could he redecorate, he could provide his own artwork as well.

THE END?

Unlike this book, the Discworld series shows no sign of ending. After writing this book, we bought the second book involving Moist von Lipwig, *Making Money*, and are reading it, hence the lack of information about it in this book. There is a rumor of another Tiffany Aching book (not sure when that will be released). How many more Discworld books will the prolific Mr. Pratchett write? Will there be another Rincewind, City Watch, or Lancre witch book? We hope so! When you've got a jones for Discworld, there's no such thing as too many books.

BIBLIOGRAPHY

This bibliography is by no means exhaustive. For authors like Terry Brooks, Robert Jordan, Arthur Conan Doyle, Neil Gaiman, Jasper Fforde, Jim Butcher, Ursula LeGuin, Raymond Feist, Terry Goodkind, Mercedes Lackey, George MacDonald, C. S. Lewis, Christopher Paolini, Charles Dickens, William Shakespeare, Tad Williams, Juliet Marillier, Anne McCaffrey, and Ngaio Marsh, who have multiple books to their credit or books in their series not printed as of the publication of this book, we chose to list only one to three titles in a particular series. After all, we had to save room for Terry Pratchett's books!

BOOKS

Alighieri, Dante. *The Divine Comedy*. New York: Vintage Books, 1950.

Asbjørnsen, Peter Christen, and Jørgen Moe. *Norwegian Folk Tales*. Translated by Pat Shaw Iversen and Carl Norman. New York: Viking, 1960.

Barrie, J. M. *Peter Pan*. New York: Charles Scribner's Sons, 1911.

Baum, L. Frank. *The Wonderful Wizard of Oz*. New York: HarperTrophy, 1987 [afterword]; originally published in 1899.

Beagle, Peter S. *The Last Unicorn*. New York: Penguin/Roc, 1968, 1991.

Bishop, Morris. *The Horizon Book of the Middle Ages*, edited by Norman Kotker. Boston: Houghton Mifflin, 1968.

Brewer, Dr. E. Cobham. *Brewer's Dictionary of Phrase & Fable*, Ivor H. Evans. 14th ed. New York: Harper & Row, 1989, 1981, 1978, 1975, 1974, 1971, 1970, 1963, 1959.

———. *Brewer's Dictionary of Phrase & Fable: The Classic Edition*. New York: Tess Press.

Brooks, Terry. *The Sword of Shannara*. New York: Ballantine, 1977.

Butcher, Jim, *Storm Front*, book 1 of The Dresden Files. New York: Penguin, 2000.

Chandler, Raymond. *The Big Sleep* in *The Raymond Chandler Omnibus*. New York: Alfred A. Knopf, Inc., 1939.

Collins, Wilkie. *The Moonstone*. New York: Random House/Modern Library Classics, 1991. Originally published in 1868.

———. *The Woman in White*. New York: Knopf/Everyman's Library, 1991. Originally published in 1860.

The Complete Work of Michelangelo. New York: Reynal and Company, 1965.

Crossley-Holland, Kevin. *The Norse Myths*. New York: Pantheon Books, 1980.

Dickens, Charles. *Bleak House*. New York: Bantam Books edition, 1983. Originally published in 1852–53.

Doyle, Arthur Conan. *A Study in Scarlet and the Sign of Four*. New York: Berkley Books edition, 1975.

Earl, Polly Anne. *Palm Beach: An Architectural Legacy*. New York: Rizzoli International Publications, Inc., 2002.

Feist, Raymond. *Magician: Apprentice*, book 1 of the Riftwar Saga. New York: Bantam Spectra reissue, 1993.

———. *Magician: Master*, book 2 of the Riftwar Saga. New York: Bantam, 1982.

Fforde, Jasper. *The Fourth Bear*. New York: Viking/Penguin, 2006.

Fitzgerald, Percy. *Chronicles of Bow Street Police-Office*. Montclair, NJ: Patterson Smith, 1888, 1972.

Gaiman, Neil. *The Sandman: Preludes and Nocturnes*. Illustrated by Sam Kieth, Mike Dringenberg, and Malcolm Jones III. New York: DC Comics, 1991.

Gardner's Art Through the Ages. 6th ed. New York: Harcourt Brace Jovanovich, Inc., 1975.

Gibson, Michael. *Gods, Men & Monsters from the Greek Myths*. Illustrated by Giovanni Caselli. New York: Schocken Books, 1977.

Gies, Frances and Joseph. *Daily Life in Medieval Times*. New York: Black Dog & Leventhal Pub., 1969, 1974, 1990.

Goodkind, Terry. *Wizard's First Rule*. New York: Tor/Tom Doherty Associates, 1994.

Grimm, Jacob and Wilhelm. *Grimm's Complete Fairy Tales*. New York: Nelson Doubleday, 1954.

Guerber, H. A. *The Myths of Greece and Rome*. London: George G. Harrap & Co., Ltd., 1907, 1938.

Haney, Seamus. *Beowulf: A New Verse Translation*. New York: W. W. Norton & Co., 2000.

Hoffmann, Heinrich. *Der Struwwelpeter*. Translated by Mark Twain. Frankfurt: Insel Verlag, 1985, 1996. Originally published in 1845.

Homer. *The Iliad*. New York: Barnes & Noble Classics. 1942, 1970 by Walter J. Black, Inc., and 1993.

———. *The Odyssey*. New York: Barnes & Noble Classics, 1993.

Huygen, Wil, and illustrated by Rien Poortvliet. *Gnomes*. New York: Harry Abrams, 1976.

Jordan, Robert. *The Eye of the World*, book 1 of the Wheel of Time series. New York: Tor/Tom Doherty Associates, 1990.

Kalindjian, Claudia, and the editors at DC Comics. *Batman Begins: The Official Movie Guide*. New York: Time, Inc., 2005.

Kemp, Martin. *Leonardo*. Oxford: Oxford University Press, 2004.

Klause, Annette Curtis. *Blood and Chocolate*. New York: Bantam/Laurel Leaf, 1997.

Lackey, Mercedes. *The Fairy Godmother (A Tale of the Five Hundred Kingdoms)*. New York: Luna, 2004.

———, and James Mallory. *The Outstretched Shadow*, book 1 of The Obsidian Trilogy. New York: Tor/Tom Doherty Associates, 2003.

———, and James Mallory. *To Light a Candle*, book 2 of The Obsidian Trilogy. New York: Tor/Tom Doherty Associates, 2003.

———, and James Mallory. *When Darkness Falls*, book 3 of The Obsidian Trilogy. New York: Tor/Tom Doherty Associates, 2003.

Lang, Andrew, ed. *The Arabian Nights Entertainments*. New York: Dover Publications, Inc., 1969; originally published in 1898.

Leavitt, Martine. *Keturah and Lord Death*. Asheville, NC: Front Street, 2006.

LeGuin, Ursula. *A Wizard of Earthsea*. Berkeley, CA: Parnassus Press, 1968.

———. *The Farthest Shore*. New York: Simon Pulse, 1972.

Lewis, C. S. *The Lion, the Witch and the Wardrobe*. New York: HarperTrophy, 1950.

————. *The Screwtape Letters*. New York: Bantam edition, 1982. Originally published in 1942.

Lloyd Webber, Andrew. *Andrew Lloyd Webber's The Phantom of the Opera*. Milwaukee: Hal Leonard Publishing, 1987.

MacDonald, George. *Phantastes*. Grand Rapids, MI: Wm. B. Eerdmans, 2000. Originally published in 1858.

————. *The Princess and the Goblin*. Mahwah, NJ: Watermill Press edition, 1985.

Machiavelli, Niccolò. *The Prince*. Translated by W. K. Marriott. New York: Dutton/Everyman's Library edition, 1958.

Mair, A. W. *Hesiod: The Poems and Fragments*. Oxford: Clarendon Press, 1908. Please note that this file was downloaded from http://oll.libertyfund.org/Home3/Book.php?recordID=0606.

Marillier, Juliet. *The Dark Mirror*. New York: Tor/Tom Doherty Associates, 2004.

————. *Wildwood Dancing*. New York: Random House/Alfred A. Knopf Books for Young Readers, 2007.

Marsh, Ngaio. *Death in a White Tie*. New York: Jove, 1938.

McCaffrey, Anne. *Dragonsdawn*. New York: Del Rey/Ballantine, 1988.

McCready, Stuart, ed. *The Discovery of Time*. Naperville, IL: Source Books, Inc., 2001.

McKinley, Robin. *The Door in the Hedge*. New York: Penguin/Firebird, 1981, 2003.

————. *Spindle's End*. New York: Penguin/Firebird, 2000.

————. *Sunshine*. New York: Penguin/Jove Reprint, 2004.

Melling, O. R. *The Hunter's Moon*, book 1 of The Chronicles of Faerie. New York: Amulet Books, 2005.

Meyer, Stephenie. *Twilight* (book 1). New York: Little, Brown and Co., 2005.

————. *New Moon* (book 2). New York: Little, Brown, 2006.

Morrissey, Jake. *The Genius in the Design: Bernini, Borromini, and the Rivalry That Transformed Rome*. New York: William Morrow, 2005.

Niven, Larry. *Ringworld*. New York: Holt, Rinehart and Winston, 1970.

Orchard, Andy. *Dictionary of Norse Myth and Legend*. London: Cassell, 1997.

Page, Michael, and Robert Ingpen. *The Time-Life Encyclopedia of Things that Never Were*. New York: Viking-Penguin, 1985.

Paolini, Christopher. *Eldest*. New York: Alfred A. Knopf, 2005.

————. *Eragon*. New York: Alfred A. Knopf, 2003.

Pavlík, Milan. Introduction in *Dialogue of Forms*. Photographs by Vladimír Uhrer. New York: St. Martin's Press, 1975.

Peat, F. David. *From Certainty to Uncertainty: The Story of Science and Ideas in the Twentieth Century*. Washington, D.C.: Joseph Henry Press, 2002.

Perry, George. *The Complete Phantom of the Opera*. New York: Henry Holt, 1987.

Pratchett, Terry. "Cult Classic" essay in *Meditations on Middle-Earth*, edited by Karen Haber. New York: St. Martin's Press, 2001.

————. *Truckers*, book 1 of the Bromeliad. New York: Delacorte Press. 1989.

The books of Discworld in series in order of publication in the United States:

————. *The Color of Magic*. New York: HarperTorch, 1983.

————. *The Light Fantastic*. New York: HarperTorch, 1986.

————. *Equal Rites*. New York: HarperTorch, 1987.

————. *Mort*. New York: HarperTorch, 1987.

————. *Sourcery*. New York: HarperTorch, 1988.

————. *Wyrd Sisters*. New York: HarperTorch, 1988.

————. *Pyramids*. New York: HarperTorch, 1989.

————. *Guards! Guards!* New York: HarperTorch, 1989.

————. *Eric*. New York: HarperTorch, 1990.

————. *Moving Pictures*. New York: HarperTorch, 1990.

————. *Reaper Man*. New York: HarperTorch, 1991.

————. *Witches Abroad*. New York: HarperTorch, 1991.

————. *Small Gods*. New York: HarperTorch, 1992.

————. *Lords and Ladies*. New York: HarperTorch, 1992.

————. *Men at Arms*. New York: HarperTorch, 1993.

————. *Interesting Times*. New York: HarperPrism, 1994.

————. *Soul Music*. New York: HarperPrism, 1995.

————. *Maskerade*. New York: HarperTorch, 1995.

————. *Hogfather*. New York: HarperTorch, 1996.

————. *Feet of Clay*. New York: HarperTorch, 1996.

————. *Jingo*. New York: HarperTorch, 1997.

————. *The Last Continent*. New York: HarperTorch, 1998.

————. *Carpe Jugulum*. New York: HarperTorch, 1998.

————. *The Fifth Elephant*. New York: HarperTorch, 2000.

————. *The Truth*. New York: HarperTorch, 2000.

————. *Thief of Time*. New York: HarperTorch, 2001.

————. *The Last Hero*. Illustrated by Paul Kidby. New York: HarperCollins, 2001.

————. *The Amazing Maurice and His Educated Rodents*. New York: HarperTrophy, 2001.

———. *Night Watch*. New York: HarperTorch, 2002.

———. *The Wee Free Men*. New York: HarperTrophy, 2003.

———. *Monstrous Regiment*. New York: HarperCollins, 2003.

———. *A Hat Full of Sky*. New York: HarperCollins, 2004.

———. *The Art of the Discworld*. Illustrated by Paul Kidby. New York: Harper-Collins, 2004.

———. *Going Postal*. New York: HarperTorch, 2004.

———. *Thud!* New York: HarperTorch, 2005.

———. *Wintersmith*. New York: HarperTempest, 2006.

Rapoport, Amos. *House Form and Culture*. Englewood Cliffs, NJ: Prentice Hall, Inc., 1969.

Rybczynski, Witold. *The Look of Architecture*. Oxford, UK: Oxford University Press, 2001.

Scoppettone, Sandra. "Vivid Villains" in *Writing Mystery: A Handbook by the Mystery Writers of America*. Cincinnati: Writer's Digest Books, 1992.

Shakespeare, William. *As You Like It*. New York: Signet Classics, 1963.

———. *The Tragedy of Hamlet*. New York: Washington Square Press, 1992.

———. *The Tragedy of Macbeth*. New York: Signet Classics, 1963.

Stead, Philip John, ed. *Pioneers in Policing*. Montclair, NJ: Patterson Smith Pub., 1977.

Steel, Duncan. *Marking Time*. New York: John Wiley & Sons Inc., 2000.

Stoker, Bram. *Dracula* in *The Annotated Dracula* with introduction, notes, and bibliography by Leonard Wolf. New York: Clarkson N. Potter, Inc., introduction, notes, and bibliography, 1975. *Dracula* © 1897.

Tinterow, Gary, and Henri Loyrette. *Origins of Impressionism*. New York: The Metropolitan Museum of Art/Harry Abrams, 1994.

Tolkien, J. R. R. *The Fellowship of the Ring*, book 1 of *The Lord of the Rings*. New York: Ballantine Books, 1955, 1965.

———. *The Two Towers*, book 2 of *The Lord of the Rings*. Boston: Houghton Mifflin, 1954, 1965, 1966.

———. *The Return of the King*, book 3 of *The Lord of the Rings*. Boston: Houghton Mifflin, 1955, 1965, 1966.

———. *Smith of Wooton Major*. Boston: Houghton Mifflin, 1967.

———. *The Silmarillion*. Boston: Houghton Mifflin, 1977.

Verlet, Pierre, Michael Florisoone, Adolf Hoffmeister, and François Tabard. *The Book of Tapestry: History and Technique*. New York: The Vendome Press, 1965.

Vogler, Christopher. *The Writer's Journey: Mythic Structure for Writers*. 2nd ed. Studio City, CA: Michael Wiese Productions, 1988.

Wesley, Kathryn. *The 10th Kingdom* (novel based on a screenplay by Simon Moore). New York: Kensington/Hallmark Entertainment, 2000.

White, T. H. *The Book of Merlyn*. Austin, TX: University of Texas Press, 1977.

————. *The Once and Future King*. New York: G. P. Putnam's Sons, 1939, 1940, 1958.

Williams, Garnett P. *Chaos Theory Tamed*. Washington, D.C.: Joseph Henry Press, 1997.

Williams, Tad. *The Dragonbone Chair*, book 1 of the Memory, Sorrow, and Thorn series. New York: DAW, 1989.

Williamson, John. *The Oak King, the Holly King, and the Unicorn*. New York: Harper & Row, 1986.

Willis, Connie. *To Say Nothing of the Dog*. New York: Bantam, 1998.

WEB SITES

- Constitution Society—http://www.constitution.org
- David Paton—http://www.davidpaton.com/index.shtml
- *Encyclopedia Britannica*—http://www.britannica.com
- Equal Employment Opportunity Commission—http://www.eeoc.gov/policy/vii.html
- IMDB LOTR quote site—http://imdb.com/title/tt0120737/quotes
- L-space: http://www.lspace.org/about-terry/interviews/book-case.html
- *Lord of the Rings* quotes—http://www.tk421.net/lotr/film/rotk/02.html
- PDF book of *Mabinogion*, translated by Lady Charlotte Guest—http://www.wyldwytch.com/weavings/reading_room/books/celtic/mab.htm
- Mystery Guide's Web site—http://www.mysteryguide.com
- Super Seventies lyrics—http://www.superseventies.com
- Wikipedia, the free encyclopedia—http://en.wikipedia.org/wiki
- Writing World's mystery guides—http://www.writing-world.com/mystery

PERIODICALS

Publishers Weekly, February 12, 2007

INDEX

ABOUT THE AUTHORS

Carrie Pyykkonen is anxiously waiting for a lifetimer that grants extra time while living in Wheaton, Illinois, with her husband, two children, four cats (two are visitors), and a dog named Wilfred. She has dabbled in writing due to Linda's nagging, volunteers by wearing a long garment called an alb, and spends a lot of money on animal food. (Please buy more books so sweet little Samantha can eat.) This is her second book project that involves talking animals and fantastical creatures for which she still has no use. She plans on spending more time photographing her animals in pink dresses and parasols.

Linda Washington is a freelance writer living in Carol Stream, Illinois, who has authored or coauthored thirty-eight books. She still mooches food from the Pyykkonens on Sundays and keeps adding to her increasingly large library of nonsense books, DVDs, and music. She became a huge fan of Terry Pratchett, thanks to (see dedication). She aspires to find the perfect cookie, own her own flying machine, and flee the newest trend of her friends, which is to acquire odd pets.